美国总统竞选演说精选

Selected Campaign Speeches of the American Presidents

汉英对照　王建华 / 主编

图书在版编目(CIP)数据

美国总统竞选演说精选:英汉对照/王建华主编.
—南昌:江西人民出版社,2008.2(2014.9重印)
ISBN 978-7-210-03750-7

Ⅰ.美… Ⅱ.王… Ⅲ.①英语—汉语—对照读物②总统—演说—汇编—美国 Ⅳ.H319.4;D

中国版本图书馆CIP数据核字(2007)第195342号

美国总统竞选演说精选(英汉对照)

王建华 主编

江西人民出版社出版发行

南昌市红星印刷有限公司印刷 新华书店经销
2008年2月第1版 2014年9月第5次印刷
开本:787毫米×1092毫米 1/16 印张:19.25
字数:250千
ISBN 978-7-210-03750-7 定价:35.00元

江西人民出版社 地址:南昌市三经路47号附1号
邮政编码:330006 传真电话:6898827 电话:6898815(发行部)
网址:www.jxpph.com
E-mail:jxpph@tom.com web@jxpph.com
(赣人版图书凡属印刷、装订错误,请随时向承印厂调换)

前 言

四年一度的美国总统选举是一道奇特的风景。从春季拉开预选的帷幕,到夏季召开民主、共和两党代表大会,再到秋季展开巡回竞选活动,直到法定的全国大选日（11月第一个星期二）,在差不多9个月的时间里,民主、共和两党都不遗余力,其他小党虽为点缀也不甘示弱,而寂寞难耐的独立派人士,也会使尽浑身解数。演讲、集会、民意测验此起彼伏,广告、口号、空头诺言铺天盖地,新闻、谣传、小道消息不胫而走。以致一位美国前总统不无担忧地说:"美国人除了竞选,无所事事。"

本书汇集了美国政界名流为问鼎白宫而发表的演说共24篇。这些演说可分为两类,一类是在政党代表大会上接受总统候选人提名后所发表的演说,另一类是候选人在巡游各地时所发表的演说。前者比较严密,篇幅较长,演说者往往遵照大会的旨意,提出日后的执政口号或施政蓝图,如罗斯福的"新政"、肯尼迪的"新边疆"、约翰逊的"伟大社会"等等;后者篇幅较短,更注重即兴发挥,更具有针对性,如杜鲁门挖苦对手的演说,肯尼迪的辩论演说,里根的广播演说,老布什的庆功演说,等等。但无论属于哪一类,它们的共同目的只有一个,那就是利用一切可以利用的手段,甚至不择手段,使自己立于不败,使对手相形见绌,最大限度地争取选民和赢得选票。

本书是专为广大演说爱好者和所有对美国问题感兴趣的人设计的。它是一个窗口,可以一睹美国竞选者的风采及其驾驭语言的技巧;它是一面镜子,可以折射出美国政坛的激烈倾轧、美国竞选的特点和弊端;它又是一部文献集,可以用历史事实来评判竞选者的言论,并探寻美国两党制的运行轨迹。

上海社会科学院信息研究所研究员

中国美国史研究会理事

王建华

目 录

亚伯拉罕·林肯
与道格拉斯法官第二次大辩论开场演说 ——2

西奥多·罗斯福
人民当家作主的权利 ——17

赫伯特·胡佛
两种政治哲学之间的竞争 ——22

富兰克林·罗斯福
我保证为美国人民实施新政 ——33
请大家投我信任票 ——54

哈里·杜鲁门
"神医"杜威和共和党的老唱片 ——67

德怀特·艾森豪威尔
共和党代表未来 ——81

约翰·肯尼迪
新边疆就在这里 ——92
与尼克松第一次辩论开场演说 ——107

林登·约翰逊
我接受你们的提名 ——112

理查德·尼克松
为美国选择新领导人的时候来到了 ——119
为了那个孩子 ——131

CONTENTS

Abraham Lincoln
Opening Speech at His Second Debate with Judge Douglas ———2

Theodore Roosevelt
The Right of the People to Rule ———17

Herbert Hoover
A Contest Between Two Philosophies of Government ———22

Franklin Roosevelt
Pledge to a New Deal for the American People ———33
I Am Asking Your Vote of Confidence ———54

Harry Truman
"Doctor" Dewey and His Republican Old Phonograph Records ———67

Dwight Eisenhower
The Republican Party Is the Party of the Future ———81

John Kennedy
The New Frontier Is Here ———92
Opening Remarks at His First Presidential Debate with Nixon ———107

Lyndon Johnson
I Accept Your Nomination ———112

Richard Nixon
It's Time for New Leadership for the United States of America ———119
For That One Child ———131

杰拉尔德·福特
让我们来改变美国国会 ——140

吉米·卡特
我们即将拥有的美国 ——158

罗纳德·里根
本次竞选运动的主要问题 ——169
美国的未来掌握在你们的手中 ——181

乔治·H.布什
使美国变得更安全、更强大 ——186
在得克萨斯州休斯敦"1992胜利庆功宴"上的讲话 ——196

比尔·克林顿
新的誓约 ——205
机会共享,责任共担 ——217

乔治·W.布什
开创一个有责任心的时代 ——223
2000年大选获胜演讲 ——248

巴拉克·奥巴马
美国的承诺 ——257
在选举夜庆祝胜利集会上的讲话 ——281

附录 美国历届总统谈竞选 ——293

Gerald Ford
Let's Change the United States Congress — 140

Jimmy Carter
The America That We Will Have — 158

Ronald Reagan
The Major Issue of This Campaign — 169
America's Future Will Be in Your Hands — 181

George H. Bush
To Make America Safer and Stronger — 186
Remarks at a Victory '92 Dinner in Houston, Texas — 196

Bill Clinton
The New Covenant — 205
Opportunity for All and Responsibility from All — 217

George W. Bush
Ushering in an Era of Responsibility — 223
2000 Victory Speech — 248

Barrack Obama
The American Promise — 257
Remarks at the Election Night Rally Celebrating Victory — 281

Appendix Remarks on Campaiguing by the U.S. Presidents — 293

与道格拉斯法官第二次大辩论开场演说

亚伯拉罕·林肯[*]

1858 年 8 月 27 日

上星期六,道格拉斯法官和我进行了第一次公开辩论。他先说一个小时,我说一个半小时,他再答复半个小时。今天的顺序正好相反。我先说一个小时,他说一个半小时,我再答复半

---

[*] 美国第 16 任总统(1861—1865),共和党人,曾领导人民投入南北战争,挽救了联邦,重新统一了美国。1865 年遇刺。1858 年,在伊利诺伊州与民主党风云人物斯蒂芬·道格拉斯竞选参议员席位,展开了 7 次"树桩式"大辩论。辩论集中于一个问题:奴隶制。两人在辩论中平分秋色,道格拉斯赢得参议员席位,而林肯也名声大振,为两年后竞选总统做好了准备。

Abraham Lincoln

August 27, 1858

Opening Speech at His Second Debate with Judge Douglas

On Saturday last, Judge Douglas and my self first met in public discussion. He spoke one hour, I an hour and a half, and he replied for half an hour. The order is now reversed. I am to speak an hour, he an hour and a half, and then I am to reply

个小时。上次在奥塔瓦辩论时,道格拉斯法官在开场演说中向我明确提出了7个问题。我在一个半小时里谈到了他的演说内容,而且我以为,我已经附带回答了他的第一个问题。当时我明确表示,我将回答他的其余问题,唯一条件是他也应回答我提出的同等数量的问题。他对我的建议没有反应。在后来半个小时的答复中,他也只字不提我的建议,而是至少花了一半时间来对付我,好像我曾拒绝回答他的问题。我这样说对他并非不公平。现在我提议,我将回答他的任何问题,条件是他也要回答我的问题,数量不会超过他提出的问题。我给他一个机会作出响应。这位法官一言不发。好,我告诉大家,无论他是否回答我的问题,我都将回答他的问题;我在回答之后,再提一些问题供他考虑。

自从1856年5月共和党在布卢明顿成立以来,我一直认为自己作为党员受到了党纲的约束。我如果在回答任何问题时超出了党纲范围,应当完全由我个人负责。

for half an hour. At Ottawa, in the course of his opening argument, Judge Douglas proposed to me seven distinct interrogatories. In my speech of an hour and a half, I attended to some other parts of his speech, and incidentally, as I thought, answered one of the interrogates then. I then distinctly intimated to him that I would answer the rest of his interrogatories on condition only that he should agree to answer as many for me. He made no intimation at the time of the proposition, nor did he in his reply allude at all to that suggestion of mine. I do him no injustice in saying that he occupied at least half of his reply in dealing with me as though I had refused to answer his interrogatories. I now propose that I will answer any of the interrogatories, upon condition that he will answer questions from me not exceeding the same number. I give him an opportunity to respond. The judge remains silent. I now say that I will answer his interrogatories, whether he answers mine or not and that after I have done so, I shall propound mine to him.

I have supposed myself, since the organization of the Republican party at Bloomington in May, 1856, bound as a party man by the platforms of the party then and since. If in any interrogatories which I shall answer I go beyond the scope of what is within these platforms, it will be perceived that no one is responsible but myself.

说了这些以后,我来逐一回答法官的问题。这些问题已刊登在《芝加哥时报》上。为了不致出错,我把这些问题和我的答案都记了下来。

问题一:"我希望知道,林肯今天是不是和他在1854年时一样,赞成无条件废除《逃奴追缉法》①?"

答:我现在不赞成,过去也从来不赞成无条件废除《逃奴追缉法》。

问题二:"我希望他回答,他今天是不是和1854年时一样,反对接纳更多的蓄奴州加入联邦,即使人民需要?"

答:我现在不反对,过去也从来不反对接纳更多的蓄奴州加入联邦。

问题三:"我想知道,他是不是反对接纳一个新的州带了一部被该州人民认为

---

①1793年曾有过《逃奴追缉法》,1850年重新制订,明确授予奴隶主追回逃奴的权利。

Having said this much I will take up the judged interrogatories as find them printed in the *Chicago Times*, and answer them seriatim. In order that there may be no mistake about it, I have copied the interrogatories in writing, and also my answers to them.

Question 1. "I desire to know whether Lincoln today stands as he did in 1854, in favor of the unconditional repeal of the fugitive-slave law?"

Answer. I do not now, nor ever did, stand favor of the unconditional repeal of the fugitive-slave law.

Q. 2. "I desire him to answer whether he stands pledged today as he did in 1854, against the admission of any more slave States into the Union, even if the people want them?"

A. I do not now, nor ever did, stand pledged against the admission of any more slave States into the Union.

Q. 3. "I want to know whether he stands pledged against the admission of a new State into the Union with such a constitution as the people of that State

订得合理的宪法①加入联邦？"

答：我不反对接纳一个新的州带了一部被该州人民认为订得合理的宪法加入联邦。

问题四："我想知道，他现在是不是主张在哥伦比亚特区废除奴隶制？"

答：我现在不主张在哥伦比亚特区废除奴隶制。

问题五："我希望他回答，他是不是主张禁止各州之间的奴隶贸易？"

答：我不主张禁止各州之间的奴隶贸易。

问题六："我希望知道，他是不是主张禁止合众国各准州实行奴隶制，无论是在《密苏里妥协案》规定的界线②以北，还是以南？"

答：我如果不是明确地至少也是含蓄地认为，国会有禁止各准州实行奴隶制

---

①指州宪法。
②该法案于1820年通过，规定北纬36°30′以北的新领土不准实行奴隶制。

may see fit to make?"

A. I do not stand pledged against the admission of a new State into the Union with such a constitution as the people of that State may see fit to make.

Q. 4. "I want to know whether he stands today pledged to the abolition of slavery in the District of Columbia?"

A. I do not stand today pledged to the abolition of slavery in the District of Columbia.

Q. 5. "I desire him to answer whether he stands pledged to the prohibition of the slave trade between the different States?"

A. I do not stand pledged to the prohibition of the slave-trade between the different States.

Q. 6. "I desire to know whether he stands pledged to prohibit slavery in all the Teritories of the United States, North as well as South of the Missouri Compromise line?"

A. I am impliedly, if not expressly, pledged to a belief in the right and

的权利和义务。

问题七:"我希望他回答,他是不是反对获得新的领地,除非该领地已禁止了奴隶制?"

答:一般地说,我不反对光明正大地获得领地;具体地说,反对与否要看获得领地以后会不会加重我们之间的奴隶制问题。

好了,我的朋友们,看看这些问答就可以知道,到现在为止,我只不过回答了我不主张这个,或不主张那个。除此以外,法官没有问更多的东西。我是严格按照问题来回答的,并且老老实实回答说,问到我的各点,没有一点是我坚决主张的。但我无意束缚于他的提问形式,而要至少从中挑出几个问题,谈谈我的真实看法。

关于第一个问题——《逃奴追缉法》问题,我过去毫不犹豫地说过,现在也毫不犹豫地说,我认为,根据合众国宪法,南方各州人民享有该法规定的权利。这样

duty of Congress to prohibit slavery in all the United States Territories.

Q. 7. "I desire him to answer whether he is opposed to the acquisition of any new territory unless slavery is first prohibited therein?"

A. I am not generally opposed to honest acquisition of territory; and, in any given case, I would or would not oppose such acquisition, accordingly as I might think such acquisition would or would not aggravate the slavery question among ourselves.

Now, my friends, it will be perceived upon an examination of these questions and answers, that so far I have only answered that I was not pledged to this, that, or the other. The judge has not framed his interrogatories to ask me anything more than this, and I have answered in strict accordance with the interrogatories, and have answered truly that I am not pledged at all upon any of the points to which I have answered. But I am not disposed to hang upon exact form of his interrogatory. I am the really disposed to take up at least some of these questions, and state what I really think upon them.

As to the first one, in regard to the fugitive-slave law, I have never hesitated to say, and I do not now hesitate to say, that I think, under the Constitution of the United States, the people of the Southern States are entitled to a congressional fugitive-slave law. Having said that, I have had nothing to say in regard to the

说了以后,我对现行的《逃奴追缉法》就没有什么要说的了,不过我认为它本来应该那样制定,以便排除异议,不至于减少效力。鉴于目前并不急于修改或修正那条法令,我不愿把它作为有关奴隶制这个大问题的一个新的煽动性问题提出来。

关于第二个问题——我是否主张接纳更多的蓄奴州加入联邦,我非常坦率地告诉你们,要我对那个问题避而不谈,我会感到非常遗憾。我将非常乐于知道再没有一个蓄奴州获准加入联邦;[掌声]但是我必须补充说,任何一个准州如果在作为准州期间把奴隶制排除在外,人民在制订宪法时有公平的机会和干净的土地,不受奴隶制实际存在的影响,居然出乎意外地制订出一部蓄奴宪法,我看没有别的选择,只有让它们加入联邦。

对第三个问题的回答和刚才一样,我认为这个问题和第二个问题相同。

关于第四个问题——在哥伦比亚特区废除奴隶制。对于这个问题,我的主意

existing fugitive-slave law, further than that I think it should have been framed so as to be free from some of the objections that pertain to it, without lessening its efficiency. And in as much as we are not now in an agitation in regard to an alteration or modification of that law, I would not be the man to introduce it as a new subject of agitation upon the general question of slavery.

In regard to the other question, of whether I am pledged to the admission of any more slave states into the Union, I state to you very frankly that I would be exceedingly sorry ever to be put in a position of having to pass upon that question. I should be exceedingly glad to know that there would never be another slave State admitted into the Union; but I must add that if slavery shall be kept out of the Territories during the territorial existence of any given Territory, and then the people shall, having a fair chance and a clear field, when they come to adopt the Constitution, do such an extraordinary thing as to adopt a slave constitution, uninfluenced by the actual presence of the institution among them, I see no alternative if we own the country, but to admit them into the Union.

The third interrogatory is answered by the answer to the second, it being, as I conceive, the same as the second.

The fourth one is in regard to the abolition of slavery in the District of Columbia.

已定。我将非常乐于看到哥伦比亚特区废除奴隶制。我以为国会有宪法规定的权力去废除奴隶制。但作为一名国会议员,我将不以我目前的看法来力争在哥伦比亚特区废除奴隶制,除非具备以下条件:第一,要逐步进行;第二,要由特区合格的投票人以多数票通过;第三,要给予不愿废除奴隶制的奴隶主以补偿。有了这三个条件,我承认我将非常乐于看到国会在哥伦比亚特区废除奴隶制,用亨利·克莱①的话来说,"从我们的首都清除民族的污点"。

关于第五个问题——我必须在这儿说,关于废除各州之间的奴隶贸易问题,我可以老老实实地回答,我目前没有任何主张。我对这个问题没有考虑成熟,还没有资格提出一种主张,并按照这个主张行事。换句话说,这个问题从未突出地摆在我面前,促使我去研究我们到底有没有宪法所赋予的权力这样做。我如果有足够

---

① 辉格党领袖,曾任国务卿、参议员。

In relation to that, I have my mind very distinctly made up. I should be exceedingly glad to see slavery abolished in the District of Columbia. I believe that Congress possesses the constitutional power to abolish it. Yet as a member of Congress, I should not with my present views be in favor of endeavoring to abolish slavery in the District of Columbia unless it would be upon these conditions: First, that the abolition should be gradual; second, that it should be on a vote of the majority of qualified voters in the District; and third, that compensation should be made to unwilling owners. With these three conditions, I confess I would be exceedingly glad to see Congress abolish slavery in the District of Columbia, and, in the language of Henry Clay, "sweep from our capital that foul blot upon our nation."

In regard to the fifth interrogatory, I must say here that as to the question of the abolition of the slave-trade between the different States, I can truly answer, as I have, that I am pledged to nothing about it. It is a subject to which 1 have not given that mature consideration that would make me feel authorized to state a position so as to hold myself entirely bound by it. In other words, that question has never been prominently enough before me to induce me to investigate whether we really have the constitutional power to do it. I could investigate it if

时间，就可以研究一下并得出结论，但是我坦率地告诉各位和道格拉斯法官，我还没有这样做过。然而我必须说，即使我认为国会确有宪法赋予的权力去废除各州之间的奴隶贸易，我还是不赞成行使那种权力，除非按照类似我关于在哥伦比亚特区废除奴隶制所提出的那些稳健的原则去做。

关于我是否希望在合众国各准州禁止奴隶制，我已经回答得很完全、很明确，再作任何解释也不能使我的回答变得更清楚。所以，关于是否除非先在新领地禁止奴隶制否则就反对获得任何新领地，我的回答是：除了我已经写下的答案以外，我无法再通过解释或进一步说明来补充任何东西。

其实，在所有这些问题上，法官明白我的意思，而且有我的讲话记录。我想，他本以为我会在一个场合持一些见解，在另一场合又持另一些见解——他本以为我不敢在一个场合说出我在另一场合说过的话。我今天在这儿所说的话，我想是对

I had sufficient time to bring myself to a conclusion upon that subject, but I have not done so, and I say so frankly to you here and to Judge Douglas. I must say, however, that if I should he of opinion that Congress does possess the constitutional power to abolish the slave-trade among the different States, I should still not be in favor of the exercise of that power unless upon some conservative principle as I conceive it, akin to what I have said in relation to the abolition of slavery in the District of Columbia.

My answer as to whether I desire that slavery should be prohibited in all the Territories of the United States is full and explicit within itself, and cannot be made clearer by any comments of mine. So I suppose in regard to the question whether I am opposed to the acquisition of any more territory unless slavery is first prohibited therein, my answer is such that I could add nothing by way of illustration, or making myself better understood, than the answer which I have placed in writing.

Now in all this the judge has me, and he has me on the record. I suppose he had flattered himself that I was really entertaining one set of opinions for one place and another set for another place that I was afraid to say at one place what I uttered at another. What I am saying here I suppose I say to a

和伊利诺伊州听众一样强烈倾向于废奴主义的广大听众说的,而且我以为,如果我的话会触犯一些人,使他们与我为敌,那么这些话也会触犯这里的一些听众。

接下来,我要向法官提几个我到目前为止所想到的问题。我准备好新问题以后,还会分批提出。现在我要提问了,只有四个问题。

问题一:如果堪萨斯人民在达到规定的大约9.3万人口之前,使用完全无可非议的手段,通过一部州宪法,并且要求联邦接纳,你会投票赞成接纳吗?

问题二:合众国一个准州的人民,在州宪法制订之前,能违反合众国任何公民的意愿,以任何合法方式把奴隶制排除在其范围之外吗?①

问题三:如果合众国最高法院裁定,各州不能把奴隶制排除在该州范围之外,

---

① 这个问题使对手进退两难。因为道格拉斯既主张在新领土是否实行奴隶制问题上实行"人民主权论",即由人民投票决定;又赞成最高法院对"斯科特判例"的裁定,即认为禁止在准州实行奴隶制为违宪。

---

vast audience as strongly tending to Abolitionism as any audience in the State of Illinois, and I believe I am saying that which, if it would be offensive to any persons and render them enemies to myself, would be offensive to persons in this audience.

I now proceed to propound to the judge the interrogatories so far as I have framed them. I will bring forward a new installment when I get them ready. I will bring them forward now, only reaching to number four.

Question 1. If the people of Kansas shall, by means entirely unobjectionable in all other respects, adopt a State constitution, and ask admission into the Union under it, before they have the requisite number of inhabitants,—some ninety-three thousand,— will you vote to admit them?

Q. 2. Can the people of a United States Territory, in any lawful way, against the wish of any citizen of the United States, exclude slavery from its limits prior to the formation of a State constitution?

Q. 3. If the Supreme Court of the United States shall decide that States cannot exclude slavery from their limits, are you in favor of acquiescing in, adopting,

你会默认、采纳并沿用这个裁定,把它作为一个政治行动准则吗?

问题四:你赞成获得更多的领地,而不管这会在奴隶制问题上对国家产生怎样的影响吗?

道格拉斯法官在奥塔瓦向我提出问题之前读过一份决议,称这份决议是1854年在斯普林菲尔德首届伊利诺伊州共和党大会上通过的,而特朗布尔法官和我都参加了这次会议。他坚持认为,我和特朗布尔法官,或许还有整个共和党,都对这份决议所包含的原则负有责任;我明白,他提的那些问题就是从这份决议演绎出来的,他想把这份决议用作一份权威材料。

今天我要在这里说,我之所以不回答他的问题,是因为这些问题完全来源于他所读的那份决议;我之所以回答了,是因为道格拉斯法官自以为提出这些问题很适当。我现在不知道,过去也从来不知道,我对那份决议负有什么责任。

and following such decision as a rule of political action?

Q. 4. Are you in favor of acquiring additional territory, in disregard of how such acquisition may affect the nation on the slavery question?

As introductory to these interrogatories which Judge Douglas propounded to me at Ottawa, he read a set of resolutions which he said Judge Trumbull and myself had participated in adopting, in the first Republican State convention, held at Springfield, in 1854. He insisted that I and Judge Trumbull, and perhaps the entire Republican party, were responsible for the doctrines contained in the set of resolutions which he read, and I understand that it was from that set of resolutions that he deduced the interrogatories which he propounded to me using these resolutions as a sort of authority for propounding those questions to me.

Now I say here today that I do not answer his interrogatories because of their springing at all from that set of resolutions, which he read. I answered them because Judge Douglas thought fit to ask them. I do not now, nor ever did, recognize any responsibility upon myself in that set of resolutions.

上次在答复他时我作过保证，我与此事全然无关。我今天在这里再说一遍，我与那份决议绝无半点关系。我相信，事情已经弄清楚了。原来，那些决议从未在斯普林菲尔德的任何大会上通过。原来，那些决议从未在我所参加过的任何大会或公众集会上通过。

除此之外，我还相信，在1854年秋，斯普林菲尔德并没有举行过自称为州共和党大会的会议；不过，确实有一个"大会"，或者说一群人自称的"大会"，并确实通过了某些决议。我对那群人的集会虽有一个大概的了解，但对该大会的议程和通过什么决议却不甚了了。所以，当道格拉斯法官朗读一份决议时，我确实弄不清楚，只以为曾通过了什么决议。我当时并没有问这个问题，因为我无法想象，道格拉斯法官不知道确有其事竟能大发议论。我当时满足于否认——因为我确实能够否认——同这些决议有任何关系，而不是去否定或肯定它们是斯普林菲尔德会议

When I replied to him on that occasion, I assured him that I never had anything to do with them. I repeat here today, that I never in any possible form had anything to do with that set of resolutions. It turns out, I believe, that those resolutions were never passed at any convention held in Springfield. It turns out that they were never passed at any convention or any public meeting that I had any part in.

I believe it turns out, in addition to all this, that there was not, in the fall of 1854, any convention holding a session in Springfield calling itself a Republican State convention, yet it is true there was a convention, or assemblage of men calling themselves a convention, at Springfield, that did pass some resolutions. But so little did I really know of the proceedings of that convention, or what set of resolutions they had passed, though having a general knowledge that there had been such an assemblage of men there, that when Judge Douglas read the resolutions, I really did not know but that they had been the resolutions passed then and there. I did not question that they were the resolutions adopted. For I could not bring myself to suppose that Judge Douglas could say what he did upon this subject without knowing that it was true. I contented myself, on that occasion, with denying, as I truly could, all connection with them, not denying or affirming whether they

通过的决议。现在有结果了。原来他拿到的是凯恩县某次大会或公众集会所通过的决议。

我希望在这里说,公平而又公正地说,我根本不认为这个发现使我得到了解脱。我与斯普林菲尔德大会有多大关系,就与凯恩县大会有多大关系;我对前者的决议负有多少责任,就对后者的决议负有多少责任——确切地说,我对二者的责任都等于零,这就像我无需对月球上通过什么决议负任何责任一样。

我在竞选中提到这段异乎寻常的往事,除了想说明以上问题外,还有一个目的。在上次辩论中,道格拉斯法官不是把这件事作为他所相信的事实,而是完全把它作为一件真事提出来的,以期用自己的坦诚来担保此事的真实性。

当全部真相大白之后,当我们考虑到道格拉斯法官是何许人——合众国的一位著名参议员、占有这个职位已达12年之久、其品格与普通参议员不可同日而语、

---

were passed at Springfield. Now it turns out that he had got hold of some resolutions passed at some convention or public meeting in Kane County.

I wish to say here that I don't conceive that in any fair and just mind this discovery relieves me at all. I had just as much to do with the convention in Kane County as that at Springfield. I am just as much responsible for the resolutions Kane County as those at Springfield, the amount of the responsibility being exactly nothing in either case; no more than there would be in regard to a set of resolutions passed in the moon.

I allude to this extraordinary matter in this canvass for some further purpose than anything yet advanced. Judge Douglas did not make his statement upon that occasion as matters that he believed to be true, but he stated them roundly as being true, in such form as to pledge his veracity for their truth.

When the whole matter turns out as it does, and when we consider who Judge Douglas is,—that he is a distinguished Senator of the United States; that he has served nearly twelve years as such; that his character is not at all limited as an ordinary senator of the United States, but that his name has become of world-wide

其名声举世皆知——下面这个情况就显得极其异乎寻常了：他竟然把公正待人和谨慎待己的训诫忘得一干二净，以致不顾风险，断定稍作调查就会证明自己大错特错的事实。为了解释他的行为，我只能假设，他的鬼才虽然使他受益终生，虽然使他获得了有目共睹的、令人吃惊的硕果，例如居然使一大批好人怀疑起美德能否战胜邪恶——但是，我只能假设，他的鬼才终于打定主意要抛弃他了。

我可以补充说，法官在这次竞选中还有一个异乎寻常的特点。他习惯于在几乎所有演说中指责对手——指责我和其他很多人荒谬绝伦。我现在要问，他能不能从特朗布尔法官的任何言谈中，或从我的任何言谈中，找出一点证据，就像我们在这件事上证明了他的庸俗不堪一样。

我的时间很快就要用完了，所以有些问题我就不谈了。但是请允许我告诉大家，道格拉斯法官像他在以前几个场合说过的那样，上一次又提到了林肯的粗

renown,—it is most extraordinary that he should so far forget all the suggestions of justice to an adversary, or of prudence to himself, as to venture upon the assertion of that which the slightest investigation would have shown him to be wholly false. I can only account for his having done so upon the supposition that that evil genius which has attended him through his life, giving to him an apparent astonishing prosperity, such as to lead very many good men to doubt there being any advantage in virtue over vice I say I can only account for it on the supposition that that evil genius has at last made up its mind to forsake him.

And I may add that another extraordinary, feature of the judged conduct in this canvass—made more extraordinary by this incident—is, that he is in the habit, in almost all the speeches he makes, of charging falsehood upon his adversaries, myself and others. I now ask whether he is able to find in anything that Judge Trumbull, for instance, has said, or in anything that I have said, a justification at all compared with what we have, in this instance, for that sort of vulgarity.

I pass one or two points I have because my time will very soon expire, but I must be allowed to say that Judge Douglas recurs again, as he did upon one

暴——一个像林肯这样的微不足道的人的粗暴——林肯竟然武断地指责大批国会议员,指责最高法院和两位总统,指责他们阴谋把奴隶制推向全国。我要说的是,首先,我没有武断地进行过此类指责。我仅仅把能够说明问题的证据摆了出来,让别人也能看得懂,我说了我所认为的它们能证明的东西,我也给了大家判断这种证明是否成立的方法。我的确这样做了。我根本没有武断地指责过什么人。在这里,我希望他注意我上星期六在奥塔瓦提到的一件事,此事表明,他几乎对上述同样的人——除了亲爱的自己——进行了几乎同样的指责。我请他稍微注意一下我提到的那件事:他本人发现,人民把奴隶制排除出自己地区的权利"正在遭到致命打击",他从华盛顿《联合报》"经授权"而发表的文章中找到了证据。

我要问,经过了谁的授权?他还从利康普顿宪法①中找出了同样的或类似的条

---

① 1857年堪萨斯准州的蓄奴派在利康普顿制订的一部维护奴隶制的宪法,后遭否决。

or two other occasions, to the enormity of Lincoln—an insignificant individual like Lincoln—upon his ipse dixit ipsedixit charging a conspiracy upon a large number of members of Congress, the Supreme Court, and two President, to nationalize slavery. I want to say that, in the first place, I have made no charge of this sort upon my ipse dixit. I have only arrayed the evidence tending to prove it, and presented it to the understanding of other,. saying what I think it proves, but giving you the means of judging whether it proves it or not. This is precisely what I have done. I have not placed it upon my ipsedixitipse dixit at all. On this occasion, I wish to recall his attention to a piece of evidence which I brought forward, that Ottawa on Saturday, showing that he had made substantially the same charge against substantially the same persons, excluding his dear self from the category. I ask him to give some attention to the evidence which I brought forward, that he himself had discovered a "fatal blow being struck" against the right of the people to exclude slavery from their limits, which fatal blow he assumed as in evidence in a article in the Washington Union, published "by authority."

I ask by whose authority? He discovers a similar or identical provision in the

文。这些条文是谁制订的？是宪法制订者。谁倡议的？是全国各地想根据这个宪法把堪萨斯纳入联邦的所有鼓吹者。

我已提请他注意他用来证明那个致命打击的证据，以及他用来支持他的指责的事实；他的做法，同他所认为的我的极其可耻的做法并无不同。他的矛头不只是指向报刊编辑，而且是指向总统、内阁、支持利康普顿宪法的国会议员以及所有制订该宪法的人。请再次允许我提醒他，本人的武断也许不能与他的武断相媲美，但或多或少减弱了他对我的提醒所具有的力量，致使我粗暴地对他进行了同样的指责。

该你说了，道格拉斯法官。

王建华　译

Lecompton constitution. Made by whom? The framers of that constitution. Advocated by whom? By the members of the party in the nation, who advocated the introduction of Kansas into the Union under the Lecompton constitution.

I have asked his attention to the evident that he arrayed to prove that such a fatal blow was being struck, and to the facts which he brought forward in support of that charge —being identical with the one which he thinks villainous in me. He pointed it not at a newspaper editor merely, but at the President and his cabinet, and the members of Congress advocating the Lecompton constitution, and those framing that instrument. I must again be permitted to remind him, that although my ipsedixitipse dixit may not be as great as his, yet it somewhat reduces the force of his calling my attention to the enormity of my making a like charge against him.

Go on, Judge Douglas.

人民当家作主的权利

西奥多·罗斯福*

1912年3月20日

现在，摆在美国人民面前的首要问题可以简要地阐述为：美国人民是否适合自我管理、自我统治、自我约束？我相信他们是可以做到的，而我的对手却并不认同。我相信人民有当家作主的权利。我相信美国的大多数普通民众在进行日常自我

---

* 美国第26任总统(1901—1909)。共和党人，原为副总统，1901年接任遇刺身亡的麦金莱总统出任总统，1904年击败民主党、社会党等6个政党的总统候选人获连任。卸任后，1912年创建进步党参选总统未果。本篇摘自他作为进步党总统候选人在纽约市卡内基大厅发表的著名演说。

Theodore Roosevelt

March 20, 1912

The Right of the People to Rule

The great fundamental issue now before our people can be stated briefly. It is, are the American people fit to govern themselves, to rule themselves, to control themselves? I believe they are. My opponents do not. I believe in the right of the people to rule. I believe that the majority of the plain people of the United States will, day in and day out, make fewer mistakes

管理时，比试图管理他们的少数人——无论他们多么训练有素——犯的错误要少。我还相信，美国人民总的来说能够自我约束，并能够从错误中吸取经验。我们的对手只在口头上信奉这一学说，而事实上，他们不择手段地使人民当家作主的信仰徒有虚名。

我领导这场斗争不是为了轰轰烈烈的壮丽场面，我之所以这么做，是因为这场斗争必须有人来领导，否则它根本就不会发生。我乐意与温和、理性的保守派共事，只要他们坚定不移地走向光明。但是，如果他们迟疑不决，背弃光明，与反对势力沆瀣一气，我必定与他们分道扬镳。美国人民不能走回头路，我们必须坚定不移地朝着进步的目标前进。

如果美国人民能够研究一下兄弟共和国的历史，那将是一件好事。法国125年来所蒙受的所有痛苦，皆源于其人民荒唐地分裂成两大阵营：非理性的保守派和

in governing themselves than any smaller class or body of men, no matter what their training, will make in trying to govern them. I believe, again, that the American people are, as a whole, capable of self-control, and of learning by their mistakes. Our opponents pay lip-loyalty to this doctrine; but they show their real beliefs by the way in which they champion every device to make the nominal rule of the people a sham.

I am not leading this fight as a matter of aesthetic pleasure. I am leading because somebody must lead, or else the fight would not be made at all. I prefer to work with moderate, with rational, conservatives, provided only that they do in good faith strive forward toward the light. But when they halt and turn their backs to the light, and sit with the scorners on the seats of reaction, then I must part company with them. We the people cannot turn back. Our aim must be steady, wise progress.

It would be well if our people would study the history of a sister republic. All the woes of France for a century and a quarter have been due to the folly of her people in splitting into the two camps of unreasonable conservatism and

同样非理性的激进派。要是大革命前夕的法国能够听从杜尔哥①的建议,并大力支持的话,那么一切都会顺利发展。然而,那些拥有特权的受益者,波旁王朝②的反动分子,目光短浅的极端保守势力,却拒绝了杜尔哥的建议。之后他们发现,取代杜尔哥的人物是罗伯斯庇尔③。他们摆脱了所有的束缚和改革,获得了20年的自由,而他们所付出的代价是如旋风般席卷而至的红色恐怖。于是,恐怖活动中不受约束的偏激分子诱发了盲目的反动势力,暴动和骚乱接踵而至,暴力的极端势力和暴力的波旁势力交替而来,法国人民经受了痛苦的磨难,他们的目标随之灰飞烟

---

① 杜尔哥(1727—1781),18世纪后半叶法国古典经济学家、重农学派最重要的代表人物之一。
② 指波旁家族在法国建立的王朝(1589—1792,1814—1830),因其祖先受爱玛主教的封地在波旁堡而得名。
③ 罗伯斯庇尔(1758—1794),法国大革命时期著名政治活动家、雅各宾派专政期间的主要当权者。

unreasonable radicalism. Had pre-Revolutionary France listened to men like Turgot, and backed them up, all would have gone well. But the beneficiaries of privilege, the Bourbon reactionaries, the shortsighted ultra-conservatives, turned down Turgot; and then found that instead of him they had obtained Robespierre. They gained twenty years' freedom from all restraint and reform, at the cost of the whirlwind of the red terror; and in their turn the unbridled extremists of the terror induced a blind reaction; and so, with convulsion and oscillation from one extreme to another, with alternations of violent radicalism and violent Bourbonism, the French people went through misery toward a shattered goal. May we profit by the experiences of

灭。但愿我们能从远隔重洋的兄弟共和国的经验中吸取教训,坚定不移地向前迈进,避免一切不羁的极端势力;但愿我国的极端保守派牢记,正是波旁王朝的统治导致了法国大革命①;但愿那些准备投身革命的人士牢记,波旁王朝并非人民和自由的危险的敌人,罗伯斯庇尔也并非如他所说是人民和自由的朋友。

我国不存在爆发革命的危机,但是却充满了严重的不满与不安。为了消除这种状况,我们需要一切智慧、正直和深刻的信念,以便提升我们所拥有的人性和博爱。朋友们,作为美国人,我们的职责是要努力争取社会正义和产业公平,而这种正义和公平是要通过人民当家作主而获得的。这就是我们的终极目标。而实现这个终极目标所采取的手段只是权宜之计,它最终被接受或被拒绝都将取决于其在实际应用中的成败。但是,我们心中必须怀有这个崇高的目标,我们必须全心全意

---

① 指 1789 年在法国爆发的资产阶级革命。

our brother republicans across the water, and go forward steadily, avoiding all wild extremes; and may our ultra-conservatives remember that the rule of the Bourbons brought on the Revolution, and may our would-be revolutionaries remember that no Bourbon was ever such a dangerous enemy of the people and of freedom as the professed friend of both, Robespierre.

There is no danger of a revolution in this country; but there is grave discontent and unrest, and in order to remove them there is need of all the wisdom and probity and deep-seated faith in and purpose to uplift humanity we have at our command. Friends, our task as Americans is to strive for social and industrial justice, achieved through the genuine rule of the people. This is our end, our purpose. The methods for achieving the end are merely expedients, to be finally accepted or rejected according as actual experience shows that they work well or ill. But in our hearts we must have this lofty purpose, and we must strive for it in all earnestness and

地努力争取，否则我们的工作将毫无意义。为了获得成功，我们需要富有创意、远见卓识的领导者，他们胸怀远大理想，努力将理想付诸行动，能用自己的激情点燃人民的斗志。眼下，无论谁是领导者，都只是人民可以使用的一件工具，直到其耗尽一切精力为止。如果他尽忠职守，那么，即使当他精力耗尽，他也不会介怀，这样的大无畏精神，就如同为了赢得胜利而被派往前线牺牲的士兵一样。在争取正义的漫长斗争中，我们大家的口号是奉献。

王凌 译　王建华 校

sincerity, or our work will come to nothing. In order to succeed we need leaders of inspired idealism, leaders to whom are granted great visions, who dream greatly and strive to make their dreams come true; who can kindle the people with the fire from their own burning souls. The leader for the time being, whoever he may be, is but an instrument, to be used until broken and then to be cast aside; and if he is worth his salt he will care no more when he is broken than a soldier cares when he is sent where his life is forfeit in order that the victory may be won. In the long fight for righteousness the watchword for all of us is spend and be spent.

两种政治哲学之间的竞争

本次竞选不仅是两个人之间的竞争,也不仅是两个政党之间的竞争,而是两种政治哲学之间的竞争。

反对党告诉我们,必须进行一场变革,必须树立一种新的理想。他们要的变革,不是由于国民生活的正常发展而引发的

赫伯特·胡佛 *

1932 年 10 月 31 日

* 美国第 31 任总统(1929—1933),共和党人,第一位工程师出身的总统。1928 年击败民主党人史密斯,在"经济繁荣的顶峰"入主白宫,任内爆发经济危机,自由放任经济政策失灵,在 1932 年竞选连任时,不敌富兰克林·罗斯福,在经济危机的狂潮中下台。本篇发表于纽约麦迪逊广场。

Herbert Hoover

October 31, 1932

A Contest Between Two Philosophies of Government

This campaign is more than a contest between two men. It is more than a contest between two parties. It is a contest between two philosophies of government.

We are told by the opposition that we must have a change, that we must have a new deal. It is not the change that comes from normal development of national life to which

变革。他们提出要改变经过几代人的检验和斗争而建立起来的、我们国民生活的整个基础,他们要改变我们的立国原则。反对党的言外之意,是要对我国的经济体制、社会体制和政治体制进行重大变革,不然,他们的言论只不过是空话而已。我知道,在当今国忧民患之际,有很多人在问:我们的社会制度和经济体制,能否履行为美国2500万个家庭提供舒适安全的家庭生活的重要职能?我们的社会制度能否为使我国人民取得重大发展和进步做好准备?我们的政治体制能否产生并维持这种安全和进步?

这些问题正是反对党借以向畏惧和困顿的人民发出呼吁的基础,他们所提议的变革和所谓的新理想,将会破坏美国的基础。

人民在作出判断之前,应该考虑一下基本事实,想一想是否要支持那些将对先辈们奋斗150余年才建立起来的整个制度产生彻底影响的变革,而不应偏听偏

I object or you object, but the proposal to alter the whole foundations of our national life which have been built through generations of testing and struggle, and of the principles upon which we have made this Nation. The expressions of our opponents must refer to important changes in our economic and social system and our system of government; otherwise they would be nothing but vacuous words. And I realize that in this time of distress many of our people are asking whether our social and economic system is incapable of that great primary function of providing security and comfort of life to all of the firesides of 25 million homes in America, whether our social system provides for the fundamental development and progress of our people, and whether our form of government is capable of originating and sustaining that security and progress.

This question is the basis upon which our opponents are appealing to the people in their fear and their distress. They are proposing changes and so-called new deals which would destroy the very foundations of the American system of life.

Our people should consider the primary facts before they come to the judgment—not merely through political agitation, the glitter of promise, and the discouragement of temporary hardships—whether they will support changes which radically affect

信政治鼓动、诱人的承诺或因暂时困难而产生的气馁言论。我们的人民不应用反对党用来表达问题的失望态度来探讨问题。

在过去三年中,我国的经济体制遭到了不正常的冲击,暂时打乱了其正常的运作。从广义上说,这些冲击来自国外。但是我要告诉大家,我们的政体使我们能进一步采取有力的行动,阻止灾难进入我国。它还使我们能够进一步采取措施和计划,而这些措施和计划正在表明,它们能够促成复兴和进步。

反对党趁我们处于困难重重、忧虑不满四起之际,企图兴风作浪。如果我们要洞察他们所鼓吹的变革的全部含义,就务必不要被他们在大选中的陈词滥调和蛊惑人心的公开演讲所蒙蔽。调查一下反对党对不满的群体和地区的呼吁记录后,我们就能发现他们要干什么了。我们必须调查他们在上一次国会会议上由民主党控制的众议院所倡议和通过的议案。我们必须调查他们投票赞成或否决的议案。

the whole system which has been built during these six generations of the toil of our fathers. They should not approach the question in the despair with which our opponents would clothe it.

Our economic system has received abnormal shocks during the last 3 years which have temporarily dislocated its normal functioning. These shocks have in a large sense come from without our borders, and I say to you that our system of government has enabled us to take such strong action as to prevent the disaster which would otherwise have come to this Nation. It has enabled us further to develop measures and programs which are now demonstrating their ability to bring about restoration and progress.

We must go deeper than platitudes and emotional appeals of the public platform in the campaign if we will penetrate to the full significance of the changes which our opponents are attempting to float upon the wave of distress and discontent from the difficulties through which we have passed. We can find what our opponents would do after searching the record of their appeals to discontent, to group and sectional interest. To find that, we must search for them in the legislative acts which they sponsored and passed in the Democratic-controlled House of Representatives in the last session of Congress. We must look into both

我们必须调查他们的总统和副总统候选人是否拒绝批准这些议案。如果他们不拒绝，我们必然得出结论：他们也是其中一分子，他们必定是所提议的大变革的重要组成部分。

除此之外，我们还必须进一步调查候选人本人提出了哪些革命的变革。

让我们花一点时间，看一看现在有人提议应予改革的美国政治体制、社会体制和经济体制。我们的制度是美利坚民族的产物，是我们所建立、世界全部历史上无与伦比的先进国家的经历的产物。这种制度是美国人民所特有的。这种制度完全不同于世界其他国家的制度。这是一种美国制度。这种制度建立在这样一种观念之上：只有通过有秩序的自由，并实行个人自由和机会均等，才能激发个人的创造性和进取心，进而推动进步的历程。

我们的个人主义与欧洲的个人主义有所不同。我们维护机会均等，因而维护

---

the measures for which they voted and in which they were defeated. We must inquire whether or not the Presidential and Vice-Presidential candidates have disavowed those acts. If they have not, we must conclude that they form a portion and are a substantial indication of the profound changes in the new deal which is proposed.

And we must look still further than this as to what revolutionary changes have been proposed by the candidates themselves.

Now, I may pause for a moment and examine the American system of government and of social and economic life which it is now proposed that we should alter. Our system is the product of our race and of our experience in building a Nation to heights unparalleled in the whole history of the world. It is a system peculiar to the American people. It differs essentially from all others in the world. It is an American system. It is rounded on the conception that only through ordered liberty, through freedom to the individual, and equal opportunity to the individual will his initiative and enterprise be summoned to spur the march of national progress.

It is by the maintenance of an equality of opportunity and therefore of a society absolutely fluid in the movement of its human particles that our individualism departs from the individualism of Europe. We resent class distinction because

社会在人类粒子的自由运动中的绝对流动性。我们憎恨阶级差别,因为它使个人无法穿越僵化的阶层而上升,使任何一个阶层都不能由于其粒子的自由上升而活跃起来。因此,在我们的理想中,能干而有雄心的人是能够不断地从社会底层上升到领导地位的。我们反对在美国煽动阶级感情或阶级对立的任何企图。

这种个人自由本身,造就了人们通过各种方式、为了因时而生的各种目的而进行合作行动的必要性和由衷的意愿;它还允许这种自愿合作只要达到目的便自行结束,由为了新的目的而建立的新的联合所取代。

更为重要的是,一种新的观念应运而生,那就是社区内部的自愿合作。合作以完善社会组织;合作以关心贫困者;合作以增进知识、促进科学研究、促进教育;合作以促进经济生活的方方面面。这是政府之外的人民自治;这是个人自由和机会均等在我国基本制度建立以来的一个半世纪中最有力的发展。

there can be no rise for the individual through the frozen strata of classes, and no stratification of classes can take place in a mass that is livened by the free rise of its human particles. Thus in our ideals the able and ambitious are able to rise constantly from the bottom to leadership in the community. We denounce any attempt to stir class feeling or class antagonisms in the United States.

This freedom of the individual creates of itself the necessity and the cheerful willingness of men to act cooperatively in a thousand ways and for every purpose as the occasion requires, and it permits such voluntary cooperation to be dissolved as soon as it has served its purpose and to be replaced by new voluntary associations for new purposes.

There has thus grown within us, to gigantic importance, a new conception. That is the conception of voluntary cooperation within the community; cooperation to perfect the social organizations; cooperation for the care of those in distress; cooperation for the advancement of knowledge, of scientific research, of education; cooperative action in a thousand directions for the advancement of economic life. This is self-government by the people outside of the Government. It is the most powerful development of individual freedom and equality of opportunity that has taken place in the century and a half since our fundamental institutions were founded.

正是在这种合作及其责任感的进一步发展过程中,我们找到了解决很多复杂问题的办法,而不是把政府的行政管理扩大到经济生活和社会生活中去。政府的最大职能就是建立这种合作。政府的最坚决的行动应该是拒绝扩大官僚机构。通过政府的帮助,我们已经发展了大合作机构,以促进和保护个人和小企业单位的利益。联邦储备银行巩固并支持了小银行;农业局巩固并支持了农场合作;国内贷款银行动员建立了并贷款给各社团和储蓄银行;联邦土地银行使各土地抵押协会获得独立和力量;救济穷人的大动员;动员工商业采取恢复措施,等等。这几十种举措都不是社会主义的——它们是保护自由人发展的基础。这是一种合众为一的美国制度,其主要观念不是对人的兵营式的管理。而是自由人的合作。它是建立在个人对社会的责任感,地方政府对州、州对联邦政府的责任感之上的。

它是建立在一种为维护个人机会均等而设立的特殊的自治观念上的。它通过

It is in the further development of this cooperation and in a sense of its responsibility that we should find solution for many of the complex problems, and not by the extension of the Government into our economic and social life. The greatest function a government can perform is to build up that cooperation, and its most resolute action should be to deny the extension of bureaucracy. We have developed great agencies of cooperation by the assistance of the Government which do promote and protect the interests of individuals and the smaller units of business: the Federal Reserve System, in its strengthening and support of the smaller banks; the Farm Board, in its strengthening and support of the farm cooperatives; the home loan banks, in the mobilizing of building and loan associations and savings banks; the Federal land banks, in giving independence and strength to land mortgage associations; the great mobilization of relief to distress, the mobilization of business and industry in measures of recovery from this depression, and a score of other activities that are not socialism, and they are not the Government in business. The primary conception of this whole American system is not the ordering of men but the cooperation of free men. It is rounded upon the conception of responsibility of the individual to the community, of the responsibility of local government to the State, of the State to the National Government.

Now, our American system is rounded on a peculiar conception of self-

分权,引发并维护这些责任感。政府集权只会损害责任感,并将破坏国家制度。

我们的政府与以往一切政府的不同之处,不仅在于分权,还在于立法、行政、司法各政府部门之间的职能的分立。

我们的政府是建立在这样一种观念上的:在紧急关头,当种种势力脱离个人的或其他合作行动的控制、脱离地方社区和州的控制时,联邦政府所保留的权力将被用来采取行动保护社会。但是,当这些势力不复存在,就必须恢复州、地方和个人的责任。

科学发现和科学新发明的前进步伐,每年都对政府提出新问题,提出新的社会秩序问题。经常出现的问题是,面对庞大的新工具的发展,民主制度是否能够继续成为自己家园的主人,是否能够维护我们美国制度的基本原则。我认为它能够;我还认为,我国的制度已经表明,它的效率和优越性超过人类迄今所发明的任何

government designed to maintain an equality of opportunity to the individual, and through decentralization it brings about and maintains these responsibilities. The centralization of government will undermine these responsibilities and will destroy the system itself.

Our Government differs from all previous conceptions, not only in the decentralization but also in the independence of the judicial arm of the Government.

Our Government is rounded on a conception that in times of great emergency, when forces are running beyond the control of individuals or cooperative action, beyond the control of local communities or the States, then the great reserve powers of the Federal Government should be brought into action to protect the people. But when these forces have ceased there must be a return to State, local, and individual responsibility.

The implacable march of scientific discovery with its train of new inventions presents every year new problems to government and new problems to the social order. Questions often arise whether, in the face of the growth of these new and gigantic tools, democracy can remain master in its own house and can preserve the fundamentals of our American system. I contend that it can, and I contend that this American system of ours has demonstrated its validity and superiority

其他制度。面对我国历史上最大的考验——也就是我们在过去三年中所面临的紧急局势,它已经表明了这一点。

由于世界大战及其余波,欧洲许多国家暴露了政治和经济上的缺陷,并最终导致了它们制度的崩溃。与此同时,我们对经济生活和社会生活的细心调整,也受到了史无前例的冲击。对于这一点,没有人比你们纽约人了解得更清楚了,没有人比你们更清楚其中的原因了。危机如此之大,以至于很多大银行企图直接或间接地把它们的资产兑换成黄金或黄金等价物。其结果是,它们实际上已经停止行使其作为信贷机构的职能了。我们的很多公民企图把自己的资金抽逃到其他国家;他们中的很多人企图大量囤积黄金。这些仅仅表明,信任正在迅速丧失,他们不相信政府能够战胜这些力量。

然而,这些力量被战胜了——也许是在有限的范围内。这就表明,在共和党坚

over any system yet invented by human mind. It has demonstrated it in the face of the greatest test of peacetime history—that is the emergency which we have passed in the last 3 years.

When the political and economic weakness of many nations of Europe, the result of the World War and its aftermath, finally culminated in the collapse of their institutions, the delicate adjustments of our economic and social and governmental life received a shock unparalleled in our history. No one knows that better than you of New York. No one knows its causes better than you. That the crisis was so great that many of the leading banks sought directly or indirectly to convert their assets into gold or its equivalent with the result that they practically ceased to function as credit institutions is known to you; that many of our citizens sought flight for their capital to other countries; that many of them attempted to hoard gold in large amounts you know. These were but superficial indications of the flight of confidence and the belief that our Government could not overcome these forces.

Yet these forces were overcome—perhaps by narrow margins. It demonstrates what the courage of a nation can accomplish under the resolute leadership of the Republican Party. And I say the Republican Party because our opponents,

定的领导下,一个勇敢的民族能够有所作为。我之所以说共和党,是因为民主党在危机之前和危机之中没有提出什么建设性的纲领,虽然他们中有些人出于爱国心而支持我们的纲领。后来,民主党在他们把持的众议院中形成了自己的真实思想和看法。但是他们的想法具有破坏性,必须予以击败,因为它们将导致破坏而不是治愈。

尽管遇到这一切阻挠,我们仍取得了胜利。我们的政体确已证明它堪负重任。我们拯救了国家,使其免遭20余年的混乱无序和衰退;我们保护了储蓄存款和保单,为人民提供了维持家庭的难得机会。我们保持了政府的完整和美元的信誉。我们采取了种种措施,而这些措施如今正使我们获得恢复。就业、农业和商业——所有这一切都表明我们的巨大创伤正在逐步——虽然缓慢——地痊愈。

因此,我认为今天的问题是继续执行这些措施和政策,以使上述美国制度恢

before and during the crisis, proposed no constructive program, though some of their members patriotically supported ours. Later on in the critical period, the Democratic House of Representatives did develop the real thought and ideas of the Democratic Party. They were so destructive that they had to be defeated. They did delay the healing of our wounds.

Now, in spite of all these obstructions we did succeed. Our form of government did prove itself equal to the task. We saved this Nation from a generation of chaos and degeneration; we preserved the savings, the insurance policies, gave a fighting chance to men to hold their homes. We saved the integrity of our Government and the honesty of the American dollar. And we installed measures which today are bringing back recovery. Employment, agriculture, and business—all of these show the steady, if slow, healing of an enormous wound.

I therefore contend that the problem of today is to continue these measures and policies to restore the American system to its normal functioning, to repair the

复其正常的职能,愈合其所蒙受的创伤,并纠正那些将会导致这种制度失败的种种弱点和邪恶。若开始一系列深刻的变革,试图追求那些在本次大选中提出的不成熟的所谓新政,将会削弱和破坏美国的制度,并一再延误复兴的机会。

同胞们,反对党的提议意味着要在美国生活中进行一场深刻的变革——他们不是借助具体的甚至糟糕的提议,而是含沙射影、推诿回避。究其精神实质,主要是想彻底背离我们有着150年之久的、使这个国家成为世界上最伟大的国家的基础。本次大选不仅是执政党和在野党的轮流执政。它意味着决定我们国家在未来一个世纪所要采取的方向。

我的美国观是:美国是这样一片国土,在那儿,男男女女行进在有序的自由中;他们可以享受财富的恩惠,这些财富不是集中在少数人手中,而是分散在全体人民的生活中。在那儿,他们建立并保护自己的家,为他们的孩子提供美国生活的

wounds it has received, to correct the weaknesses and evils which would defeat that system. To enter upon a series of deep changes now, to embark upon this inchoate new deal which has been propounded in this campaign would not only undermine and destroy our American system but it will delay for months and years the possibility of recovery.

My countrymen, the proposals of our opponents represent a profound change in American life—less in concrete proposal, bad as that may be, than by implication and by evasion. Dominantly in their spirit they represent a radical departure from the foundations of 150 years which have made this the greatest Nation in the world. This election is not a mere shift from the ins to the outs. It means the determining of the course of our Nation over a century to come.

Now, my conception of America is a land where men and women may walk in ordered liberty, where they may enjoy the advantages of wealth not concentrated in the hands of a few but diffused through the opportunity of all, where they build and safeguard their homes, give to their children the full opportunities of American life, where every man shall be respected in the faith that his conscience and his

全部机会。在那儿，人人受到尊敬，相信良知将会指引他前进。在那里，人们的自由有保障，他们有闲暇、有冲动去寻求更加丰富的人生。这将使男男女女的能量得到释放，获得更加广阔的视野和更加远大的理想。这将导致越来越多的服务机会，不仅是我国同胞之间的相互服务，而且是我们国家对世界的服务。这将导致身体健康，精神开朗，朝气蓬勃，思想开放，目光远大，慷慨大方，富有同情心。但是这一切必须建立在我们过去经历的基础上，建立在使我们国家成为一个伟大国家的基础上。它必须是我们真正的美国制度的产物。

王　寅　译

heart direct him to follow, and where people secure in their liberty shall have leisure and impulse to seek a fuller life. That leads to the release of the energies of men and women, to the wider vision and higher hope. It leads to opportunity for greater and greater service not alone of man to man in our country but from our country to the world. It leads to health in body and a spirit unfettered, youthful, eager with a vision stretching beyond the farthest horizons with a mind open and sympathetic and generous. But that must be built upon our experience with the past, upon the foundations which have made this country great. It must be the product of the development of our truly American system.

我保证为美国人民实施新政

富兰克林·罗斯福*

1932年7月2日

诸位经受了6天折腾仍愿意留下①，我对此深表感谢。我深知，诸位和我都曾夜不能寐。我来迟了，我很懊悔，但我无法呼风唤雨，我只能庆幸自己曾在海军中受过训练。②

---

* 美国第32任总统(1933—1945)，民主党人，唯一一位任期超过2届并连任4届的总统。任内力挽经济危机狂澜，推行著名的"新政"，太平洋战争爆发后，领导美国加入反法西斯战争。他在1932年民主党大会上获得总统候选人提名后发表了此篇演说，充分表达了他要破旧立新的决心。

① 指民主党大会多次出现僵局，罗斯福在第4轮投票中才胜出。

② 指罗斯福赶乘飞机从纽约奥尔巴尼飞赴芝加哥会场，受尽逆风飞行之苦，而且晚到了几小时。

Franklin Roosevelt

July 2, 1932

Pledge to a New Deal for the American People

I appreciate your willingness after these six arduous days to remain here, for I know well the sleepless hours which you and I have had. I regret that I am late, but I have no control over the winds of Heaven and could only be thankful for my Navy training.

一个竞争总统提名的人在党的全国大会上露面,并被正式告知他已获得提名,这一举动不但史无前例,而且异乎寻常。但目前正是史无前例和异乎寻常的时刻。因此,我以打破陋习来投身我所面临的任务。这个陋习就是,候选人应当假装对事态进展一无所知,直到过了很多个星期,接到正式通知为止。

朋友们,但愿此举表达了我的一个心愿:我要以诚待人,绝不虚情假意,绝不愚蠢地对这次竞选运动的真相闭目塞听。我知道诸位已提名我为总统候选人,我来到这里,就是为了感谢大家给了我这份殊荣。

但愿这也象征着打破了传统。但愿从今以后,打破传统能成为本党的任务。我们要打破愚蠢的传统,而让共和党领导人去打破自己的诺言,他们在这方面有着高超的技艺。

让我们在此时此地下定决心,要恢复我国中断的征程,使我国重新沿着真正

The appearance before a National Convention of its nominee for President, to be formally notified of his selection, is unprecedented and unusual, but these are unprecedented and unusual times. I have started out on the tasks that lie ahead by breaking the absurd traditions that the candidate should remain in professed ignorance of what has happened for weeks until he is formally notified of that event many weeks later.

My friends, may this be the symbol of my intention to be honest and to avoid all hypocrisy or sham, to avoid all silly shutting of the eyes to the truth in this campaign. You have nominated me and I know it, and I am here to thank you for the honor.

Let it also be symbolic that in so doing I broke traditions. Let it be from now on the task of our Party to break foolish traditions. We will break foolish traditions and leave it to the Republican leadership, far more skilled in that art, to break promises.

Let us now and here highly resolve to resume the country's interrupted

的进步、公正、平等之路,沿着对所有公民不论其伟大或渺小都一律平等之路前进。在那次中断的征程上,一位不屈不挠的领袖已离开人世,但今天他的精神仍然活着。感谢上帝! 他的许多助手仍然同我们在一起,仍然在给我们提出明智的建议。让我们相信,无论我们做什么,伍德罗·威尔逊①总司令伟大的、不屈不挠的、一往无前的、不断革新的精神仍然同我们在一起。

在这次竞选活动中,我有很多问题要尽早澄清自己的立场。对于那份备受赞赏的文献,即大家已通过的、观点鲜明的政纲,我百分之百予以赞同。

我可以向大家保证,在这次竞选中,我对任何重大问题都将毫不含糊地阐明自己的立场。

在投入新的战斗之际,让我们大家永远牢记党的理想:无论从传统来说,还是

---

① 美国民主党人,第 28 任总统(1913—1921),曾领导美国参加第一次世界大战。

---

march along the path of real progress, of real justice, of real equality for all of our citizens, great and small. Our indomitable leader in that interrupted march is no longer with us, but there still survives today his spirit. Many of his captains, thank God, are still with us, to give us wise counsel. Let us feel that in everything we do there still lives with us, if not the body, the great indomitable, unquenchable, progressive soul of our Commander-in-Chief, Woodrow Wilson.

I have many things on which I want to make my position clear at the earliest possible moment in this campaign. That admirable document, the platform which you have adopted, is clear. I accept it 100 percent.

And you can accept my pledge that I will leave no doubt or ambiguity on where I stand on any question of moment in this campaign.

As we enter this new battle, let us keep always present with us some of the ideals of the Party: The fact that the Democratic Party by tradition and by the

从历史发展的逻辑来说，民主党在过去和现在都既是自由主义和进步的旗手，同时又是维护我国制度安全的保证。如果我党失去了这种号召力，朋友们请记住，由于共和党领导人的失败而引起的怨恨就会变成丧失理智的激进主义。

与前几次经济萧条不同，本次萧条中有一个重要的社会现象，那就是以往司空见惯的骚乱情况这次并不多见。

野蛮的激进主义只赢得了少数信徒。在当前物资奇缺的日子里，我国千百万人民尽管备受折磨，却始终秩序井然，满怀希望。我向同胞们表示最崇高的敬意。我们如果不能为他们提供新的转机，那不仅是辜负他们的希望，而且是误解他们的耐心。

对激进主义的危险作出反应会导致灾难。作出反应并不能阻止激进主义。这样做是一种挑战、一种挑衅。避免激进主义的危险只有一条路，即提出一种可行的

continuing logic of history, past and present, is the bearer of liberalism and of progress and at the same time of safety to our institutions. And if this appeal fails, remember well, my friends, that a resentment against the failure of Republican leadership may degenerate into unreasoning radicalism.

The great social phenomenon of this depression, unlike others before it, is that it has produced but a few of the disorderly manifestations that too often attend upon such times.

Wild radicalism has made few converts, and the greatest tribute that I can pay to my countrymen is that in these days of crushing want there persists an orderly and hopeful spirit on the part of the millions of our people who have suffered so much. To fail to offer them a new chance is not only to betray their hopes but to misunderstand their patience.

To meet by reaction that danger of radicalism is to invite disaster. Reaction is no barrier to the radical. It is a challenge, a provocation. The way to meet that danger is to offer a workable program of reconstruction, and the party to offer it

重建方案,并且应由诚实的政党提出这个方案。

只有这样,才能正确地既避免作出盲目反应,又不至于堕入想入非非的、漫不经心的、不负责任的乐观主义。

对于政府在影响经济和社会生活方面的职责,存在着两种观点。一种观点认为应帮助有天赋的少数人,并希望他们的昌盛会在某种程度上传递给劳工、农民和小业主。这种理论属于托利党人,而我希望,大多数托利分子早已在1776年就离开我国了。①

但这不是,永远也不是民主党的理论。现在不是恐惧的时候,不是对抗的时候,不是怯懦的时候。此时此地,我邀请所有名义上的共和党人同我携起手来,因为他们从良心上对自己的党的领袖的折腾和失败感到不安;同样,我也对徒有虚

---

① 指1776年美国在独立战争后摆脱了英国的殖民统治,暗喻共和党的保守政策不得人心。

is the party with clean hands.

This, and this only, is a proper protection against blind reaction on the one hand and an improvised, hit-or-miss, irresponsible opportunism on the other.

There are two ways of viewing the Government's duty in matters affecting economic and social life. The first sees to it that a favored few are helped and hopes that some of their prosperity will leak through, sift through, to labor, to the farmer, to the small business man. That theory belongs to the party of Toryism, and I had hoped that most of the Tories left this country in 1776.

But it is not and never will be the theory of the Democratic Party. This is no time for fear, for reaction or for timidity. Here and now I invite those nominal Republicans who find that their conscience cannot be squared with the groping and the failure of their party leaders to join hands with us; here and now, in equal measure, I warn those nominal Democrats who squint at the future with their

名的民主党人提出警告,因为他们对未来半信半疑,墨守成规,对新时代赋予的责任浑然不觉,他们的步调已不能与本党保持一致。

是的,美国人民今年要的是真正的选择,而不是在两个名称之间的选择。我们的党必须具有自由主义思想,必须采取有计划的行动,必须用开明的国际观点,为我国绝大多数公民谋取最大利益。

当前,萧条状况极其严重,在现代史上闻所未闻。因此,这次竞选运动的关键应该是对这一明确的事实作出解答。这是无法回避的,这是时代的决定。仅仅说全世界都发生了萧条是无济于事的——共和党领导人在解释自己屡屡违背诺言、长期毫无行动时正是这样说的。但他们对1928年的经济繁荣却另有一番解释。人民不会忘记,他们当时声称,繁荣是由共和党人总统和共和党人控制的国会所带来的国内产物。假如他们能声称自己是繁荣的开拓者,就不能否认他们也是萧条的

faces turned toward the past, and who feel no responsibility to the demands of the new time, that they are out of step with their Party.

Yes, the people of this country want a genuine choice this year, not a choice between two names for the same reactionary doctrine. Ours must be a party of liberal thought, of planned action, of enlightened international outlook, and of the greatest good to the greatest number of our citizens.

Now it is inevitable—and the choice is that of the times—it is inevitable that the main issue of this campaign should revolve about the clear fact of our economic condition, a depression so deep that it is without precedent in modern history. It will not do merely to state, as do Republican leaders to explain their broken promises of continued inaction, that the depression is worldwide. That was not their explanation of the apparent prosperity of 1928. The people will not forget the claim made by them then that prosperity was only a domestic product manufactured by a Republican President and a Republican Congress. If they claim

始作俑者。

今天，我无法阐述所有问题，而只谈几个重要问题。让我们稍微看一看最近的历史和一种简单的经济学——诸位和我以及普通人所谈论的经济学。

我们知道，在1929年以前的若干年，我国经历了一个建设和通货膨胀的周期。整整10年，我们根据弥补战争损耗①的理论发展生产，而实际上远远超出了这一限度，并超出了我们的自然增长和正常增长的限度。现在，值得回忆的是——冷酷的金融数字证实了这一点——在那段时期，尽管数字表明生产成本已极大下降，但消费者必须支付的价格却只微微下降或没有下降。公司获得了丰厚的利润，却很少用于降低价格——消费者被遗忘了；很少用于增加工资——工人被遗忘了；根本谈不上把充足的部分用于支付红利——持股人被遗忘了。

---

①指第一次世界大战给美国造成了损失。

---

paternity for the one they cannot deny paternity for the other.

I cannot take up all the problems today. I want to touch on a few that are vital. Let us look a little at the recent history and the simple economics, the kind of economics that you and I and the average man and woman talk.

In the years before 1929 we know that this country had completed a vast cycle of building and inflation; for ten years we expanded on the theory of repairing the wastes of the War, but actually expanding far beyond that, and also beyond our natural and normal growth. Now it is worth remembering, and the cold figures of finance prove it, that during that time there was little or no drop in the prices that the consumer had to pay, although those same figures proved that the cost of production fell very greatly; corporate profit resulting from this period was enormous; at the same time little of that profit was devoted to the reduction of prices. The consumer was forgotten. Very little of it went into increased wages; the worker was forgotten, and by no means an adequate proportion was even paid out in dividends—the stockholder was forgotten.

顺便说一句,在那些年,政府极少通过征税把上述利润用于慈善事业。

结果如何呢?公司获得了巨额盈余——史无前例的巨额盈余。那么,在疯狂投机的符咒的支配下,这些盈余到哪里去了呢?让我们用数字所证实的和我们所能懂的经济学来谈一谈。瞧,这些盈余主要有两大流向:其一,流向现在已徒有躯壳的不必要的新工厂;其二,直接通过公司,或间接通过银行,流向华尔街的活期借贷市场。这些都是事实。为什么要视而不见?

接着便发生了崩溃。诸位都知道崩溃的过程。对不必要的工厂所进行的投资变得不值分文。人们失去了工作;购买力枯竭了;银行害怕了,开始索债。有钱人怕失去钱。信贷业萎缩了。工业停顿了。商业衰退了。失业率直线上升。

于是,轮到我们站出来了。

在历史上,全体人民的利益从未像今天这样在同一个经济问题上如此紧密地

And, incidentally, very little of it was taken by taxation to the beneficent Government of those years.

What was the result? Enormous corporate surpluses piled up—the most stupendous in history. Where, under the spell of delirious speculation, did those surpluses go? Let us talk economics that the figures prove and that we can understand. Why, they went chiefly in two directions: first, into new and unnecessary plants which now stand stark and idle; and second, into the call-money market of Wall Street, either directly by the corporations, or indirectly through the banks. Those are the facts. Why blink at them?

Then came the crash. You know the story. Surpluses invested in unnecessary plants became idle. Men lost their jobs; purchasing power dried up; banks became frightened and started calling loans. Those who had money were afraid to part with it. Credit contracted. Industry stopped. Commerce declined, and unemployment mounted.

And there we are today.

Never in history have the interests of all the people been so united in a

联系起来。比如,诸位可以想象,我国千百万公民拥有大批财产,这些财产都以证券和抵押形式体现于信贷:各级政府包括联邦政府、州政府、市政府和县政府所发行的各种证券;工业公司和公用事业公司的证券;农场和城市的房地产抵押;最后,还有国家对铁路的巨额投资。我们应如何看待上述各个团体的安全问题呢?我们深知,在我们复杂的、互为关联的信贷结构中,任何一个信贷团体的垮台,都会导致整个结构的垮台。一个团体的危险,就是全体的危险。

我要问,华盛顿当局是如何对待上述信贷团体之间的相互关系的呢?答案非常清楚,它根本没有认识到存在着那种相互关系。我国人民要问,华盛顿当局为什么不理解,应该把所有这些团体——每一个团体,无论它处于金字塔顶层还是底层,都统一起来考虑呢?每一个团体都与其他团体休戚相关;每一个团体都会对整个金融结构产生影响。

single economic problem. Picture to yourself, for instance, the great groups of property owned by millions of our citizens, represented by credits issued in the form of bonds and mortgages—Government bonds of all kinds, Federal, State, county, municipal; bonds of industrial companies, of utility companies; mortgages on real estate in farms and cities, and finally the vast investments of the Nation in the railroads. What is the measure of the security of each of those groups? We know well that in our complicated, interrelated credit structure if any one of these credit groups collapses they may all collapse. Danger to one is danger to all.

How, I ask, has the present Administration in Washington treated the interrelationship of these credit groups? The answer is clear: It has not recognized that interrelationship existed at all. Why, the Nation asks, has Washington failed to understand that all of these groups, each and every one, the top of the pyramid and the bottom of the pyramid, must be considered together, that each and every one of them is dependent on every other; each and every one of them affecting the whole financial fabric?

朋友们,无论从治国的才能还是从治国的目标而言,都要求我们同时救济所有的人。

让我简单地谈谈税收问题——由我们大家掏腰包供各级政府开支的税收问题。

我对税收略知一二。3年来,我在美国东奔西跑进行宣传,说政府的开支——无论联邦政府、州政府还是地方政府的开支都太大了。我不会停止宣传。作为一项紧急行动计划,我们必须废除不起作用的官职。我们必须取消不必要的政府职能,取消那些对保持政府的连续性实际上无足轻重的职能。我们必须合并政府的下属部门,并且像每个公民那样,放弃再也无力承担的奢侈。

我们要在华盛顿做出榜样,以便为地方政府指明节俭之路。让我们牢记:在各州向联邦交纳的每一美元税收中,有40美分纳入了华盛顿特区的财政开支,只有

Statesmanship and vision, my friends, require relief to all at the same time.

Just one word or two on taxes, the taxes that all of us pay toward the cost of Government of all kinds.

I know something of taxes. For three long years I have been going up and down this country preaching that Government—Federal and State and local—costs too much. I shall not stop that preaching. As an immediate program of action we must abolish useless offices. We must eliminate unnecessary functions of Government—functions, in fact, that are not definitely essential to the continuance of Government. We must merge, we must consolidate subdivisions of Government, and, like the private citizen, give up luxuries which we can no longer afford.

By our example at Washington itself, we shall have the opportunity of pointing the way of economy to local government, for let us remember well that out of every tax dollar in the average State in this Nation, 40 cents enter the treasury in Washington,

10或12美分汇入州的资本,而其余48美分则被地方政府,即被市、镇和县政府花费掉了。

朋友们,我要向你们并通过你们建议,各级政府不分大小都不可借债度日,合众国总统及其内阁必须树立榜样。

说到明确地树立榜样,我要祝贺大会勇敢地、大无畏地把绝大多数与会者对第18条修正案①的真实想法写入了原则宣言。本次大会要求取消该条修正案;你们的候选人要求取消该条修正案;我坚信,美利坚合众国也要求取消该条修正案。

现在谈一谈失业问题,顺便提一提农业问题。我赞成实施某种公共工程,作为刺激就业的另一项应急措施,也作为支付此种工程费用的证券的担保;但我也已

---

① 即美国宪法第 18 条修正案,长期名存实亡,1933 年被废除。该条修正案规定:"禁止在合众国及其所辖一切领土内酿造、出售和运送作为饮料的致醉酒类,并禁止该类酒进口或出口。"

D. C., 10 or 12 cents only go to the State capitals, and 48 cents are consumed by the costs of local government in counties and cities and towns.

I propose to you, my friends, and through you, that Government of all kinds, big and little, be made solvent and that the example be set by the President of the United States and his Cabinet.

And talking about setting a definite example, I congratulate this convention for having had the courage fearlessly to write into its declaration of principles what an overwhelming majority here assembled really thinks about the 18th Amendment. This convention wants repeal. Your candidate wants repeal. And I am confident that the United States of America wants repeal.

And now one word about unemployment, and incidentally about agriculture. I have favored the use of certain types of public works as a further emergency means of stimulating employment and the issuance of bonds to pay for such public works, but I have pointed out that no economic end is served if we

经指出,如果我们并非为了必要目的而建设,那么任何经济手段也无济于事。当然,如果通过发行证券来筹集资金,这种工程就应尽可能做到自给自足。为了尽可能扩大受益面,我们必须采取坚决的步骤来压缩所需的工作日。

让我们运用我们的常识和企业意识吧。仅举一个例子,①我们知道,通过植树造林,把成千上万公顷荒地改造成林地,这个宏伟计划,无论对于解决失业问题还是农业问题,都是一个大有希望的应急救济措施。仅在密西西比河以东,在那些杂草丛生的被废弃的农场和采伐过的林地,就有上千万公顷土地。欧洲各国都有明确的土地政策,而且这些政策已持续了几代人之久。而美国却没有。正因为如此,我们才面对着土壤受侵蚀和森林遭灾害的景象。显而易见,经济上的远见卓识和眼前的就业问题都要求我们在这一大片土地上植树造林。

---

① 以下所谈,后来成为著名的田纳西河流域工程的组成部分。

merely build without building for a necessary purpose. Such works, of course, should insofar as possible be self-sustaining if they are to be financed by the issuing of bonds. So as to spread the points of all kinds as widely as possible, we must take definite steps to shorten the working day and the working week.

Let us use common sense and business sense. Just as one example, we know that a very hopeful and immediate means of relief, both for the unemployed and for agriculture, will come from a wide plan of the converting of many millions of acres of marginal and unused land into timberland through reforestation. There are tens of millions of acres east of the Mississippi River alone in abandoned farms, in cut-over land, now growing up in worthless brush. Why, every European Nation has a definite land policy, and has had one for generations. We have none. Having none, we face a future of soil erosion and timber famine. It is clear that economic foresight and immediate employment march hand in hand in the call for the reforestation of these vast areas.

这样做就能解决100万人的就业问题。这种公共工程是自给自足的,能通过发行证券来筹集资金,因为大批农作物的成长为投资者提供了足够的安全感。

不错,我有一个非常明确的、用这种方法提供就业机会的方法。

我用过这个方法,今天我正在纽约州使用这个方法。我知道,民主党能在全国卓有成效地采用这个方法。它将使人们重新行动起来,它也是我们将采取行动的一个例子。

作为救济农业的另一项措施,我们完全知道——但我们是否已如此明确地说过——应该立即废除那些为减少农产品剩余,而迫使联邦政府进入农产品购销和投机市场的法律条文。坚持这些条文的人正是那些要求政府不干预企业的人。切实可行地帮助农民的办法是,一方面要减轻压在他们肩上的、使他们穷困潦倒的负担;另一方面要采取措施减少市场上的剩余农产品。我们的目标是根据世界农

In so doing, employment can be given to a million men. That is the kind of public work that is self-sustaining, and therefore capable of being financed by the issuance of bonds which are made secure by the fact that the growth of tremendous crops will provide adequate security for the investment.

Yes, I have a very definite program for providing employment by that means.

I have done it, and I am doing it today in the State of New York. I know that the Democratic Party can do it successfully in the Nation. That will put men to work, and that is an example of the action that we are going to have.

Now as a further aid to agriculture, we know perfectly well—but have we come out and said so clearly and distinctly? —we should repeal immediately those provisions of law that compel the Federal Government to go into the market to purchase, to sell, to speculate in farm products in a futile attempt to reduce farm surpluses. And they are the people who are talking of keeping Government out of business. The practical way to help the farmer is by an arrangement that will, in addition to lightening some of the impoverishing burdens from his back, do something toward the reduction of the surpluses of staple commodities that hang on the market. It should be our aim to add to the world prices of staple products

作物价格，采取合理的关税保护措施，使农业也得到工业那样的保护。

我能肯定，我国农民由此就可以立即获得收益，而作为一种交换条件，他们最终也会同意妥善地安排生产，以减少农产品剩余，而且今后不必依赖向国外倾销来维持国内价格。别的国家已取得那样的成果，美国为什么不能呢？

总的来说，农场领导人和农业经济学家都已同意，根据这个原则而制定的计划是可取的，是恢复农业的第一步。它本身并不是一个完整的计划，但从长远来看，它将有助于驱除农产品剩余的阴影，避免世界性倾销的持久威胁。

农民最终能自愿地减少农产品剩余是我们的目标之一。但是，长期存在的农产品剩余和目前的压力，使我们有必要采取措施来医治目前的创伤。

这样一个计划，我的朋友们，不需要政府花钱，也不会使政府干预企业或从事投机。

the amount of a reasonable tariff protection, to give agriculture the same protection that industry has today.

And in exchange for this immediately increased return I am sure that the farmers of this Nation would agree ultimately to such planning of their production as would reduce the surpluses and make it unnecessary in later years to depend on dumping those surpluses abroad in order to support domestic prices. That result has been accomplished in other Nations; why not in America, too?

Farm leaders and farm economists, generally, agree that a plan based on that principle is a desirable first step in the reconstruction of agriculture. It does not in itself furnish a complete program, but it will serve in great measure in the long run to remove the pall of a surplus without the continued perpetual threat of world dumping.

Final voluntary reduction of surplus is a part of our objective, but the long continuance and the present burden of existing surpluses make it necessary to repair great damage of the present by immediate emergency measures.

Such a plan as that, my friends, does not cost the Government any money, nor does it keep the Government in business or in speculation.

至于这个法规①的具体措辞,我相信民主党已做好准备,按照负责的农场团体所同意的任何意见办理。这是一个十分有效的原则,我再次要求大家行动起来。

关于农民我还要说几句。我知道,这个大厅里每一位住在城里的代表都明白我为什么要强调农民。因为我国有一半人口,即有5000多万人依靠农业;而且,我的朋友们,如果这5000万人没有钱——没有现金来买城里生产的东西,城市也要蒙受同样的或更大的痛苦。

因此,我们今年打算使选民们懂得,这个国家不仅是独立的国家,而且,如果我们要存在下去,就一定要成为相互依存的国家——乡镇和城市、北方和南方、东部和西部。这就是我们的目标,这个目标将会被我国人民所理解,无论他们居住在哪里。

①即日后实施的《农业调整法》。

As to the actual wording of a bill, I believe that the Democratic Party stands ready to be guided by whatever the responsible farm groups themselves agree on. That is a principle that is sound; and again I ask for action.

One more word about the farmer, and I know that every delegate in this hall who lives in the city knows why I lay emphasis on the farmer. It is because one-half of our population, over 50,000,000 people, are dependent on agriculture; and, my friends, if those 50,000,000 people have no money, no cash, to buy what is produced in the city, the city suffers to an equal or greater extent.

That is why we are going to make the voters understand this year that this Nation is not merely a Nation of independence, but it is, if we are to survive, bound to be a Nation of interdependence—town and city, and North and South, East and West. That is our goal, and that goal will be understood by the people of this country no matter where they live.

实际上,我国那一半依靠农业的人口的购买力已经荡然无存。农场抵押今天已接近100亿美元,每年应付的利息多达5600万美元。但事情还没有完。地方政府的奢侈和无效率,引起了额外的税收重负。我们最迫切的任务应该是减轻由抵押而产生的利息重负。

对于我国城乡的小企业主,我打算也这样做。我们能够减轻他们的重负,开发他们的购买力。朋友们,把高利率的幽灵赶走吧!把逾期未付的幽灵尽快赶走吧!我们要拯救家庭和家宅,让成千上万个有自尊心的家庭安居乐业,把萦绕我们脑际的危及安全的恐惧赶走。

综观无数件印刷品,无数次演说、反诘、辩护,以及华盛顿和各州随心所欲构想出来的无数个计划,一个既重要又简单的事实就变得显而易见:在共和党人担任领导的过去10年间,通过关税手段,一个1.2亿人口的国家已在其边境周围建起

Yes, the purchasing power of that half of our population dependent on agriculture is gone. Farm mortgages reach nearly ten billions of dollars today and interest charges on that alone are $560,000,000 a year. But that is not all. The tax burden caused by extravagant and inefficient local government is an additional factor. Our most immediate concern should be to reduce the interest burden on these mortgages.

I aim to do the same thing, for the small home-owner in our cities and villages. We can lighten his burden and develop his purchasing power. Take away, my friends, that spectre of too high an interest rate. Take away that spectre of the due date just a short time away. Save homes; save homes for thousands of self-respecting families, and drive out that spectre of insecurity from our midst.

Out of all the tons of printed paper, out of all the hours of oratory, the recriminations, the defenses, the happy-thought plans in Washington and in every State, there emerges one great, simple, crystal-pure fact that during the past ten years a Nation of 120,000,000 people has been led by the Republican leaders to erect an impregnable barbed wire entanglement around its borders

了固若金汤的铁丝网工事,把自己同全世界人民隔离了开来。我完全赞同本次大会政纲中所作的关税声明。它将对美国企业和劳工起到保护作用。我们过去的行动已招致外国的报复。我提议向这些国家发出邀请,大家捐弃前嫌,友好地进行谈判,为复兴世界贸易而制订计划。

到企业主的家里看看吧,他知道关税给自己带来了什么。到工厂工人的家里看看吧,他知道为什么货物积压滞销。到农民的家里看看吧,他知道关税如何使自己毁于一旦。

我们终于睁大了眼睛。美国人民终于准备承认共和党领导人错了,而民主党是对的。

我的纲领——我只能谈及上述要点——建立在一个简单的道德原则之上。这就是:国家的福利和健全首先应以人民大众的意愿和需要为转移,要看人民大众

through the instrumentality of tariffs which have isolated us from all the other human beings in all the rest of the round world. I accept that admirable tariff statement in the platform of this convention. It would protect American business and American labor. By our acts of the past we have invited and received the retaliation of other Nations. I propose an invitation to them to forget the past, to sit at the table with us, as friends, and to plan with us for the restoration of the trade of the world.

Go into the home of the business man. He knows what the tariff has done for him. Go into the home of the factory worker. He knows why goods do not move. Go into the home of the farmer. He knows how the tariff has helped to ruin him.

At last our eyes are open. At last the American people are ready to acknowledge that Republican leadership was wrong and that the Democracy is right.

My program, of which I can only touch on these points, is based upon this simple moral principle: the welfare and the soundness of a Nation depend first upon what the great mass of the people wish and need; and second, whether or not

的意愿和需要是否得到了满足。

美国人民最需要什么？我认为他们最需要两件东西：一是工作和随之而来的所有的道德和精神价值；二是合情合理的安全感——使自己和妻子儿女获得安全感。这两件东西比任何言词更重要，比任何事实更重要。它们是精神价值的体现，它们应该是我国重新建设的方向。实现这些价值是我的纲领和目标。我们在现职领导人的领导下未能实现这些价值。

共和党领导人告诫我们：经济规律是神圣的，不可侵犯的，不可逆转的；经济规律引起了无法预防的恐慌。不过，当他们滔滔不绝地侈谈经济规律时，人民却在忍饥挨饿。我们必须坚持一个事实：经济规律不是天生的，而是人类造就出来的。

是的，当——不是假如——我们得到机会，联邦政府就会勇敢地掌握领导权，开始救济工作。几年来，华盛顿一会儿把头埋入沙堆，说什么缺衣少食的贫民并不

they are getting it.

What do the people of America want more than anything else? To my mind, they want two things: work, with all the moral and spiritual values that go with it; and with work, a reasonable measure of security—security for themselves and for their wives and children. Work and security—these are more than words. They are more than facts. They are the spiritual values, the true goal toward which our efforts of reconstruction should lead. These are the values that this program is intended to gain; these are the values we have failed to achieve by the leadership we now have.

Our Republican leaders tell us economic laws—sacred, inviolable, unchangeable—cause panics which no one could prevent. But while they prate of economic laws, men and women are starving. We must lay hold of the fact that economic laws are not made by nature. They are made by human beings.

Yes, when—not if—when we get the chance, the Federal Government will assume bold leadership in distress relief. For years Washington has alternated between putting its head in the sand and saying there is no large number of

多,一会儿又说如果存在贫民,各州政府就应该关心。他们早在两年半以前就应该做现在想做的事,但他们一拖再拖,日复一日,周复一周,月复一月,直到有良心的美国人要求采取行动为止。

我认为,地方政府虽应一如既往地对救济负起主要责任,但对于广大人民的福利,联邦政府过去一直负有、现在仍然负有责任。联邦政府不久就要承担起那种责任。

现在,我想简单谈谈未来4个月的计划。我来到这里,而不是等候正式通知,这一举动已清楚表明,我们将废除开支昂贵的仪式。朋友们,我们将立即开动、今晚就开动所有必要的机器,向全国各地的选举团充分阐述各种问题。

作为一个伟大的州的州长①,我本人还有重要的职责,在目前时刻,这些职责

---

① 罗斯福在竞选总统时为纽约州州长(1928—1932)。

---

destitute people in our midst who need food and clothing, and then saying the States should take care of them, if there are. Instead of planning two and a half years ago to do what they are now trying to do, they kept putting it off from day to day, week to week, and month to month, until the conscience of America demanded action.

I say that while primary responsibility for relief rests with localities now, as ever, yet the Federal Government has always had and still has a continuing responsibility for the broader public welfare. It will soon fulfill that responsibility.

And now, just a few words about our plans for the next four months. By coming here instead of waiting for a formal notification, I have made it clear that I believe we should eliminate expensive ceremonies and that we should set in motion at once, tonight, my friends, the necessary machinery for an adequate presentation of the issues to the electorate of the Nation.

I myself have important duties as Governor of a great State, duties which in these times are more arduous and more grave than at any previous period. Yet I

比以往任何时候都更加光荣和艰巨。然而我相信,我将能够对我国若干地方做几次短访,首要目的就是与各党派、各行业的人们开展对话,直接研究全国各地的实际状况和需要。

我再说一句:人类每经历一次危机、忧伤和灾难,都会共同获得更丰富的知识、更高尚的礼仪、更纯洁的目的。我们必将能度过一个思想涣散、道德败落的时期,必将能度过一个在人际和国际关系方面自私自利的时代。我们不要只责备政府,我们同样也要责备自己。让我们坦率承认,许多人对金钱顶礼膜拜,而投机获利、好逸恶劳的思想已使我们误入歧途。为了重新确立高尚的标准,我们必须抛弃错误的预言家,寻找符合自己愿望的新领袖。

在我国现代史上,两大政党的根本区别从未像今天这样突出。共和党领导人不仅在物质方面失败了,而且在提出目标方面也失败了,因为他们在灾难时期不

feel confident that I shall be able to make a number of short visits to several parts of the Nation. My trips will have as their first objective the study at first hand, from the lips of men and women of all parties and all occupations, of the actual conditions and needs of every part of an interdependent country.

One word more: Out of every crisis, every tribulation, every disaster, mankind rises with some share of greater knowledge, of higher decency, of purer purpose. Today we shall have come through a period of loose thinking, descending morals, an era of selfishness, among individual men and women and among Nations. Blame not Governments alone for this. Blame ourselves in equal share. Let us be frank in acknowledgment of the truth that many amongst us have made obeisance to Mammon, that the profits of speculation, the easy road without toil, have lured us from the old barricades. To return to higher standards we must abandon the false prophets and seek new leaders of our own choosing.

Never before in modern history have the essential differences between the two major American parties stood out in such striking contrast as they do today. Republican leaders not only have failed in material things, they have failed in national vision, because in disaster they have held out no hope, they have pointed out no path for the people below to climb back to places of security and of safety

能展示希望,不能为人民指出一条可以返回安全场所的道路。

在过去年代被政府遗忘的、全国各地的男男女女正看着这里,看着我们,期待着我们能提供指导,提供更公平的机会来共享国家的财富。

在农场、在大都会、在小城市、在村庄,千百万公民满怀着希望,希望传统的生活标准和思想准则并没有一去不复返。他们的希望不能、也绝不会落空。

我向你们保证,也向自己保证,我要为美国人民实施新政。让所有聚集在这儿的人都献出自己的能力和勇气,做新秩序的倡导者。这不仅是一场政治运动,这也是战斗的号令。帮助我吧!不仅为了赢得选票,而且为了赢得这场使美国回到人民手中的改革运动。

王建华 译

in our American life.

Throughout the Nation, men and women, forgotten in the political philosophy of the Government of the last years look to us here for guidance and for more equitable opportunity to share in the distribution of national wealth.

On the farms, in the large metropolitan areas, in the smaller cities and in the villages, millions of our citizens cherish the hope that their old standards of living and of thought have not gone forever. Those millions cannot and shall not hope in vain.

I pledge you, I pledge myself, to a new deal for the American people. Let us all here assembled constitute ourselves prophets of a new order of competence and of courage. This is more than a political campaign; it is a call to arms. Give me your help, not to win votes alone, but to win in this crusade to restore America to its own people.

请大家投我信任票①

富兰克林·罗斯福

1940年11月2日

今晚,我很高兴能在克利夫兰②通过这么多听众和老朋友,向美国人民传递一个信息。

①本篇演说常被誉为罗斯福一生中"最雄辩、最动人"的演说。面对第二次世界大战的烽火和国内孤立主义情绪,他冷静阐述了美国外交政策和"新政"的成就,深情描绘了美国的未来,并委婉表达了三连任的愿望,充分展现了一个政治家驾驭局势的卓越才能。
②俄亥俄州东北部一港口城市。

Franklin Roosevelt

November 2, 1940

I Am Asking Your Vote of Confidence

Tonight in Cleveland, I am happy, through this great audience of my old friends, to give this message to America.

在过去7年里,我有幸担任美国人民的领袖——这是一份崇高的荣誉,也是一种庄严的职责。7年来,美国人民已经走出萧条和失望的荒原,踏上了前进的坦途。

他们阔步前进,一直来到了未来的门槛——我们的希望将要成真,真正的自由、繁荣与和平将要实现。

我想把这一前进势头再保持4年。为此,我请大家投我信任票。

我们这一代美国人生逢历史重要时刻。

由于国际风云的激荡①,我们中间有少数人提出了一个疑问:这是不是所说的故事的结尾?现在是否该合上这本叫民主的书,把它放到时间老人积满灰尘的书架上?

我的回答是:我们所知道的民主的一切优点——它的自由、它作为一种生活

---

①指德、意、日法西斯挑起了第二次世界大战。

For the past seven years I have had the high honor and the grave responsibility of leadership of the American people. In those seven years, the American people have marched forward, out of a wilderness of depression and despair.

They have marched forward right up to the very threshold of the future—a future which holds the fulfillment of our hopes for real freedom, real prosperity, real peace.

I want that march to continue for four more years. And for that purpose, I am asking your vote of confidence.

This generation of Americans is living in a tremendous moment of history.

The surge of events abroad has made some few doubters among us ask: Is this the end of a story that has been told? Is the book of democracy now to be closed and placed away upon the dusty shelves of time?

My answer is this: All we have known of the glories of democracy—its

方式所带来的效率、它为满足普通人的愿望所具备的能力——所有这一切,只是为一个更伟大、更辉煌的未来写下了序篇。

我们这些当代美国人——全体美国人——都是这本生气勃勃的民主巨著中的人物。

然而我们也是这本书的作者。现在,未来的篇章究竟讲述倒退,还是讲述继续前进,就要看我们说什么了。

我相信美国人民会说:"向前进!"

我们看看今天的欧洲旧大陆。那是一片丑恶的大陆,仇恨、贪婪和恐惧已毒害了那片大陆。我们可以看到,战争这剂毒药如何造成了无可挽回的后果。

我们看看自己居住的国家。这是一个伟大的国家,一代又一代热爱和平的、待人友好的男男女女建设了她。他们心中怀着一个信念:凡努力工作者,就一定能过

---

freedom, its efficiency as a mode of living, its ability to meet the aspirations of the common man—all these are merely an introduction to the greater story of a more glorious future.

We Americans of today—all of us—we are characters in this living book of democracy.

But we are also its author. It falls upon us now to say whether the chapters that are to come will tell a story of retreat or a story of continued advance.

I believe that the American people will say: "Forward!"

We look at the old world of Europe today. It is an ugly world, poisoned by hatred and greed and fear. We can see what has been the inevitable consequence of that poison—war.

We look at the country in which we live. It is a great country, built by generations of peaceable, friendly men and women who had in their hearts faith

上美好的生活。

我们知道,我们决心保卫自己的国家,并决心与邻邦一起保卫本半球。我们的国防无比坚强。我们的国力与日俱增。

我们的外交方针是要在对外交往中表达我国政府的决心和我国人民的意志。在过去几年,对外交往已变得比以往任何时候都更加困难、更加复杂。

我们的外交方针没有任何秘密可言——对美国人民不是秘密,对世界各国政府也不是秘密。过去,我已多次不但用语言,而且用行动说明了这个方针。今天,让我这样来重申:我国外交方针的首要目标是把我国置于战争之外。与此同时,我们力求把外国政府的概念拒于国门之外。

这就是我们为什么要自强,这就是我们为什么要召集全国的后备队。

第二,我们的目标是尽可能使战争远离整个西半球海岸。我国的方针是要增

that the good life can be attained by those who will work for it.

We know that we are determined to defend our country—and with our neighbors to defend this Hemisphere. We are strong in our defense. Every hour and every day we grow stronger.

Our foreign policy is shaped to express the determination of our Government and the will of our people in our dealings with other nations. Those dealings, in the past few years, have been more difficult, more complex than ever before.

There is nothing secret about our foreign policy. It is not a secret from the American people–and it is not a secret from any Government anywhere in the world. I have stated it many times before, not only in words but in action. Let me restate it like this: The first purpose of our foreign policy is to keep our country out of war. At the same time, we seek to keep foreign conceptions of Government out of the United States.

That is why we make ourselves strong; that is why we muster all the reserves of our national strength.

The second purpose of this policy is to keep war as far away as possible from the shores of the entire Western Hemisphere. Our policy is to promote such

进与拉丁美洲各共和国以及与加拿大的友好关系,使欧洲和亚洲列强①知道,它们不可能在我们这个半球挑拨离间。如果大家从北到南走一走,就会知道这一方针已取得实际成功。

最后,我国的方针是尽可能从物质上援助大西洋彼岸和太平洋彼岸仍在抵抗侵略的国家。

让我毫不含糊地声明,我们不想犯绥靖主义的致命错误。

因为美国人民决心要为自己维护言论自由的权利、宗教自由的权利、集会自由的权利以及构成所有这些权利基础的、通过自由选举来选择政府官员的权利。

我们要维护自由——通过反击外部进犯和打击内部腐败来捍卫自由。我们将反对各种独裁势力,不管它们披上什么伪装和画皮。

---

① 指德国、意大利和日本。

friendly relations with the Latin-American Republics and with Canada, that the great powers of Europe and Asia will know that they cannot divide the peoples of this hemisphere one from another. And if you go from the North Pole to the South Pole, you will know that it is a policy of practical success.

Finally, our policy is to give all possible material aid to the nations which still resist aggression, across the Atlantic and Pacific Oceans.

And let me make it perfectly clear that we intend to commit none of the fatal errors of appeasement.

For Americans are determined to retain for themselves the right of free speech, free religion, free assembly and the right which lies at the basis of all of them—the right to choose the officers of their own Government in free elections.

We intend to keep our freedom—to defend it from attacks from without and against corruption from within. We shall defend it against the forces of dictatorship, whatever disguises and false faces they may wear.

但是，我们已经懂得，单有自由是不够的。

言论自由对一个无话可说的人毫无用处。

信仰自由对一个失去信仰的人毫无用处。

民主须能为公民提供自由，又能为公民提供机会，这样的民主才是有活力的。

我们这一代人在过去几年里已看到，这种能动的民主制在美国获得了新生。

美国人民已经勇敢地面对我国近代以来最严峻的问题。

"新政"是你们——美国人民的创造。

你们为我国找不到工作的自由人提供了工作。

闲散人员获得了机会，或修筑公路，或建设民宅，或治理河流，或为农场、家庭和工业提供电力。

你们运用政府的力量，使我国的土地不再荒芜，农作物价格不再下降，使众多

But we have learned that freedom in itself is not enough.

Freedom of speech is of no use to a man who has nothing to say.

Freedom of worship is of no use to a man who has lost his God.

Democracy, to be dynamic, must provide for its citizens opportunity as well as freedom.

We of this generation have seen a rebirth of dynamic democracy in America in these past few years.

The American people have faced with courage the most severe problems of all of our modern history.

The New Deal has been the creation of you, the American people.

You provided work for free men and women in America who could find no work.

Idle men were given the opportunity on roads to be built, homes to be erected, rivers to be harnessed, power to be made for farm and home and industry.

You used the powers of Government to stop the depletion of the top soil of

家庭和农场保住了抵押品赎回权。

你们使工人的集体谈判权成为法律,并建立了执行那种权力的机构。

你们注意到了青少年和老年问题。你们从工厂和商店带回了孩子,宣布任何人无权剥削童工的劳动;你们给了这些孩子机会,让他们从身体和思想上做好准备,迎接更完善、更光辉的未来。你们为这片国土上的青年人提供了工作和受教育的机会。你们为老年人提供了安全和休闲。

在我国民主向前迈进的那些年里,本政府同你们一起工作,为你们而工作。政府有时会遇到障碍。但是,在全体人民的支持和提议下,我们一如既往地重新向前迈进。

现在,有些人要求我们在跑道上停下脚步,要求我们向后转,回到我们走过的荒原。

America, to stop decline in farm prices, to stop foreclosures of homes and farms.

You wrote into the law the right of working men and women to bargain collectively, and you set up the machinery to enforce that right.

You turned to the problems of youth and age. You took your children out of the factory and shop and outlawed the right of anyone to exploit the labor of those children; and you gave to those children the chance to prepare in body and spirit the molding of an even fuller and brighter day for themselves. For the youth of the land you provided chances for jobs and for education. And for old age itself you provided security and rest.

During those years while our democracy moved forward, your Government has worked with you and for you. Your Government has at times been checked. But always, with the aid and the counsel of all the people, we have resumed our march.

Now we are asked to stop in our tracks. We are asked to turn about, to march back into the wilderness from which we came.

我们当然不会倒退。我们之所以不倒退,因为我们是开拓、探索、实验和冒险传统的继承人。我们不会被怀疑民主的人吓倒,我们不会后撤。

我们当然将继续加强我国社会和政治生活中的生气勃勃的改革,并且使民主与发展现代工业生产并驾齐驱。

我们当然将继续利用科技天才们创造出来的良好条件——不是给少数人享受,而是为了全体美国人的福利。

因为通向坚强的民主制之路就在这里。

我们当然要保护并改善国土,包括土壤、森林、河流以及上帝赐予合众国人民的一切资源。

我们当然要通过民主教育和实施健康计划,继续增进我国人民体质和精神素质。

因为通向坚强的民主制之路就在这里。

Of course we will not turn backward. We will not turn back because we are the inheritors of a tradition of pioneering, exploring, experimenting and adventuring. We will not be scared into retreating by threats from the doubters of democracy.

Of course we shall continue to strengthen all these dynamic reforms in our social and economic life; to keep the processes of democracy side by side with the necessities and possibilities of modern industrial production.

Of course we shall continue to make available the good things of life created by the genius of science and technology—to use them, however, not for the enjoyment of the few but for the welfare of all.

For there lies the road to democracy that is strong.

Of course we intend to preserve and build up the land of this country—its soil, its forests and its rivers—all the resources with which God has endowed the people of the United States.

Of course we intend to continue to build up the bodies and the minds of the men, women and children of the Nation—through democratic education and a democratic program for health.

For there lies the road to democracy that is strong.

我们当然要继续努力保护企业和财产的私有制,使其免遭金融垄断的破坏。

我们当然将继续努力,防止经济专制和政治专制。

我们当然要继续加强我国的道德建设——不是要盲从某些领袖,而是要对美国及其民主赖以诞生的、根深蒂固的道德原则充满信心。

因为通向坚强的民主制之路就在这里。

我国的进步和防务都要求团结一致。我们需要每一个美国人给予合作,包括工人、工厂的伟大的组织者和技师、农民、专业人员,包括所有的母亲、父亲和青年,总之,包括所有热爱美国稍微胜过热爱自己的人。

如果得到所有这些人的帮助,我们就可以保证:这样一个计划能够使我国蒸蒸日上,自由而坚强,能够使我国成为世界的明灯和各国人民的慰藉。

一切邪恶势力都不能压倒我们。

Of course we intend to continue our efforts to protect our system of private enterprise and private property, but to protect it from monopoly of financial control.

Of course we shall continue our efforts to prevent economic dictatorship as well as political dictatorship.

Of course we intend to continue to build up the morale of this country, not as blind obedience to some leader, but as the expression of confidence in the deeply ethical principles upon which this Nation and its democracy were founded.

For there lies the road to democracy that is strong.

The progress of our country, as well as the defense of our country, requires national unity. We need the cooperation of every single American—our workers, the great organizers and technicians in our factories, our farmers, our professional men and women, our mothers, our fathers, our youth—all the men and women who love America just a little bit more than they love themselves.

And if we can have the assistance of all these, we can promise that such a program can make this country prosperous and free and strong—to be a light of the world and a comfort to all people.

And all the forces of evil shall not prevail against it.

我们这一代美国人肩负着使命,那就是向全世界指出一条通向未来之路。我们祈望所有热爱自由的人——这个世界上所有受苦受难、我们寻求为之照亮道路的普通人——都能加入我们的行列。

我看到这样一个美国,那里的工人不会在风华正茂时被一脚踢开,那里的人们不会世世代代受穷,那里的穷苦农民不会变成无家可归的流浪汉,那里的青年不会在垄断的淫威下乞讨工作。

我看到这样一个美国,她的江河、盆地和湖泊,她的山脉、溪流和平原,她的高山和地下自然资源,都作为全体人民的合法财产而受到保护。

我看到这样一个美国,那里的小企业真正有机会发展壮大。

我看到这样一个美国,那里的全体人民有极好的接受文化教育的机会。

我看到这样一个美国,那里的农业收入将受到重视和保护,政府决心保证农

It is the destiny of this American generation to point the road to the future for all the world to see. It is our prayer that all lovers of freedom may join us—the anguished common people of this earth for whom we seek to light the path.

I see an America where factory workers are not discarded after they reach their prime, where there is no endless chain of poverty from generation to generation, where impoverished farmers and farm hands do not become homeless wanderers, where monopoly does not make youth a beggar for a job.

I see an America whose rivers and valleys and lakes—hills and streams and plains—the mountains over our land and nature's wealth deep under the earth—are protected as the rightful heritage of all the people.

I see an America where small business really has a chance to flourish and grow.

I see an America of great cultural and educational opportunity for all its people.

I see an America where the income from the land shall be implemented and protected by a Government determined to guarantee to those who hoe it a fair

民在国民收入中享有公平的份额；贸易和私营企业将继续运转，为国家生产货物；任何企业都不因受制于严厉的垄断而停止发展；全国每一个企业主，不论大小，都可经营合法企业而得到公平的回报，获得合理的利润。

我看到这样一个美国，那里的劳工界太平无恙。工人真正获得了自由，并且——通过不受外力控制或内部独裁者控制的强大工会——能与企业主和经理一起，在会议桌旁占有合适的一席之地。由于自身的力量和法律的保障，他们的尊严和安全得到了保证。进入暮年之人能够安度余生，养老金和保险金将理所当然地颁发给这些为国为家忙碌了一生的人。

我看到这样一个美国，她为自由事业而献身，她因宽容和宗教信仰而团结一致，她的人民愿为和平作出奉献，他们因身心都已获得安全和无所畏惧，对自己的力量充满信心。

share in the national income. An America where the wheels of trade and private industry continue to turn to make the goods for America. Where no businessman can be stifled by the harsh hand of monopoly, and where the legitimate profits of legitimate business are the fair reward of every businessman—big and little—in all the Nation.

I see an America with peace in the ranks of labor. An America where the workers are really free and—through their great unions undominated by any outside force, or by any dictator within—can take their proper place at the council table with the owners and managers of business. Where the dignity and security of the working man and woman are guaranteed by their own strength and fortified by the safeguards of law. An America where those who have reached the evening of life shall live out their years in peace and security. Where pensions and insurance for these aged shall be given as a matter of right to those who through a long life of labor have served their families and their nation as well.

I see an America devoted to our freedom—unified by tolerance and by religious faith—a people consecrated to peace, a people confident in strength because their body and their spirit are secure and unafraid.

在这些年里,当我们的民主在很多战场上向前推进时,我有此殊荣担任你们的总统。人生最大的愿望莫过于此。

这是一项艰巨的任务,一项需要日夜操劳的任务。

完成任务之余,有两个最重要的想法一直在我的脑海中翻腾:一是在我们的国土上维持和平;二是为我国普通人的利益让民主力量发挥作用。

目前,一场特大风暴正在来临,它将使世界事务变得更加艰难。那场风暴虽然不是起源于我们这片土地,却是我想继续与人民休戚与共,直到我们抵达前方明确而稳固的立足之地的真正原因。

我们会成功的——在下一个4年任期结束前会成功。

我们会成功的;我们希望世界也会成功。

到那个任期结束时,将会产生另外一位总统,以后还会有很多位总统。我想,

During these years while our democracy advanced on many fields of battle, I have had the great privilege of being your President. No personal ambition of any man could desire more than that.

It is a hard task. It is a task from which there is no escape day or night.

And through it all there have been two thoughts uppermost in my mind—to preserve peace in our land; and to make the forces of democracy work for the benefit of the common people of America.

There is a great storm raging now, a storm that makes things harder for the world. And that storm, which did not start in this land of ours, is the true reason that I would like to stick by these people of ours until we reach the clear, sure footing ahead.

We will make it—we will make it before the next term is over.

We will make it; and the world, we hope, will make it, too.

When that term is over there will be another President, and many more Presidents in the years to come, and I think that, in the years to come, that word "resident"

在将来,"总统"将成为一个鼓舞世界各地普通人的词。

我国的未来属于我们美国人。

未来要由我们设计,要由我们建设。

我们在建设那个未来时将证明,我们曾以无比坚强的信念,战胜过历史上最令人恐惧的风暴。

我们在未来的岁月里将创造历史——为未来勾画新的轮廓。我们将确保这个未来是自由的未来。

我们的心愿将永远是普通人的心愿——他们从未放弃对民主的信仰,从未放弃对家庭、家乡和祖国的热爱。

普通人的精神就是和平的精神和良好的心愿。这是上帝的精神。而相信上帝,这就是全美国的力量所在。

王建华　译

will be a word to cheer the hearts of common men and women everywhere.

Our future belongs to us Americans.

It is for us to design it; for us to build it.

In that building of it we shall prove that our faith is strong enough to survive the most fearsome storms that have ever swept over the earth.

In the days and months and years to come, we shall be making history—hewing out a new shape for the future. And we shall make very sure that that future of ours bears the likeness of liberty.

Always the heart and the soul of our country will be the heart and the soul of the common man—the men and the women who never have ceased to believe in democracy, who never have ceased to love their families, their homes and their country.

The spirit of the common man is the spirit of peace and good will. It is the spirit of God. And in His faith is the strength of all America.

"神医"杜威和共和党的老唱片

哈里·杜鲁门 *

1948 年 10 月 23 日

我认为总统竞选是民主进程中最重要的组成部分,借此机会,可以把存在的问题摆出来,进行讨论,作出决定。我是个竞选老手,我享受这项运动。

如果我的对手有勇气站出来讨论问题,那就更是个享受。

---

* 美国第 33 任总统(1945—1953),民主党人,1945 年出任副总统,罗斯福逝世后接任总统,4 年后连任。本篇是他在匹兹堡发表的著名演说,惟妙惟肖地把竞争对手杜威比作包治百病的"神医",把第 80 届国会比作带有裂口的"老唱片",淋漓尽致地嘲讽对手拿不出治国良策,只会空口说白话。

Harry Truman
October 23, 1948

"Doctor" Dewey and His Republican Old Phonograph Records

I think a Presidential campaign is one of the most important elements in our democratic process. It's a chance to get things out in the open and discuss them and make decisions. I am an old campaigner, and I enjoy it.

You know, I would enjoy this campaign a lot more if my opponent had the courage to discuss the issues. The American

这些问题与每位国人息息相关,因此,国人有权利知道我和我的对手在这些问题上的立场。

大家清楚我的立场,但共和党候选人却拒绝表明自己的立场。

我的对手在进行一场特别的竞选。他把自己标榜为一个"神医",包治人间百病。

现在,让我们美国人民来会会这位"神医"。这是4年一次的例行检查。

我们进了医生的诊所。

"医生,"我们说,"我们没什么不舒服。"

"果真如此?你最近难道没有病魔缠身?"

"确实没有,"我们说,"当然也有一些问题,比如物价过高,还有住房、教育、社会安全以及其他一些问题。"

"这很糟糕,你们不应该有这么多问题。"

people have the right to know where I stand and where my opponent stands on the issues that affect every person in this country.

Now, the people know where I stand. But the Republican candidate refuses to tell where he stands.

My opponent is conducting a very peculiar campaign. He has set himself up as some kind of doctor with a magic cure for all the ills of mankind.

Now, let's imagine that we, the American people, are going to see this doctor. It's just our usual routine checkup which we have every 4 years.

Now, we go into this doctor's office.

And, "Doctor," we say, "we're feeling fine."

"Is that so?" says the doctor, "You have been bothered much by issues lately?"

"Not bothered, exactly," we say. "Of course, we've had a few. We've had the issues of high prices, and housing, and education, and social security, and a few others."

"That's too bad," says the doctor. "You shouldn't have so many issues."

"是吗？"我们说，"我们认为这些问题是政治健康的标志。"

"完全不是。你们不应该考虑这些问题。你们所需要的是我独创的止痛糖浆——我把它叫作'一致'。"

然后医生凑近了些。

"嗯，你看上去确实不怎么好。"他说。

"看上去好才怪呢。医生，我从没感到好过，我没有更多的钱，也没有光明的前程，我这是得了什么病？"

"我从来不和病人讨论问题，你需要的是大手术。"医生面无表情地说。

"这严重吗，医生？"我们问。

"不，不太严重，"他说，"只是我要把你的器官整个儿拿掉，换上共和党执政。"

这就是共和党的竞选。他们不讨论问题，却坚持要动大手术。

"Is that right?" we say. "We thought that issues were a sign of political health."

"Not at all," says the doctor. "You shouldn't think about issues. What you need is my brand of soothing syrup—I call it 'unity.'"

Then the doctor edges up a little closer.

And he says, "Say, you don't look so good."

We say to him, "Well, that seems strange to me, Doc. I never felt stronger, never had more money, and never had a brighter future. What is wrong with me?"

Well, the doctor looks blank and he says, "I never discuss issues with a patient. But what you need is a major operation."

"Will it be serious, Doe?" we say.

"Not so very serious," he says. "It will just mean taking out the complete works and putting in a Republican administration."

Now, that's the kind of campaign you have been getting from the Republicans. They won't talk about the issues, but they insist that a major operation is necessary.

请看这位共和党候选人关于本届政府"失败"的云山雾罩的谈话。这些话,让我颇感迷惑。

我在想这样一个事实:我们的国民收入现在每年达到了2200亿——是1932年的5倍。这难道是他所谓的"失败"?

他或许担心公司利润。1932年,公司损失了30亿美元。但现在公司利润以每年190亿的速度递增。这难道是他所谓的"失败"?

他或许担心我们对那些自由国家所作的承诺,能否保证他们不受共产主义的侵犯。事实证明我们做到了。这难道是他所谓的"失败"?

几天前就在这里,在匹兹堡,这位共和党候选人假惺惺地对本届政府对待劳工的方式感到不满,说1946年劳工处境恶劣。以此为借口,他搬出了塔夫脱—哈特

Take this vague talk of the Republican candidate about the "failures" of the present administration. That puzzled me for a little bit.

I thought of the fact that our national income is now running at the rate of over \$220 billion a year—over five times as much as it was in 1932. Is that what he calls a failure?

Or perhaps he was worried about the profits of the corporations. In 1932, corporations lost \$3 billion. Now corporate profits are running at the rate of \$19 billion a year. Is that what he calls a failure?

Perhaps he was thinking about our mighty undertakings to assist the free nations of the world to protect themselves against the inroads of communism. These efforts are proving successful. Is that what he calls a failure?

In his speech here in Pittsburgh just a few days ago, the Republican candidate pretended to be upset about the way my administration has treated labor—about the terrible condition that labor was in 1946. That's the excuse he

莱法案。①

好,让我们仔细看看:

1946年更多的人有了工作。工会更加健康,成员也比以往任何时期多。1946年工人创造了比以往任何一个和平年代更多的物质财富。

1946年不会是完美的。但在作出任何抱怨之前,共和党最好睁开眼看看1932年——上届共和党执政的最后一年。

共和党候选人谈到1946年因罢工损失的工作日。1946年的工业产值是1932年的3倍,因罢工损失的工作日比1932年少一半。

共和党不愿谈1932年——我们也不责怪他们,但在选举日开始投票的那一刻,你们肯定会记起这一年。

---

① 1947年由参议员塔夫脱和众议员哈特莱提出的一项劳资关系法案。

gives for the passage of the Taft-Hartley law.

All right, let's examine that.

In 1946, more people had jobs than ever before in the history of the country. Unions were healthier and had more members than ever before. And the workingmen and women of the United States produced more goods in 1946 than in any previous peacetime year.

The world wasn't perfect in 1946. But before any Republican begins complaining about that, he had better take a look at 1932—the last Republican year.

The Republican candidate talks about the workdays lost from strikes in 1946. Our industrial production in 1946 was three times as much as it was in 1932. And the days lost from strikes in 1946 were less than 1 1/2 percent of the total days worked that year.

Republicans don't like to talk about 1932—and I don't blame them. But it is a good year for you to remember when you start out to vote on election day.

在匹兹堡,共和党候选人谈到了我执政期间工人所受的苦,接着,他告诉大家谁是救世主。

你们猜是谁?是共和党。

你们认为他们会如何拯救我们?他们用的是塔夫脱—哈特莱法案。

共和党候选人抱着塔夫脱—哈特莱法案,昂首阔步——一切的一切统统都解决了。没有任何人可以再有任何怀疑。

在赞扬塔夫脱—哈特莱法案时,他又用了习惯用的方式——空口说白话。他想告诉大家,是塔夫脱—哈特莱法案将从事左翼活动的人赶出了劳动工会。

如果大家想知道他的声明有多少可信度,那就请去问贝尔·格林,去问菲利浦·默里①。他们会告诉你们,是谁从工会中清除了左翼分子,是通过工会自身——

---

① 两人均为劳工领袖。

When the Republican candidate finished telling you, here in Pittsburgh, how labor had suffered under my administration, he told you who had come to the rescue of labor.

Now, who do you think it was? It was the Republicans.

Now, how do you suppose they did it? They did it with the Taft-Hartley Act.

The Republican candidate marched up proudly and embraced the Taft-Hartley law. No workingman can have any doubt about that any more.

And in praising the Taft-Hartley law, he displayed his characteristic tendency of claiming credit where no credit is due. He tried to tell you that it is the Taft-Hartley Act that is driving the Communists out of labor unions.

Now, if you want to know how much truth there is in this claim, ask Bill Green—ask Phil Murray. They will tell you who got the Communists out. It's being

最为美国化的方式。

就在这里,在匹兹堡的演说中,共和党候选人以其特有的谦虚,承认他打算领导这个国家乃至整个世界走出所有困境。他作了太多的承诺。

他张开嘴,闭上眼,吞下了第80届共和党国会的糟糕记录。

4年前这位共和党议员在全国各地游说,说他赞成民主党所做的,但他可以做得更好。他说他不反对全国劳工关系法案、工资与工时法、社会保障法以及"所有其他旨在保护和提高美国劳动人民福利的联邦法案"——但他可以做得更好。

由于这样或那样的原因,美国人民在1944年没有相信他。

今年,这位候选人又回来了。他在重弹老调:他喜欢我们民主党的法案,但他可以做得更好。

这听上去像是同一架老唱机里播放着老唱片,今年他这张唱片裂了口,指针

done in the good American way—the unions are doing it themselves.

Now in this speech the Republican candidate made here in Pittsburgh, he admitted, with characteristic modesty, that he is going to lead the country—and, indeed, the whole world—out of all its troubles. And he made a lot of promises.

He opened his mouth and he closed his eyes, and he swallowed the terrible record of that good-for-nothing Republican Both Congress.

Now, 4 years ago this same Republican Presidential candidate went around the country saying that he was in favor of what the Democrats had done, but he could do it better. He said he was in favor of the National Labor Relations Act, the Wage and Hour Act, the Social Security Act, and "all the other Federal statutes designed to promote and protect the welfare of the American workingmen and women"—but he could do it better.

For some reason or other the American people did not believe him in 1944.

This year the same candidate is back with us, and he is saying much the same thing; that he likes the Democratic laws, but that he can run them better than we can.

It sounds to me like the same old phonograph record; but this year the

被卡住,发出了嘎嘎吱吱的怪音,这个裂口来自共和党人控制的、"无所作为"的第80届国会。

1948年当这位候选人说"我会做得更好"时,这个裂口就冒出来说"我们反对"。因此,今年共和党唱出的调子就不那么和谐,其可信度比1944年还要差。

这位候选人说:"现今法律规定的最低工资太低,需要提高。"不错,在这点上,我们与这位候选人一致,事实上我们已走在了他的前面。

过去的两年里,我一次次地敦促共和党第80届国会,将最低工资额由目前的每小时40美分,提高到至少75美分。但共和党国会——老唱片上那个裂口大叫"没门儿,我们反对"。最低工资因此还是老样子。

让我们听听这位候选人在匹兹堡从老唱片里播放出的另一支老调子。

他说:"为失业者,为老年人,我们将彻底改革社会保障体系,扩大其覆盖面,

record has a crack, and the needle gets stuck in that crack every once in a while. Now the crack in the soothing syrup of that record was provided by the Republican 80th "do-nothing" Congress.

Now, in 1948, every time the Republican candidate says, "I can do it better," up comes an echo from the crack which says, "We're against it." So the sounds coming out of the Republican Party this year are not very harmonious. And they are even less believable than they were in 1944.

The candidate said, and I quote: "The present minimum wage set by law is far too low and it will be raised." Now, that's fine. I am glad he said that. We're right with the candidate on that. In fact, we are 'way out ahead of him.

Time and time again in the last 2 years I urged the Republican "do-nothing" 80th Congress to raise the minimum wage from the present 40 cents an hour to at least 75 cents an hour. But that Republican Congress—that crack in the record—said, "Nothing doing—we're against it." And the minimum wage stayed where it was.

Now, let's look at another song on the record the candidate played for you here in Pittsburgh.

That Republican candidate for President said: "We will overhaul the Social Security System for the unemployed and the aged, and go forward to extend its

增加福利。"尽管有些含糊,但很动听。这是这位候选人口头上说的。那么事实上共和党对社会保障体系采取的立场又如何呢?

作为总统,我尽各种努力促使共和党国会扩大社会保障范围,增加社会福利,但国会做了什么呢?他们砍掉了近100万人的社会福利保障。

你们相信什么?是竞选许诺,还是共和党的所作所为?

唱片上的裂口又一次出卖了他们,裂口说:"我们反对。"

我曾给国会7月的会议提出建议,指出我们迫切需要将老年人的保险福利至少提高50%。目前,每一位老人平均保险金额每月还不到40美元。

共和党国会没有任何行动——这位候选人也同样无动于衷。

在共和党国会的会议上,他一言不发。现在参加竞选,他突然对增加社会福利来劲了。我想问诸位:"你们能相信如此的竞选许诺吗?"

coverage and increase its benefits." Now, that sounds good, although it's a little vague. But that's the candidate speaking. Where do the Republicans actually stand on social security?

As your President, I made every effort to get the Republican 80th Congress to extend social security coverage and increase social security benefits. What did that Congress do? They took social security benefits away from nearly a million people.

What do you believe—campaign promises, or plain facts of Republican action?

Now, again that cracked record gives them away. It says, "We're against it."

In my recommendations to the special "do-nothing" session of Congress in July, I pointed out the desperate need to increase old-age insurance benefits at least 50 percent. At the present time the average insurance benefit payment for an old couple is less than $40 a month.

The Republican Congress did nothing about it—and neither did the Republican candidate for President.

He was silent as the tomb while the Congress was in session. Now, while he's campaigning, he suddenly takes quite an interest in increasing social security benefits. And I ask you: "Can you believe that kind of a campaign promise?"

请看看他在匹兹堡演说中作出的另一个许诺,这位候选人说,"我们将把劳工部在内阁中的地位提高到与贸易部、农业部相同,这将为全国福利作出巨大贡献"。说得很动听,是不是?

对照第80届共和党国会的所作所为,这个许诺真是荒谬至极。第80届国会从劳工部收回了调停局的权力,收回了美国劳工部的权力。它还砍掉了劳动统计局拨款的一半——很明显是为了阻止统计局将生活费用问题公之于众。这就是过去两年里共和党为劳工部做的好事。

请记住,这位候选人说他为第80届国会的所作所为而骄傲。可唱片上的裂口又一次出卖了他们。

这里还有一个许诺。在匹兹堡这位候选人说,"我们将把一个新的、充满活力的领导班子引入联邦调停局,以解决各种纷争,从而避免罢工"。

Take another promise in that Pittsburgh speech. The Republican candidate said: "We will make the Labor Department equal in actual Cabinet status to Commerce and Agriculture. It will make an important contribution to the national welfare." Doesn't that sound nice?

That promise is ridiculous in the face of what the Republicans in the 80th Congress did. The Republican 80th Congress stripped the Mediation and Conciliation Service from the Labor Department. The Republican 80th Congress cut the appropriations for the Bureau of Labor Statistics almost in half—apparently to prevent the Bureau from showing what's happening to the cost of living. That's the plain factual record of what the Republicans have done to the Labor Department in the last 2 years.

Remember, the Republican candidate has said he is proud of the record of the 80th Congress. But that crack in the record gives them away.

Here's another one of his promises. Here in Pittsburgh, the Republican candidate said: "We will bring a new and vigorous leadership to the Federal Conciliation and Mediation Service so that major disputes are settled before they become strikes."

这真是个独到的许诺,调停局现在的负责人,是一位著名的企业家,名叫席勒斯·诚。诚先生在调停方面的工作受到广泛赞扬。我想这位候选人在此事上有些糊涂。

再看看另一个许诺。还是在匹兹堡,这位候选人说,"我们将给工会以更多的权力,并强化劳资双方协议的制订过程。"也就在同一次演说中,他曾说过要尽力支持塔夫脱—哈特莱法案。

因此,这位候选人就陷进了他与共和党国会之间的裂口。他作许诺,国会则唱反调。

他还许诺过:我们将始终如一地加强反托拉斯法以遏制商业垄断。

这真是滑稽透顶,共和党向来以支持大财团垄断而声名狼藉。他们的作为就是很好的明证。他们不顾我的反对,从反托拉斯法中删去了铁路垄断,还拒绝通过

Now that's a very, very peculiar promise. The present director of the Mediation Service is a well-known industrial leader named Cyrus Ching. Mr. Ching has been widely praised for his work in mediation. I think the Republican candidate is a bit confused here.

Let me take another campaign promise, here in Pittsburgh. The Republican candidate said right here: "We will encourage unions to grow in responsibility and strengthen the processes of collective bargaining." And he said it in the very same speech in which he went all out for the Taft-Hartley law.

Now, in this case, the candidate has fallen in the crack with the Republican Congress. He makes a promise, but the record says they're both against it.

Here's another promise by the Republican candidate: "We will vigorously and consistently enforce and strengthen our antitrust laws against business monopolies."

Now that's really fantastic. The Republican Party is notoriously favorable toward big business monopolies. The record of the Republican 80th Congress furnishes plenty of proof. They passed over my veto a bill to exempt railroads from antitrust laws. And

我所建议的、堵塞反垄断法漏洞的欧默哈尼-基弗维尔①议案。

面对国会如此作为,这位候选人现在却满脸真诚地声称,共和党将加强反垄断法。

他还作了更多的许诺!他说过,"我们将以合理的价格,向人民提供像样的住房,来解决住房危机"。但在整整两年中,我做过各种努力,督促共和党为解决住房危机而通过塔夫脱-艾伦德-瓦格纳议案。共和党却没有行动。面对上到州长、市长,下到退伍军人、平民百姓的恳求、敦促,共和党却拒绝通过住房议案。而我已经给了他们四次机会。

但现在——在竞选半道上,这位共和党候选人却斗胆承诺,共和党会在住房问题上采取行动。然而,看不到议案黑字落在白纸上,我是不会相信的。

①美国律师,曾任众议员和参议员,并主持调查州际集团商务犯罪的参议院特别委员会,支持民权立法。

at the same time they refused to pass, as I recommended, the O'Mahoney-Kefauver bill to plug loopholes in the antitrust laws.

In the face of that record, the candidate now claims that the Republicans will strengthen the antitrust laws.

But here's another—here's another! He said: "We will break the log jam in housing so that decent houses may be provided at reasonable cost for the people." For 2 solid years I tried in every way I knew to get the Republican Both Congress to break the log jam in housing by passing the Taft-Ellender-Wagner bill. The Republicans would not act. In the face of pleading and urging from Governors and Mayors, from veterans and plain people all over the country, the Republican Congress refused to pass the housing bill. And I gave them four chances to do it.

But now—now in the middle of the campaign—the Republican candidate has the gall to promise that the Republicans will take action on housing. I certainly wouldn't have believed it if I hadn't seen it in print.

请允许我从这不可思议的匹兹堡演说中再引用另一个竞选许诺。"我们保证,"这位候选人说,"飞涨的物价不会影响到美国家庭的衣食住行。"我简直无话可说。

美国的每一位公民都知道,共和党第80届国会一次次拒绝通过限制高物价的法律。1947年11月、1948年1月、1948年7月,我都曾要求共和党国会对通货膨胀采取措施。

他们毫无作为。共和党这位候选人同样无动于衷。每次的国会会议从头至尾都在敷衍、阻碍反通货膨胀法,而这位议员却一言不发。

但现在——游说人民投他的票时,这位候选人说共和党将对高物价采取行动。我看,作此诺言似乎为时已晚。

这位候选人说,"我,也拥护",但共和党的唱片唱出的仍是"我反对"。

Let me quote just one more campaign promise from that incredible Pittsburgh speech. "We will make sure," said the Republican candidate, I quote: "we will make sure that soaring prices do not steal food and clothing and other necessities from American families." Now that one completely stops me.

Everybody in this country knows that the Republican 80th Congress refused, time and time again, to pass the laws we need to stop high prices. In November 1947, in January 1948, in July 1948, I asked that Republican Congress to act against inflation.

They didn't do a thing about it. And neither did the Republican candidate. All through the time when the Congress was in session, stalling and blocking anti-inflation legislation, the Republican candidate was silent as the grave.

But now that he's trying to persuade the people to vote for him—the Republican candidate says the Republicans will do something about high prices. It looks to me as though it's a little late in the game for that promise, anyway.

Now, the candidate says: "Me, too." But the Republican record still says, "We're against it."

"我拥护"和"我反对"这两个词儿是这次共和党竞选的真实写照。

朋友们,这并不好笑。它是灾难,对普通公民来说是一场灾难。

这种不坚定的含糊其辞的谈话,这种狡黠的沉默和彻头彻尾的假话,是对投票者智慧的侮辱。他以为,他可以永远愚弄所有的人——或大多数人。

对这次竞选,你们不必相信诺言,因为你们有唱片。

你们不一定只放唱片上共和党的一面,可以翻过来——翻到我们民主党这面——它不会说,"我们反对"。它说"你们给我们一个机会,我们就能够做到"。我们这一面是胜利进行曲——11月2日将是人民的胜利、人民的政党——民主党的胜利。

石淑芳　译

These two phrases, "me, too," and "we're against it," sum up the whole Republican campaign.

My friends, it isn't funny at all. It's tragic, tragic for the everyday citizen.

This soft talk and double talk, this combination of crafty silence and resounding misrepresentation, is an insult to the intelligence of the American voter. It proceeds upon the assumption that you can fool all the people–or enough of them—all the time.

In this campaign you don't have to rely on promises. This time, you have the record.

You don't have to play just the Republican side of that record. Turn it over. Our side—the Democratic side—doesn't say, "We're against it." It says, "And we will do it—if you will give us a chance." Our side is the Victory March a victory on November 2d for all the people and for the people's party—the Democratic Party.

共和党代表未来

德怀特·艾森豪威尔[*]

1956年8月23日

女士们、先生们,当亚伯拉罕·林肯在1860年获得提名,一个委员会赶往伊利诺伊州斯普林菲尔德他的家中把消息告诉他时,他只回答了两句话。然后,当他的朋友和邻居们在街上等候,点起篝火照亮了五月的夜空,林肯只说了句,"现在,我不

---

[*] 美国第34任总统(1953—1961),共和党人。第二次世界大战中任欧洲盟军最高司令官,曾指挥诺曼底登陆。本篇是他在旧金山接受总统候选人提名后,发表的纲领性演说。在共和党诞生100周年之际,他抚今思昔,侃侃而谈,陈述了他所认为的"共和党代表着未来"的5条理由。

Dwight Eisenhower

August 23, 1956

The Republican Party Is the Party of the Future

Ladies and gentlemen, when Abraham Lincoln was nominated in 1860, and a committee brought the news to him at his home in Springfield, Illinois, his reply was two sentences long. Then, while his friends and neighbors waited in the street, and while bonfires lit up the May evening, he said simply, "And now I will not longer defer the pleasure of

可再拖延这份愉悦了,我要与你们每一个人握手"。

我真希望我现在也能够那样做——讲一两句话,并与你们所有的人握手。假如我能够那样做,我首先要一个个地感谢你们——感谢你们对我寄予的信任,感谢你们对我满怀信心。然后,就像林肯在篝火的照耀下在他的朋友们中间穿行一样,我也会不时地在你们中间停留片刻,听你们谈谈首先想到的问题。

我能肯定,有一个问题是压倒一切的。这个问题是:未来会怎样?

今天探讨这一问题正合时宜。因为本次大会适逢共和党百年诞辰,而百年庆典不仅是回顾峥嵘岁月的场合,更是展望未来的时刻。

人们在元旦那一天不禁会想:"一年后我会在哪里?"同样道理,共和党人今天也会自然而然地问:"今年大选会怎样?今后一百年会怎样?"

我的回答是:假如我们这些站在20世纪弧光灯下的人,与当年站在19世纪篝

---

taking you, and each of you, by the hand."

I wish I could do the same—speak two sentences, and then take each one of you by the hand. If I could do so, I would first thank you individually for your confidence and your trust. Then, as I am sure Lincoln did as he moved among his friends in the light of the bonfires, we could pause and talk a while about the questions that are uppermost in your mind.

I am sure that one topic would dominate all the rest. That topic is: the future.

This is a good time to think about the future, for this convention is celebrating its one hundredth anniversary. And a centennial is an occasion, not just for recalling the inspiring past, but even more for looking ahead to the demanding future.

Just as on New Year's Day we instinctively think, "I wonder where I will be a year from now," so it is quite natural for the Republican Party to ask today, "What will happen, not just in the coming election, but even one hundred years from now?"

My answer is this: If we and our successors are as courageous and forward-looking and as militantly determined, here under the klieg-lights of the twentieth century,

火旁的林肯及其同僚们一样勇敢无畏,一样高瞻远瞩,一样坚定不移,那么共和党就能继续向前发展,不仅在今年的大选中,而且到它的二百周年诞辰之际甚至以后,它都能得到美国人民的信任和拥戴。

当然,在本次大会召开期间,我们对1956年的兴趣超过了对2056年的兴趣。但问题在于,我们今天制定的方针只有经受住明天的考验,才能证明是正确的。

伟大的挪威人易卜生①曾经写道:"我坚信,谁与未来有最紧密的联系,谁就站在正确的一边。"②

今天,我想阐明一个论点是正确的,这个论点就是:共和党是代表未来的政党。

---

① 剧作家、诗人,以社会问题剧著称,对世界各国戏剧发展有深远影响。著名作品有《玩偶之家》《群鬼》等。
② 引自易卜生1882年1月3日致布兰德斯的信。

---

as Abraham Lincoln and his associates were in the bonfire-light of the nineteenth, the Republican Party will continue to grow in the confidence and affection of the American people, not only to November next, but indeed to, and beyond, its second centennial.

Now, of course, in this convention setting, you and I are momentarily more interested in November 1956 than in 2056. But the point is this: Our policies are right today only as they are designed to stand the test of tomorrow.

The great Norwegian, Henrik Ibsen once wrote: "I hold that man is in the right who is most clearly in league with the future."

Today I want to demonstrate the truth of a single proposition: The Republican Party is the Party of the Future.

为什么说共和党是代表未来的政党?我可以摆出5条理由。

首先,因为共和党是坚持长期原则,而不是注重短期权宜之计的政党。

据说有一位前任总统认为,他在决策时必须像橄榄球比赛中的四分卫那样——等到上一局比赛有了结果,他才为下一局制定出好的方案。这个办法用来管理球队也许不错,但用来管理政府却不行。

那么,政府制定宏观计划为什么要以原则为基础,而不能以朝三暮四的政治机会主义为基础呢?为什么这样做如此重要呢?

因为政府的所作所为,必然对全国人民的日常生活和他们的计划产生深远的影响。如果政府不以恒久的原则作为行动指南,国家政策就会产生摇摆和混乱,使成千上万的个人、家庭和企业无所适从,而他们的未来计划和种种冒险正是我国的活力所在。

Now, the first reason of the five I shall give you why the Republican Party is the Party of the Future is this:

First: Because it is the Party of long-range principle, not short-term expediency.

One of my predecessors is said to have observed that in making his decisions he had to operate like a football quarterback—he could not very well call the next play until he saw how the last play turned out. Well, that may be a good way to run a football team, but in these days it is no way to run a government.

Now, why is it so important that great governmental programs be based upon principle rather than upon shifting political opportunism?

It is because what government does affects profoundly the daily lives and plans of every person in the country. If governmental action is without the solid guidelines of enduring principle, national policies flounder in confusion. And more than this, the millions of individuals, families and enterprises, whose risk-taking and planning for the future are our country's very life force, are paralyzed by uncertainty, diffidence and indecision.

有原则的变革意味着进步,无原则的反复变化意味着混乱。

第二条理由,因为共和党是注重现在及将来的事实和问题的政党,而不是注重过去的事实和问题的政党。

20多年前,我们的对手在经济萧条问题上找到了进攻的战场,并获得了多次政治胜利。但经济周期并没有被消灭。20世纪30年代以来,世界仍然在前进,经济景气取代了经济萧条,人们掌握并验证了许多能防止严重经济衰退的新方法,并迎来了一连串新问题,然而,我们的对手却念念不忘经济萧条时期,这使他们对当今的迫切需要视而不见。

现在和未来为联邦政府和地方政府都带来了新的挑战:供水、公路、保健、住房、电力、和平使用原子能,等等。我们有三分之二人口居住在大城市,因此,都市的组织和再发展问题必须给予高度重视。但最重要的莫过于优先考虑发展第一流

Change based on principle is progress. Constant change without principle becomes chaos.

My second reason for saying that the Republican Party is the Party of the Future is this: It is the Party which concentrates on the facts and issues of today and tomorrow, not the facts and issues of yesterday.

More than twenty years ago, our opponents found in the problems of the depression a battleground on which they scored many political victories. Now, economic cycles have not been eliminated. Still, the world has moved on from the 1930's: good times have supplanted depression; new techniques for checking serious recession have been learned and tested and a whole new array of problems has sprung up. But their obsession with a depression still blinds many of our opponents to the insistent demands of today.

The present and the future are bringing new kinds of challenge to federal and local governments: water supply, highways, health, housing, power development, and peaceful uses of atomic energy. With two-thirds of us living in big cities, questions of urban organization and redevelopment must be given high priority.

的教育事业,以满足学龄人口的迅速增长。

共和党属于所有的青年人、中年人和老年人。它呼吁:让我们不要为过去而纠缠不休,让我们都能着眼于现在和将来的问题,着眼于与我国人民的长期福利紧密相关的问题。

第三,我们说共和党是代表未来的政党,是因为它使人民团结一致,而不是使人民四分五裂。

共和党蔑视那种为达到浅薄的政治目的而在党派之间挑拨离间的伎俩;共和党人认为,"合众为一"不仅是硬币上的一个词语,而是我们的行动准则。

早在1856年,我们的党就开始把工人、小农场主、小企业主作为中坚力量。它还吸引了许多少数民族群体、学者、作家,就更不必提各种改革家了,如自由土壤

Highest of all, perhaps, will be the priority of first-class education to meet the demands of our swiftly growing school-age population.

The Party of the young and of all ages says: Let us quit fighting the battles of the past, and let us all turn our attention to these problems of the present and future, on which the longterm well-being of our people so urgently depends.

Third: The Republican Party is the Party of the Future because it is the party that draws people together, not drives them apart.

Our Party detests the technique of pitting group against group for cheap political advantage. Republicans view as a central principle of conduct—not just as a phrase on nickels and dimes–that old motto of ours: "E pluribus unum"—"Out of many—One."

Our Party as far back as 1856 began establishing a record of bringing together, as its largest element, the working people and small farmers, as well as the small businessmen. It attracted minority groups, scholars and writers, not to mention

党人①、独立民主党人、辉格党人、"温和的亨克派成员"②、绝对戒酒主义者、素食主义者以及超验主义者!

在100年以后的今天,各种职业、各种年龄、各个种族、各种收入的所有美国人,又都聚集到共和党的旗帜之下。他们从共和党制定的具有广泛性、前瞻性、务实性和战斗性的纲领之中,看到了稳步走向美好未来的最大希望。有些反对派人士把共和党称为"单一利益的政党"。它确实是一个单一利益的政党,而这个单一利益,指的就是美国所有男人、女人和儿童的利益!可以肯定地说,只要共和党继续是这种单一利益的政党——一个代表大众利益的政党——它就将继续是代表未来的政党。

---

①建于1848—1854年间,反对奴隶制,提出了"自由土壤、自由言论、自由劳动和自由人民"的政治口号。
②19世纪40年代纽约州民主党内同情共和党的一个派别。

reformers of all kinds, Free-Soilers, Independent Democrats, Conscience Whigs, "soft Hunkers," teetotalers, vegetarians, and transcendentalists!

Now, a hundred years later, the Republican Party is again the rallying point for Americans of all callings, ages, races and incomes. They see in its broad, forward-moving, straight-down-the road, fighting program the best promise for their own steady progress toward a bright future. Some opponents have tried to call this a "one-interest party." Indeed it is a one-interest party; and that one interest is the interest of every man, woman and child in America! And most surely, as long as the Republican Party continues to be this kind of one-interest party—a one-universal-interest party—it will continue to be the Party of the Future.

第四,共和党之所以代表未来,是因为它能够把自由的、创造性的人民热情最充分地调动起来,并以最快的速度完成所需要完成的工作。

共和党人已经证明,政府在给人民的日常生活送去温暖和关怀的同时,能够消除那种"大哥正在看着你"式的家长主义干预。个人——尤其是理想主义的年轻人——对于联邦包办一切的做法并没有信心。他在寻找机会,也应得到机会;他和他的同伴们都热切地想参与补偏救弊的工作。

在当今繁荣和进步的时代,我们必须时时提防沾沾自喜。是的,形势很不错,但仍有成千上万件工作要做,仍有无数的痛苦需要安抚,仍有很多不公正现象需要消除,以便为所有年轻的改革者们提供职业。

我们需要他们每一个人!共和党人们,独立派人士们,有眼光的民主党人们,大家一起来努力吧!

And now the fourth reason: The Republican Party is the Party of the Future because it is the party through which the many things that still need doing will soonest be done—and will be done by enlisting the fullest energies of free, creative, individual people.

Republicans have proved that it is possible for a government to have a warm, sensitive concern for the everyday needs of people, while steering clear of the paternalistic "Big-Brother-is-watching-you" kind of interference. The individual—and especially the idealistic young person—has no faith in a tight federal monopoly on problem-solving. He seeks and deserves opportunity for himself and every other person who is burning to participate in putting right the wrongs of the world.

In our time of prosperity and progress, one thing we must always be on guard against is smugness. True, things are going well; but there are thousands of things still to be done. There are still enough needless sufferings to be cured, enough injustices to be erased, to provide careers for all the crusaders we can produce or find.

We want them all! Republicans, independents, discerning Democrats—come on in and help!

共和党是100年前创建的,它坚信,在一个由自由人构成的国度里,人人都享有平等、公正和机会。

共和党在社会公正方面取得了许多令人瞩目的成就,而不仅仅是说说而已。记录表明,三年来,由于它采取了广泛而有效的措施,使我国在社会公正和机会平等方面已经取得了真正的进展,这些进展比以往20年的总和还要多。

第五,代表未来的政党必须彻底献身于和平事业,因为没有和平,也就没有未来。

正是根据这个道理,美国在1953年提出了和平利用原子能的计划,此后又做了大量工作,使这种新科学为各友好国家所利用,为人民造福。同样,我们为促进有效的裁军也作出了不懈的努力,这样,人们就可以满怀信心地把精力用于建设,而不是浪费在建造毁灭性的机器。

我比任何人都更清楚地认识到,打仗的是年轻人,花好几年时间参加军训和

One hundred years ago the Republican Party was created in a devout belief in equal justice and equal opportunity for all in a nation of free men and women.

What is more, the Republican Party´s record on social justice rests, not on words and promises, but on accomplishment. The record shows that a wide range of quietly effective actions, has brought about more genuine progress toward equal justice and opportunity in the last three years than was accomplished in all the previous twenty put together.

Finally, a Party of the Future must be completely dedicated to peace, as indeed must all Americans. For without peace there is no future.

It was in the light of this truth that the United States proposed its Atoms for Peace Plan in 1953, and since then has done so much to make this new science universally available to friendly nations in order to promote human welfare. In the same way, we have worked unceasingly for the promotion of effective steps in disarmament so that the labor of men could with confidence be devoted to their own improvement rather than wasted in the building of engines of destruction.

No one is more aware than I that it is the young who fight the wars, and

服役的也是年轻人。因此,他们的长辈所允诺的"让我们这一代人享有和平"是不够的,和平也应该属于他们那一代人,属于他们的孩子。确实,我的朋友们,真正意义上的和平现在只有一种,那就是世世代代的永久和平。

同胞们,我所描述的时代是可以到来的。但不是通过革命,不是通过在派别之间挑拨离间,而是通过16800万自由美国人的雄心、判断、热情和果敢。只要他们一起努力,与国外朋友们一起努力,朝着和平世界的共同理想一起努力,这个时代必将来临。

1858年,在共和党代表大会上,林肯用《圣经》里的一句话作为他的开场白:"一城一家自相纷争,必站立不住。"①

今天的世界就好比一个自相纷争的家庭。

---

① 《圣经·新约全书·马太福音》,第12章第25节。

it is the young who give up years of their lives to military training and service. It is not enough that their elders promise "Peace in our time"; it must be peace in their time too, and in their children's time; indeed, my friends, there is only one real peace now, and that is peace for all time.

My friends, the kind of era I have described is possible. But it will not be attained by revolution. It will not be attained by the sordid politics of pitting group against group. It will be brought about by the ambitions and judgments and inspirations and dare of 168 million free Americans working together and with friends abroad toward a common ideal in a peaceful world.

Lincoln, speaking to the Republican State Convention in 1858, began with the biblical quotation, "A house divided against itself cannot stand."

Today the world is a house divided.

然而,林肯在引用《圣经》之后——这一点有时被人们忘了——他却对灾难深重的祖国寄予希望:"我不希望这个家败落,但我的确希望它结束不和状态。"

一个世纪以后,我们对开国元勋们赋予我们的命运,也必须怀有同样的眼光、同样的战斗精神和同样深邃的宗教信仰,而我们对当今四分五裂的世界,也必须寄予同样的希望——在上帝的护佑下,只要我们作出不懈努力,那么,人人过上好日子,拥有美好愿望的新时代就一定会到来。

一位美国哲人说过:"每一个明天都有两个把手。我们要么抓住焦虑的把手,要么抓住信念的把手。"

朋友们,现在,我怀着坚定的信念,深信共和党的目标和原则与这种未来"有紧密的联系",我谦卑而自信地接受你们给予我的美国总统的提名。

王建华　译

But—as is sometimes forgotten—Lincoln followed this quotation with a note of hope for his troubled country: "I do not expect the house to fall," he said, "but I do expect it will cease to be divided."

A century later, we too must have the vision, the fighting spirit, and the deep religious faith in our Creator's destiny for us, to sound a similar note of promise for our divided world; that out of our time there can, with incessant work and with God's help, emerge a new era of good life, good will and good hope for all men.

One American put it this way: "Every tomorrow has two handles. We can take hold of it with the handle of anxiety or the handle of faith."

My friends, in firm faith, and in the conviction that the Republican purposes and principles are "in league" with this kind of future, the nomination that you have tendered me for the Presidency of the United States I now—humbly but confidently—accept.

新边疆就在这里

约翰·肯尼迪*

1960年7月15日

我怀着强烈的责任感和坚定的决心接受诸位提名。

我怀着由衷感激之心,毫无保留地接受提名。我只有一个义务——义不容辞地、全身心地致力于使我党重新获得胜利,使我国重新变得伟大。

我还感激诸位提供了一份关于我党政纲的雄辩声明。如此

---

* 美国第35任总统(1961—1963),民主党人,经选举产生的最年轻总统(43岁)。任内推出"新边疆"施政纲领,但执政仅千日便遇刺身亡。本篇是他在洛杉矶接受民主党总统候选人提名时发表的演说,提出了他日后的重要施政方针——新边疆。

John Kennedy

July 15, 1960

The New Frontier Is Here

With a deep sense of duty and high resolve, I accept your nomination.

I accept it with a full and grateful heart—without reservation—and with only one obligation—the obligation to devote every effort of body, mind and spirit to lead our Party back to victory and our Nation back to greatness.

I am grateful too, that you have provided me with such

雄辩地作出的保证必须履行。"人的权利"——每一个人的尊严所不可或缺的公民权和经济权——实际上是我们的目标,我们的首要原则。这是一个我可以满腔热情、满怀信心地施展才干的政纲。

最后,我庆幸自己在今后几个月能依靠众人相助:依靠一位杰出的竞选伙伴——林登·约翰逊,他使我们对候选人名单的意见趋于一致,给我们的政纲带来了力量;依靠一位当代最雄辩的政治家——阿德莱·史蒂文森;依靠一位我们国家、我们民族所需要的伟大发言人——斯图亚特·赛明顿;依靠那位富有战斗精神的活动家——哈里·杜鲁门,我欢迎他的支持。

现在,我感到安然,因为他们再次站在我这一边。相对我们的共和党对手,我感到自豪,因为他们显然势单力薄,竟然没有一个挑战者有能力、有勇气公开召集会议。

an eloquent statement of our Party´s platform. Pledges which are made so eloquently are made to be kept. "The Rights of Man,"—the civil and economic rights essential to the human dignity of all men—are indeed our goal and our first principles. This is a platform on which I can run with enthusiasm and conviction.

And I am grateful, finally, that I can rely in the coming months on so many others—on a distinguished running mate who brings unity to our ticket and strength to our Platform, Lyndon Johnson—on one of the most articulate statesmen of our time, Adlai Stevenson—on a great spokesman for our needs as a Nation and a people, Stuart Symington—and on that fighting campaigner whose support I welcome, President Harry S. Truman.

I feel a lot safer now that they are on my side again. And I am proud of the contrast with our Republican competitors. For their ranks are apparently so thin that not one challenger has come forth with both the competence and the courage to make theirs an open convention.

我充分意识到这样一个事实:民主党提名具有我这种信仰的人,是冒着很多人视为极大的新的风险的——至少,是1928年以来的新风险①。但我这样认为:民主党再次置信于美国人民,置信于美国人民作出自由、公正判断的能力;同时,你们置信于我,置信于我能够自由、公正地作出判断,维护宪法和我的就职誓言,抛开一切可能的、直接或间接的宗教压力和责任,为国家利益行使总统职权。

14年来,我支持公众教育,支持政教完全分离,抵制任何一方在任何问题上的压力,这些记录现在该有目共睹了。

我希望,鉴于这个国家所面临的、实际存在的种种关键问题,没有一个美国人会仅仅因为我的宗教关系而投票支持我或反对我,以致白白浪费了自己的公民

---

① 1928年大选时,民主党曾提名天主教徒艾尔弗雷德·史密斯为总统候选人,结果被共和党人赫伯特·胡佛击败。

I am fully aware of the fact that the Democratic Party, by nominating someone of my faith, has taken on what many regard as a new and hazardous risk—new, at least since 1928. But I look at it this way: the Democratic Party has once again placed its confidence in the American people, and in their ability to render a free, fair judgement—to uphold the Constitution and my oath of office—and to reject any kind of religious pressure or obligation that might directly or indirectly interfere with my conduct of the Presidency in the national interest.

My record of fourteen years supporting public education—supporting complete separation of church and state—and resisting pressure from any source on any issue should be clear by now to everyone,

I hope that no American, considering the really critical issues facing this country, will waste his franchise by voting either for me or against me solely on account of my religious affiliation. It is not relevant. I want to stress, what some

权。我想强调的是,某些政治领袖或宗教领袖关于这个问题可能说过的话是不恰当的;在其他国家或其他时候可能有过的攻击是不恰当的;可以想见的种种强加于我的压力,如果有的话,也是不恰当的。我现在要告诉诸位,因为你们有权知道:我将作为一个美国人,一个民主党人和自由人,亲自制定每一项维护公共利益的政策。

然而无论如何,我们所追求的在11月的胜利都将来之不易。这一点,我们心里都很明白。我们清楚地知道,各种势力将联手反对我们。我们知道,为了他们的候选人,他们将乞灵于亚伯拉罕·林肯的名字——尽管事实上,他们的政治生涯似乎经常表明,他们对谁都不宽容,对谁都怨恨。

我们知道,要同一个站在所有已知问题的已知方面说话或表决的人竞选①,谈

---

① 指竞选对手尼克松曾任8年副总统,因而相对来说处于有利地位。

---

other political or religious leader may have said on this subject. It is not relevant what abuses may have existed in other countries or in other times. It is not relevant what pressures, if any, might conceivably be brought to bear on me. I am telling you now what you are entitled to know: that my decisions on any public policy will be my own—as an American, a Democrat and a free man.

Under any circumstances, however, the victory that we seek in November will not be easy. We all know that in our hearts. We recognize the power of the forces that will be aligned against us. We know they will invoke the name of Abraham Lincoln on behalf of their candidate—despite the fact that the political career of their candidate has often served to show charity toward none and malice toward for all.

We know that it will not be easy to campaign against a man who has spoken or voted on every known side of every known issue. Mr. Nixon may feel it is his

何容易。尼克松先生可能感到,继新政和公平施政之后,现在轮到他了——可是,在他发牌之前,最好有人切一下牌。

这里所说的"有人",可能是数百万曾投票支持艾森豪威尔总统,但是对他未来的、自封的继承人犹豫不决的美国人。因为,历史学家告诉我们,理查一世①不适合接替大胆的亨利二世②的位置;理查·克伦威尔③不适合继承他叔叔的衣钵。他们在未来还可以加上一句:理查德·尼克松不适合承袭德怀特·艾森豪威尔的事业。

也许他能够继续贯彻党的政策,制定尼克松、本森、德克森和戈德华特之流的政策。可是,这个国家承受不了这种奢华。也许,我们养得起一个继承哈定④的柯立

---

① 英国金雀花王朝国王,1189—1199年在位,亨利二世第三子,在位期间穷兵黩武,征敛日增。
② 英国国王,1154—1189年在位,金雀花王朝建立者。
③ 英国护国公奥利弗·克伦威尔的长子,就职数日后被迫宣布退位。
④ 美国第29任总统(1921—1923),共和党人,任内贪污舞弊盛行,丑闻不断。

turn now, after the New Deal and the Fair Deal—but before he deals, someone had better cut the cards.

That "someone" may be the millions of Americans who voted for President Eisenhower but balk at his would-be, self-appointed successor. For just as historians tell us that Richard I was not fit to fill the shoes of bold Henry II—and that Richard Cromwell was not fit to wear the mantle of his uncle—they might add in future years that Richard Nixon did not measure to the footsteps of Dwight D. Eisenhower.

Perhaps he could carry on the party policies—the policies of Nixon, Benson, Dirksen and Goldwater. But this Nation cannot afford such a luxury. Perhaps we could better afford a Coolidge following Harding. And perhaps we could afford a

芝①。也许，我们养得起一个继承菲尔莫尔②的皮尔斯③。

可是，继布坎南④之后，这个国家需要一个林肯；继塔夫脱⑤之后，我们需要一个威尔逊；继胡佛之后，我们需要富兰克林·罗斯福；继历时8年靠药物诱发的半醒半睡之后，这个国家需要强大的、有创造力的民主党领导白宫。

但是，我们不仅仅是同尼克松先生竞选。我们的任务不仅仅是——登录共和党的失败。那并不十分必要。因为被迫离开农场的家庭会知道如何投票，无须我们告诉他们。失业矿工和纺织工人会知道如何投票。不享受保健医疗的老年人，没有像

---

①美国第 30 任总统(1923—1929)，共和党人，任内推行不干涉工商事务的政策和孤立主义的外交政策。
②美国第 13 任总统(1850—1853)，辉格党人，政绩平平。
③美国第 14 任总统(1853—1857)，民主党人，任内主张加快开发西部，扩大美国领土和增加商业利益。
④美国第 15 任总统(1857—1861)，民主党人，被认为是一个软弱无能、力求妥协的总统。
⑤美国第 27 任总统(1909—1913)，共和党人，生性保守，遇事谨慎寡断。

Pierce following Fillmore.

But after Buchanan, this nation needed a Lincoln—after Taft, we needed a Wilson—after Hoover we needed Franklin Roosevelt. And after eight years of drugged and fitful sleep, this nation needs strong, creative Democratic leadership in the White House.

But we are not merely running against Mr. Nixon. Our task is not merely one of itemizing Republican failures. Nor is that wholly necessary. For the families forced from the farm will know how to vote without our telling them. The unemployed miners and textile workers will know how to vote. The old people without medical care—the families without a decent home—the parents of children without adequate

样住房的家庭,没有足够食物或学校的儿童的父母,他们都知道变革的时候到了。

但是我认为,美国人民希望从我们这儿得到的不仅仅是愤怒的呐喊和攻击。时势严峻,挑战紧迫,赌注太大,以致不允许有通常那种热衷于政治辩论的激情。我们今天在这里,不是要诅咒黑暗,而是要点燃指引我们穿过黑暗、通往安康未来的蜡烛。正如温斯顿·丘吉尔20余年前就职时所说:"我们如果对现在和过去纠缠不休,就有失去将来的危险。"

今天,我们关注的必须是将来。因为世界正在变化。旧的时代正在结束,旧的方式将行不通了。

在国外,权力平衡正在发生变化,出现了新的、更可怕的武器——新的、不确定的国家——人口和物质匮乏带来了新的压力。据说,世界的三分之一可能是自由的——三分之一是残酷镇压的牺牲品——其余三分之一则为贫困、饥饿和妒忌

food or schools—they all know that it's time for a change.

But I think the American people expect more from us than cries of indignation and attack. The times are too grave, the challenge too urgent, and the stakes too high—to permit the customary passions of political debate. We are not here to curse the darkness, but to light the candle that can guide us through that darkness to a safe and sane future. As Winston Churchill said on taking office some twenty years ago: if we open a quarrel between the present and the past, we shall be in danger of losing the future.

Today our concern must be with the future. For the world is changing. The old era is ending. The old ways will not do.

Abroad, the balance of power is shifting. There are new and more terrible weapons—new and uncertain nations—new pressures of population and deprivation. One-third of the world, it has been said, may be free—but one-third is the victim of cruel repression—and the other one-third is rocked by the pangs

的剧痛所困扰。新国家的觉醒正在释放出比原子裂变更大的能量。

与此同时,共产党势力进一步渗入亚洲,横跨中东,并且在佛罗里达海岸线以外约90英里处扩散。朋友转向中立——中立者则转向敌对。正如我们的基调演说人提醒大家的,以进入韩国开始其生涯的总统,将以离开日本而告终。

世界以往接近过战争,可是,人类顶住了对其生存的历次威胁,现在已经把足以多次消灭全部人类的力量掌握在自己手中了。

在国内,未来的、变化中的事实同样是革命性的。新政和公平施政曾经是几代人的大胆举措——可这是新的一代。

农场技术革命导致了产量激增,可我们尚未学会一方面有效地利用这一激增,另一方面保护农民在收入方面全面享有平价制度①的权利。

---

① 一种由政府采用价格补贴和生产限额以调整农产品价格,保护农民购买力的制度。

of poverty, hunger and envy. More energy is released by the awakening of these new nations then by the fission of the atom itself.

Meanwhile, Communist influence has penetrated further into Asia, stood astride in the Middle East and now festers some ninety miles off the coast of Florida. Friends have slipped into neutrality—and neutrals into hostility. As our keynoter reminded us, the President who began his career by going to Korea ends it by staying away from Japan.

The world has been close to war before—but now man, who has survived all previous threats to his existence, has taken into his mortal hands the power to exterminate the entire species some seven times over.

Here, at home, the changing face of the future is equally revolutionary. The New Deal and the Fair Deal were bold measures for their generations—but this is a new generation.

A technological revolution on the farm has led us to an output explosion—but we have not yet learned how to harness that explosion usefully, while protecting our farmers' right to full parity income.

城市人口激增使学校人满为患,郊区拥挤嘈杂,贫民窟愈加肮脏不堪。

争取人权的和平革命——要求结束我们社区生活各个方面的种族歧视——已难以接受怯懦的行政领导所强加的束缚。

医疗进步延长了老年公民的生命,却没有为他们提供在晚年本应享有的尊严和安全。自动化革命使机器在美国工矿企业中取代了人,却没有为他们带来收入,或培训,或用以支付家庭医生、食品杂货商和房东的所需费用。

我们的知识和道德力量也发生了变化——不断下降。经过 7 个干旱、饥饿的歉收年,思想的田野枯萎了。枯萎病袭击了制定规章制度的机构——一场始于华盛顿的干腐病正渗入美国各个角落,导致了贿赂心态,费用账户生活方式,分辨不清什么是合法的,什么是正确的。太多的美国人失去了方向、意志和历史目标感。

总而言之,现在已经到了由新一代领导人——一代新人来处理新问题、把握

An urban population explosion has crowded our schools, cluttered up our suburbs, and increased the squalor of our slums.

A peaceful revolution for human rights—demanding an end to racial discrimination in all parts of our community life has strained at the leashes imposed by timid executive leadership.

A medical revolution has extended the life of our elder citizens without providing the dignity and security those later years deserve. And a revolution of automation finds machines replacing men in the mines and mills of America, without replacing their incomes or their training or their needs to pay the family doctor, grocer and landlord.

There has also been a change—a slippage—in our intellectual and moral strength. Seven lean years of drought and famine have withered a field of ideas. Blight has descended on our regulatory agencies—and a dry rot, beginning in Washington, is seeping into every corner of America—in the payola mentality, the expense account way of life, the confusion between what is legal and what is right. Too many Americans have lost their way, their will, and their sense of historic purpose.

It is a time, in short, for a new generation of leadership—new men to

新机会的时候了。

在世界各地,尤其在新生国家,年轻人即将掌权——他们不为过去的传统所束缚,不被旧的恐惧、仇恨和对立遮住眼睛,能够抛掉旧的标语口号、妄想和猜忌。

共和党将被提名的候选人当然也是一个年轻人。可是,他的方法和麦金莱①一样老。他的党是过去的党。他的语言来自《穷理查年鉴》②。他们的政纲是由民主党剩余下的政纲条目拼凑而成的。他们有勇气追随我们的传统信仰。他们的保证是对原状的保证——而今天是不可能维持原状的。

因为我今晚在这儿向西而立,面对着那条曾经是最后的边疆。在我身后连绵3000英里的土地上,旧日的垦荒者们抛弃了他们的安全、舒适,乃至生命,来到西

---

① 美国第 25 任总统(1897—1901),共和党人。
② 美国 18 世纪著名政治家本杰明·富兰克林编辑的一部年鉴,书中充满言简意赅的警句和格言。

---

cope with new problems and new opportunities.

All over the world, particularly in the newer nations, young men are coming to power—men who are not bound by the traditions of the past—men who are not blinded by the old fears and hates and rivalries—young men who can cast off the old slogans and delusions and suspicions.

The Republican nominee-to-be, of course, is also a young man. But his approach is as old as McKinley. His party is the party of the past. His speeches are generalities from *Poor Richard's Almanac*. Their platform, made up of left-over Democratic planks, has the courage of our old convictions. Their pledge is a pledge to the status quo—and today there can be no status quo.

For I stand tonight facing west on what was once the last frontier. From the lands that stretch three thousand miles behind me, the pioneers of old gave up their safety, their comfort and sometimes their own lives to build a new world

部建设一个新世界。他们不是自己的疑虑的俘虏,不是自己的价格标签的囚徒。他们的座右铭不是"人人为自己",而是"一切为了共同的事业"。他们决心使新世界强大而自由,决心要克服新世界的艰难困苦,战胜从外部和内部构成威胁的敌人。

今天,有人会说,这些斗争都已结束——所有的地平线都已勘探——所有的战斗都已打赢——不再有一条美国的边疆了。

但我相信,与会者中无人会同意这些看法。因为问题没有全部解决,战斗没有全部打赢:今天我们正站在新边疆①的边缘——这是20世纪60年代的边疆,充满未知机会和风险,没有实现的希望和威胁。

伍德罗·威尔逊的新自由许诺给我们国家一种新的政治和经济体制。富兰克林·罗斯福的新政许诺给贫困者以保障和救济。可是,我所说的新边疆不是一套承

---

① 这是肯尼迪提出的施政方针,意在要求美国人民探索和解决"新边疆"面临的各种问题。

here in the West. They were not the captives of their own doubts, the prisoners of their own price tags. Their motto was not "every man for himself" but "all for the common cause." They were determined to make that new world strong and free, to overcome its hazards and its hardships, to conquer the enemies that threatened from without and within.

Today some would say that those struggles are all over—that all the horizons have been explored—that all the battles have been won—that there is no longer an American frontier.

But I trust that no one in this vast assemblage will agree with those sentiments. For the problems are not all solved and the battles are not all won—and we stand today on the edge of a New Frontier—the frontier of the 1960's—a frontier of unknown opportunities and perils, a frontier of unfulfilled hopes and threats.

Woodrow Wilson's New Freedom promised our nation a new political and economic framework. Franklin Roosevelt's New Deal promised security and succor to those in need. But the New Frontier of which I speak is not a set of

诺——而是一套挑战。它所概括的不是我打算为美国人民提供的东西,而是我打算向他们索取的东西。它所吁求的是他们的自尊,而不是他们的钱包——它所许诺的是更多的牺牲,而不是更多的保障。

但是,我要告诉诸位,新边疆就在这里,无论我们是否寻找它。在边疆的那一边,是未探索的科学和空间领域,未解决的和平与战争问题,未征服的无知和偏见角落,未解答的贫困和过剩问题。在这条边疆前退缩,寻求过去的安稳平庸,陶醉于良好意愿和漂亮言辞,是比较容易的——选择这条路的人,不应将他们的选票投给我,无论他们属于哪一个政党。

但我认为,时代需要发明、革新、想象和决定,我要求诸位都成为新边疆的新的开拓者。我号召的是心灵上的年轻人——无论他多大年纪;是所有那些响应这个神圣号召的人。"要坚强,要有勇气;你们不要害怕,也不要灰心。"

promises, it is a set of challenges. It sums up not what I intend to offer the American people, but what I intend to ask of them. It appeals to their pride, not to their pocketbook—it holds out the promise of more sacrifice instead of more security.

But I tell you the New Frontier is here, whether we seek it or not. Beyond that frontier are the uncharted areas of science and space, unsolved problems of peace and war, unconquered pockets of ignorance and prejudice, unanswered questions of poverty and surplus. It would be easier to shrink back from that frontier, to look to the safe mediocrity of the past, to be lulled by good intentions and high rhetoric—and those who prefer that course should not cast their votes for me regardless of party.

But I believe the times demand new invention, innovation, imagination, decision. I am asking each of you to be pioneers on that New Frontier. My call is to the young in heart, regardless of age—to all who respond to the Scriptural call: "Be strong and of good courage; be not afraid, neither be thou dismayed."

因为我们今天需要的是勇气,而不是自满;是领导才干,而不是推销术。而有关领导才干的唯一有效的监测标准是领导能力,强有力的领导。劳合·乔治①说过,疲惫的国家是保守的国家——而今日之美国既不能疲惫,也不能保守。

也许有人希望听到更多——对这个或那个群体作出更多的承诺,对克里姆林宫的人作出更严厉的抨击,对金色的未来作出更多的保证——到那时,税收总是很低,补助金却相当高。但是,我的承诺在你们通过的政纲中,我们的目标将不是靠豪言壮语达到;我们只有对自己充满信心,才能对未来充满信心。

因为,关于这个问题的严峻事实是,我们是在历史的转折关头站在这条边疆上的。我们必须再次证明,这个国家,抑或任何这样孕育的国家,是否能够长久存在下去;证明我们的社会,及其选择的自由、广泛的机会、抉择的范围,是否能够同

---

① 英国首相(1916—1922),自由党领袖。

For courage—not complacency—is our need today—leadership, not salesmanship. And the only valid test of leadership is the ability to lead, and lead vigorously. A tired nation, said David Lloyd George, is a Tory nation, and the United States today cannot afford to be either tired or Tory.

There may be those who wish to hear more—more promises to this group or that—more harsh rhetoric about the men in the Kremlin—more assurances of a golden future, where taxes are always low and subsidies ever high. But my promises are in the platform you have adopted. Our ends will not be won by rhetoric and we can have faith in the future only if we have faith in ourselves.

For the harsh facts of the matter are that we stand on this frontier at a turning-point in history. We must prove all over again whether this nation, or any nation so conceived, can long endure; whether our society, with its freedom of choice, its breadth of opportunity, its range of alternatives, can compete with

共产主义制度竞争。

像我们这样组织和统治的国家能否存在下去？这是一个实际问题。我们是否有魄力、有意愿？在一个我们不仅将亲眼目睹毁灭性武器的新突破，而且要亲眼目睹一场控制天空和降雨、海洋和潮汐、宇宙深处和人的内心的竞赛的时代，我们能否坚持下去？

我们是否胜任这项任务？我们是否应付得了挑战？我们是否愿意像俄国人一样为了将来而牺牲现在？抑或，我们是否必须牺牲将来以享受现在？

这就是新边疆的问题。这就是我们国家必须作出的选择。这个选择不仅存在于两个人或两个政党之间，而且存在于公众利益与私人安逸之间，国家强盛与国家衰弱之间，进步的新鲜空气与"正常状态"的、不流通的、阴湿的空气之间，坚贞不渝的献身精神与缓慢前进的平庸之间。

the Communist system.

Can a nation organized and governed such as ours endure? That is the real question. Have we the nerve and the will? Can we carry through in an age where we will witness not only new breakthroughs in weapons of destruction, but also a race for mastery of the sky and the rain, the ocean and the tides, the far side of space and the inside of men's minds?

Are we up to the task—are we equal to the challenge? Are we willing to match the Russian sacrifice of the present for the future, or must we sacrifice our future in order to enjoy the present?

That is the question of the New Frontier. That is the choice our nation must make—a choice that lies not merely between two men or two parties, but between the public interest and private comfort—between national greatness and national decline—between the fresh air of progress and the stale, dank atmosphere of "normalcy"—between determined dedication and creeping mediocrity.

全人类都在等待我们作出决定。全世界都期望看到我们将要干什么。我们不能辜负他们的信任。我们不能不尝试一下。

从新罕布什尔第一个下雪天,到召开本次大会的这个拥挤的城市,是一条漫长的道路。现在,让我们开始另一次长途旅行,把我带到全美各地你们的城市和家中。把你们的选票、你们的手、你们的声音给我。和我一起回忆以赛亚的话:"那等候耶和华的,必重新得力,他们必如鹰展翅上腾,他们奔跑却不困倦,行走却不疲乏。"①

我们面对的是即将到来的挑战。因此,我们也将侍奉上帝,请他恢复我们的力量。这样,我们就能经受考验。这样,我们就不会困乏。这样,我们就能获得胜利。

王 寅 译

---

① 《圣经·旧约全书·以赛亚书》,第40章31节。

All mankind waits upon our decision. A whole world looks to see what we will do. We cannot fail their trust, we cannot fail to try.

It has been a long road from that first snowy day in New Hampshire to this crowded convention city. Now begins another long journey, taking me into your cities and homes all over America. Give me your help, your hand, your voice, your vote. Recall with me the words of Isaiah: "They that wait upon the Lord shall renew their strength; they shall mount up with wings as eagles; they shall run and not be weary."

As we face the coming challenge, we too shall wait upon the Lord, and ask that he renew our strength, Then shall we be equal to the test. Then shall we not be weary. And then we shall prevail.

与尼克松第一次辩论开场演说①

约翰·肯尼迪

1960 年 9 月 26 日

林肯在1860年竞选时说,问题是这个国家能否以半奴隶半自由的方式存在。1960年的今天,问题是整个世界能否以半奴隶半自由的方式存在,是走向自由还是走向奴隶制。

我认为这在很大程度上取决于美国的作为,取决于她所建立的社会,取决于她所拥有的力量。

① 本篇是肯尼迪与尼克松展开的首场电视辩论会的开场演说,约 8000 万人观看了实况转播。肯尼迪精神饱满,风度翩翩,言辞犀利;而生病初愈的尼克松容颜憔悴。从此,胜利的天平开始向肯尼迪倾斜。

John Kennedy
September 26, 1960

Opening Remarks at His First Presidential Debate with Nixon

In the election of 1860, Abraham Lincoln said the question was whether this nation could exist half-slave or half-free. In the election of 1960, and with the world around us, the question is whether the world will exist half-slave or half-free, whether it will move in the direction of freedom, or whether it will move in the direction of slavery.

I think it will depend in great measure upon what we do here in the United States, on the kind of society that we build, on the kind of strength that we maintain.

因此，摆在国人面前的问题是：我们是否尽到了最大努力？是否达到了应有的实力，强大到足以保持独立，强大到能够向需要我们帮助的国家——那些得靠我们的帮助才能生存的国家——伸出援助之手？应该指出的是，我认为我们做得很不够。美国取得的进展不能令人满意。

这是一个大国，我想她能够更大，这是一个强国，我想她应该更强。

我不满意我国钢铁厂有50%的能力闲置。我不满意作为世界主要工业国之一的美国，其年经济增长率倒数第一。因为经济增长代表着一个国家的生机和活力，它可以显示我们是否有安全的防御，是否能够完成在海外的使命。

我不满的是，我们拥有价值超过90亿的食物，却仍有大批人在挨饿；有400万国人在等待政府发放每人每天价值5美分的食物，与此同时，却有许多食物在腐烂。我目睹了西弗吉尼亚的情况，就在这里，在我们的国度里，孩子们省下学校的午餐来养活他们的家人。我不能满意，因为我们没有尽到对国人应尽的责任。

Therefore, I think the question before the American people is: Are we doing as much as we can do? Are we as strong as we should be? Are we as strong as we must be if we're going to maintain our independence, and if we're going to maintain and hold out the hand of friendship to those who look to us for assistance, to those who look to us for survival? I should make it very clear that I do not think we're doing enough, that I am not satisfied as an American with the progress that we're making.

This is a great country, but I think it could be a greater country; and this is a powerful country, but I think it could be a more powerful country.

I'm not satisfied to have fifty percent of our steel-mill capacity unused. I'm not satisfied when the United States had last year the lowest rate of economic growth of any major industrialized society in the world. Because economic growth means strength and vitality; it means we're able to sustain our defenses; it means we're able to meet our commitments abroad.

I'm not satisfied when we have over nine billion dollars worth of food—some of it rotting—even though there is a hungry world, and even though four million Americans wait for a food package from the government, which averages five cents a day per individual. I saw cases in West Virginia, here in the United States, where children took home part of their school lunch in order to feed their families because I don't think we're meeting our obligations toward these Americans.

我不满的是,苏联培养的科学家和工程师是我们的两倍。

我不满的是,我们的许多教师没有得到合理的薪水,孩子们没有享受到全日制的教育。我认为我们的教育体系应该是世界一流的。

我不满的是,像吉米·霍法①这种控制美国最大工会的人,却未被绳之以法。

我不满的是,我们没有能够充分利用自然资源。我们开发了田纳西流域,建造了深峡谷以及西北部的拦河坝,但我们现有的发电能力——这一工业国能力的标志,到1975年将会被苏联超过。

上述事情的成败,关系到我们的社会将会更加强盛还是停滞不前。

只有当每个美国人都能享受到宪法所赋予的权利,我才能满足。黑人孩子上中学的机会只有白人孩子的一半,成为专业人士的机会只有三分之一,拥有一处

---

① 美国劳工领袖,国际卡车司机联合会主席,1967年以贿赂、诈骗等罪名被判刑13年,1971年获释后神秘失踪。

I'm not satisfied when the Soviet Union is turning out twice as many scientists and engineers as we are.

I'm not satisfied when many of our teachers are inadequately paid, or when our children go to school part-time shifts. I think we should have an educational system second to none.

I'm not satisfied when I see men like Jimmy Hoffa—in charge of the largest union in the United States—still free.

I'm not satisfied when we are failing to develop the natural resources of the United States to the fullest. Here in the United States, which developed the Tennessee Valley and which built the Grand Coulee and the other dams in the Northwest United States at the present rate of hydropower production—and that is the hallmark of an industrialized society—the Soviet Union by 1975 will be producing more power than we are.

These are all the things, I think, in this country that can make our society strong, or can mean that it stands still.

I'm not satisfied until every American enjoys his full constitutional rights. If a Negro baby is born, he has about one-half as much chance to get through high school as a white baby. He has about a third as much chance to be a professional man, about half as much chance to own a house. He has about

房子的机会只有一半,失业的机会却是白人的4倍。我认为我们能够做得更好。我不希望看到任何一个美国人的能力被浪费。

我知道有人会说我们想把一切都归咎于政府。完全不是。我希望个人尽到个人的义务,州尽到州的义务,国家尽到国家的义务。

过去25年里,每一次社会立法都会遇到争论,靠个别美国人不可能开发田纳西流域,但集合起来就能办到。

乔治亚州的一个棉农,或威斯康星州、明尼苏达州一个果农或乳品厂主,他们作为个人,无法顶住市场供求的压力而保护自己,但在政府有力的计划下,他们联合起来就能够做到这一点。

1700万65岁以上的老人靠每月78美元的社会救济支票生活,他们个人无法维持生计,但通过社会保障体系,他们就能够生存。

我不相信庞大的政府,但我相信办事高效的政府,我认为这是美国保证其自

---

uh—four times as much chance that he'll be out of work in his life as the white baby. I think we can do better. I don't want the talents of any American to go to waste.

I know that there are those who want to turn everything over to the government. I don't at all. I want the individuals to meet their responsibilities. And I want the states to meet their responsibilities. But I think there is also a national responsibility.

The argument has been used against every piece of social legislation in the last twenty-five years. The people of the United States individually could not have developed the Tennessee Valley; collectively they could have.

A cotton farmer in Georgia or a peanut farmer or a dairy farmer in Wisconsin and Minnesota, he cannot protect himself against the forces of supply and demand in the market place; but working together in effective governmental programs he can do so.

Seventeen million Americans, who live over sixty-five on an average Social Security check of about seventy-eight dollars a month, they're not able to sustain themselves individually, but they can sustain themselves through the social security system.

I don't believe in big government, but I believe in effective governmental action. And I think that's the only way that the United States is going to main-

由的唯一出路,是能够前进的唯一出路,我认为我们能够做得更好。要担当起时代和形势赋予我们的责任,我们也必须做得更好。

这个责任无法推卸。如果美国失败了,那么整个自由事业也将失败,我想这在很大程度上取决于我们现在的作为。

罗斯福在美洲很有口碑,这是因为他在美国名望颇高,因为美洲人感觉到美国社会行动起来了。希望我们能重树这一形象。我希望美洲人、非洲人、亚洲人开始把期盼的目光投向美国,看我们的作为,让他们注意美国总统在做什么,而不是注意赫鲁晓夫或中国共产党。这是我们这一代人的责任。

罗斯福在1933年的就职演说中曾说过,他们那一代美国人遇到了"决定命运的关键时刻",我认为我们这一代人遇到了同样的关键时刻。现在的问题是,在前所未有的严重攻势下,自由是否能保持下去,这取决于美国的作为。我认为美国到了该重新行动起来的时候了。

石淑芳　译

---

tain its freedom. It's the only way that we're going to move ahead. I think we can do a better job. I think we're going to have to do a better job if we are going to meet the responsibilities which time and events have placed upon us.

We cannot turn the job over to anyone else. If the United States fails, then the whole cause of freedom fails. And I think it depends in great measure on what we do here in this country.

The reason Franklin Roosevelt was a good neighbor in Latin America was because he was a good neighbor in the United States. Because they felt that the American society was moving again. I want us to recapture that image. I want people in Latin America and Africa and Asia to start to look to America; to see how we're doing things; to wonder what the President of the United States is doing; and not to look at Khrushchev, or look at the Chinese Communists. That is the obligation upon our generation.

In 1933, Franklin Roosevelt said in his inaugural that this generation of Americans has a rendezvous with destiny. I think our generation of Americans has the same rendezvous. The question now is: Can freedom be maintained under the most severe tack—attack it has ever known? I think in the final analysis it depends upon what we do here. I think it's time America started moving again.

我接受你们的提名

林登·约翰逊 *

1964 年 8 月 27 日

我接受你们的提名，接受领导本党今年走向胜利的重任。

今天晚上我们创造了纪录，通过了党纲，公开提出我们的党是一个为了全体美国人的政党，一个为了全体美国人的全民党。

---

* 美国第 36 任总统（1963–1969），民主党人。1961 年当选副总统，1963 年肯尼迪遇刺，接任总统，两年后获连任。任内提出"伟大社会"执政纲领，后因扩大侵越战争而失去民心。本篇发表于大西洋城召开的民主党全国代表大会。

Lyndon Johnson

August 27, 1964

I Accept Your Nomination

I accept your nomination. I accept the duty of leading this party to victory this year.

Tonight we offer ourselves—on our record and by our platform—as a party for all Americans, an all-American party for all Americans.

我们这个繁荣昌盛的民族,这个理性者的国家,没有褊狭的派性和乖戾的偏见的位置。少数人的政党永远不能满足全体人民的需要。商人党或劳工党、战争党或和平党、南方党或北方党,都不能满足全体人民的需要。

只有当一个为全体人民服务的政党为我们服务时,才能满足我们的需要。

我们都是这样一个政党——1964年的民主党的党员。

我们的成就为全体美国人谱写了一部值得骄傲的纪录。

如果有人问我们都干了些什么,就让他们看一看我们都承诺了些什么吧。因为承诺已经化为行动;而今天晚上的承诺,我向你们保证,将成为明天的行动。

我们正处在我国历史上最伟大、最持久的和平繁荣时期。今天晚上听我们讲话的美国人,几乎人人都从自己的生活中看到了结果。但是,大多数人的富裕并没有给全体人民带来富裕。那些获得这片土地慷慨馈赠的人,那些财产和权力安然

This prosperous people, this land of reasonable men, has no place for petty partisanship or peevish prejudice. The needs of all can never be met by parties of the few. The needs of all cannot be met by a business party or a labor party, not by a war party or a peace party, not by a southern party or a northern party.

Our deeds will meet our needs only if we are served by a party which serves all our people.

We are members together of such a party, the Democratic Party of 1964.

We have written a proud record of accomplishments for all Americans.

If any ask what we have done, just let them look at what we promised to do. For those promises have become our deeds. And the promises of tonight I can assure you will become the deeds of tomorrow.

We are in the midst of the largest and the longest period of peacetime prosperity in our history. And almost every American listening to us tonight has seen the results in his own life. But prosperity for most has not brought prosperity to all. And those who have received the bounty of this land—who sit tonight

在握、今晚端坐一旁的人，现在不应该不顾及邻舍们的需要。

我们的党、我们的国家，将继续向老人、病人和穷人伸出同情之手、仁义之手、慈爱之手。因为我们当中有谁敢违抗这项命令："你应该向你的兄弟，向地球上的穷人和贫困者，伸出手去。"

我们力图满足的需要、我们力图实现的希望，不仅是我们的需要、我们的希望，而且是大多数人民的需要和希望。

我们的问题很多、很严重，可是，我们的机会更多、更好。

让我把这一点讲清楚。我请求美国人民批准，不是去领导一项已经完成了的计划，也不仅仅是让事情继续发展。我请求美国人民批准我们开始。

此时此刻，这个国家、这一代人，拥有人类第一个机会去建设一个伟大的社会。在这个社会中，人类生活的意义同人类劳动所创造的奇迹相一致。

secure in affluence and safe in power—must not now turn from the needs of their neighbors.

Our party and our Nation will continue to extend the hand of compassion and the hand of affection and love to the old and the sick and the hungry. For who among us dares to betray the command: "Thou shalt open thine hand—unto thy brother, to thy poor, and to thy needy, in thy land."

The needs that we seek to fill, the hopes that we seek to realize, are not our needs, our hopes alone. They are the needs and hopes of most of the people.

Our problems are many and are great. But our opportunities are even greater.

And let me make this clear. I ask the American people for a mandate—not to preside over a finished program—not just to keep things going, I ask the American people for a mandate to begin.

This Nation—this generation—in this hour, has man's first chance to build the Great Society—a place where the meaning of man's life matches the marvels of man's labor.

我们寻求一个人人能劳有所酬,能施展才干得到满足的国家。我们寻求一个人人能追求知识,接触美好事物,享受家庭和社区温暖的国家。

我们寻求一个人人能工作的国家——在这个国家,伴随追求幸福而来的不仅是安全,而且是精神上的成就、升华和满足。

所以,让我们携起手,共同完成这项伟大的任务。

你们是否愿意今天晚上同我一起开始,一起重新建设我们的城市,使它们成为我们孩子居住的体面的地方?

你们是否愿意今天晚上同我一起,开始一项保护我们美好的土地和空气的计划?

让我们大家联合起来,使每一个美国人得以过上他所能希冀的生活,因为最后检验我们文明的,不是商品、不是枪炮,而是质量——我国人民生活的质量,以及我们所造就的男男女女。

We seek a nation where every man can find reward in work and satisfaction in the use of his talents. We seek a nation where every man can seek knowledge, and touch beauty, and rejoice in the closeness of family and community.

We seek a nation where every man can, follow the pursuit of happiness—not just security—but achievements and excellence and fulfillment of the spirit.

So let us join together in this great task.

Will you join me tonight in rebuilding our cities to make them a decent place for our children to live in?

Will you join me tonight in starting a program that will protect the beauty of our land and the air that we breathe?

So let us join together in giving every American the fullest life which he can hope for. For the ultimate test of our civilization, the ultimate test of our faithfulness to our past, is not in our goods and is not in our guns. It is in the quality—the quality of our people's lives and in the men and women that we produce.

这个目标我们能够实现。我们有资源、我们有知识。但是今天晚上我们所要寻求的是勇气。

因为今天晚上的竞争同我们在每一个历史转折关头的竞争一样。它不是自由主义者和保守主义者之间的竞争,不是政党和政党之间、政纲和政纲之间的竞争。这是勇敢和怯懦之间的竞争。这是远见卓识者和只想维持现状者之间的竞争。这是迎接未来者和看不到美好未来者之间的竞争。

这是真正的自由事业。饥饿的人,找不到工作的人,不能教育孩子的人,被匮乏压倒的人——这些人不是完全自由的。

30多年来,从社会保障制度到反贫困战争,我们勤奋工作以扩大人类自由,结果,美国人今天晚上比我们全部光荣历史上的任何一个时期都可以更加自由地按照自己的意愿生活,实现自己的抱负,满足自己的愿望,供养自己的家庭。

This goal can be ours. We have the resources; we have the knowledge. But tonight we must seek the courage.

Because tonight the contest is the same that we have faced at every turning point in history. It is not between liberals and conservatives, it is not between party and party, or platform and platform. It is between courage and timidity. It is between those who have vision and those who see what can be, and those who want only to maintain the status quo. It is between those who welcome the future and those who turn away from its promises.

This is the true cause of freedom. The man who is hungry, who cannot find work or educate his children, who is bowed by want—that man is not fully free.

For more than 30 years, from social security to the war against poverty, we have diligently worked to enlarge the freedom of man. And as a result, Americans tonight are freer to live as they want to live, to. pursue their ambitions, to meet their desires, to raise their families than at any time in all of our glorious history.

每一个美国人心中都知道,事实就是这样!

我决心在我的任期内尽我所能,率领这个伟大的可爱之邦,这个伟大的国家,团结一致,共同奋斗,去追求这个共同目标。我确实相信,我们总有一天会看到一个不分南方和北方、不分东部和西部的美国,一个不为信仰和肤色所分裂、不为猜忌和阶级所折磨的美国。

开国元勋们在建国之前就梦想着美国。拓荒者们梦想着在他们走过的荒野上建立起大都市。

我们的明天正在到来,它可能是暗淡的轮廓,也可能是美好的事物。选择权是我们的,也是你们的,因为它将是我们所敢于做的梦。

我知道,如果富兰克林·罗斯福、哈里·杜鲁门、约翰·肯尼迪今天晚上在这儿的话,他们会做些什么梦。

And every American knows in his heart that this is right.

I am determined in all the time that is mine to use all the talents that I have for bringing this great, lovable land, this great Nation of ours, together—together in greater unity in pursuit of this common purpose. I truly believe that we someday will see an America that knows no North or South, no East or West—an America that is undivided by creed or color, and untorn by suspicion or strife.

The Founding Fathers dreamed America before it was. The pioneers dreamed of great cities on the wilderness that they crossed.

Our tomorrow is on its way. It can be a shape of darkness or it can be a thing of beauty. The choice is ours, it is yours, for it will be the dream that we dare to dream.

I know what kind of a dream Franklin Delano Roosevelt and Harry S. Truman and John F. Kennedy would dream if they were here tonight.

我认为,我知道你们想做什么梦。

今天晚上,我们民主党人满怀信心地走到人民面前,提供的是答案,而不是退却;是团结,而不是分裂;是希望,而不是恐惧或者诽谤。

我们为人民提供的是选择,即把这项勇敢而仁慈的事业继续下去,使这个国家成为人类历史上最强大、最自由、最繁荣、最和平的国家。

那些力图分裂我们的人,反而有助于使我们团结起来。

对于那些向我们挑衅的人,我们转过脸不予理睬。

既然我们已经结束了我们的工作,就让我们明天转而着手新的任务,让我们开始行动吧!

王 寅 译

And I think that I know what kind of a dream you want to dream.

Tonight we of the Democratic Party confidently go before the people offering answers, not retreat; offering unity, not division; offering hope, not fear or smear.

We do offer the people a choice, a choice of continuing on the courageous and the compassionate course that has made this Nation the strongest and the freest and the most prosperous and the most peaceful nation in the history of mankind.

To those who have sought to divide us they have only helped to unite us.

To those who would provoke us we have turned the other cheek.

So as we conclude our labors, let us tomorrow turn to our new task. Let us be on our way!

为美国选择新领导人的时候来到了

理查德·尼克松 *

1968年8月8日

16年前,我站在这个大会面前,接受你们提名我为这个时代或任何时代最伟大的美国人之一——德怀特·艾森豪威尔的竞选伙伴。

8年前,我得到了接受你们提名我为美国总统候选人的最高荣誉。今晚,我再次深感光荣地接受你们提名我为美国总统

---

* 美国第37任总统(1969—1974),共和党人。任内提出尼克松主义,推行均势外交。1972年访华,开创美中关系新阶段。1974年因水门事件下台。本篇是他1968年在佛罗里达迈阿密共和党大会上接受总统候选人提名时的演说。

Richard Nixon

August 8, 1968

It's Time for New Leadership for the United States of America

Sixteen years ago I stood before this Convention to accept your nomination as the running mate of one of the greatest Americans of our time—or of any time—Dwight D. Eisenhower.

Eight years ago, I had the highest honor of accepting your nomination for President of the United States. Tonight, I again proudly accept that nomination for President of the

候选人。

但是我要告诉你们一个消息。这次与以往不同——这次我们将赢得胜利。

美国今日之所以陷入困境,其咎不在于人民,而在于领导人失职。

美国所需要的是配得上她的伟大人民的领导人。

为数众多的美国人知道——那些被遗忘的美国人①和其他美国人知道,美国必须在11月通过选举来回答的大问题是:我们究竟要不要在下一个4年中继续执行过去5年的政策。

美国人民对这个问题的回答,我对这个问题的回答都是:既然世界上这个最强大的国家可能在未来4年里仍被束缚于不知何时才能结束的越南战争,既然世界上这个最富裕的国家竟然管不好本国的经济,既然这个具有最伟大的法治传统

---

① 指属于中产阶级或劳工阶级的人。20世纪30年代,富兰克林·罗斯福总统用来指经济萧条时期受害者。

United States.

But I have news for you. This time there is a difference. This time we are going to win.

America is in trouble today not because her people have failed but because her leaders have failed.

And what America needs are leaders to match the greatness of her people.

And this great group of Americans, the forgotten Americans, and others know that the great question Americans must answer by their votes in November is this: Whether we shall continue for four more years the policies of the last five years.

And this is their answer and this is my answer to that question. When the strongest nation in the world can be tied down for four years in a war in Vietnam with no end in sight; When the richest nation in the world can't manage its own economy; When the nation with the greatest tradition of the rule of law

的国家苦于前所未有的混乱状态,既然一个世纪以来这个以机会均等著称于世的国家已因规模空前的种族暴行而疲惫不堪,既然美国总统前往国外或国内任何一个大城市时总要担心遇到抗议示威——那么,为美利坚合众国选择新领导人的时候来到了。

美国同胞们,今晚我接受这个挑战并承诺为美国提供新的领导人,而且请求你们同我一起接受挑战。

善于承诺而怯于行动的情况,我们见得够多的了。美利坚合众国拥有一个诚实的政府的时机已经到来。

所以,今晚我并不承诺黄金时代会在一个早晨出现。

我不承诺在4年甚至8年的时间里做到根除贫穷、结束歧视和消除一切战争危险。但我承诺会采取行动。我承诺对国外实行新的和平政策,对国内实行新的和

is plagued by unprecedented lawlessness; When a nation that has been known for a century for equality of opportunity is torn by unprecedented racial violence; And when the President of the United States cannot travel abroad or to any major city at home without fear of a hostile demonstration—then it's time for new leadership for the United States of America.

My fellow Americans, tonight I accept the challenge and the commitment to provide that new leadership for America. And I ask you to accept it with me.

We've had enough of big promises and little action. The time has come for honest government in the United States of America.

And so tonight I do not promise the millennium in the morning.

I don't promise that we can eradicate poverty, and end discrimination, eliminate all danger of war in the space of four, or even eight years. But, I do promise action—a new policy for peace abroad; a new policy for peace and progress and

平、进步和正义的政策。

今晚我向你们保证,我们下一届政府外交政策的首要目标就是体面地结束越南战争。我们不能停留在这一件事上。我们需要一种政策来防止出现更多的越南。我们必须对所有的维持和平机构和美国所承担的全部外交义务重新进行评价。

在过去25年中,美国给海外一些国家提供了1500多亿美元的援助。在韩国,现在又在越南,美国提供了它们所需要的绝大部分金钱、武器和人力,帮助这些国家的人民自卫和反对侵略。现在我们是一个富裕、强大、人口众多的国家。但是,美国有2亿人,自由世界有20亿人,所以我说,现在该是自由世界其他国家来承担它们在保卫世界和平与自由这个重任中应负的一份责任的时候了。

我们现在对共产主义世界领导人说,在对抗时期过去后,一个谈判时期已到来。

我们相信,这应该是一个不仅在工厂的生产力方面,而且在观念的性质方面

justice at home.

And I pledge to you tonight that the first priority foreign policy objective of our next Administration will be to bring an honorable end to the war in Vietnam. We shall not stop there—we need a policy to prevent more Vietnams. All of America's peace-keeping institutions and all of America's foreign commitments must be re-appraised.

Over the past twenty-five years, America has provided more than one-hundred and fifty billion dollars in foreign aid to nations abroad. In Korea and now again in Vietnam, the United States furnished most of the money, most of the arms; most of the men to help the people of those countries defend themselves against aggression. Now we are a rich country. We are a strong nation. We are a populous nation. But there are two hundred million Americans and they're two billion people that live in the Free World. And I say the time has come for other nations in the Free World to bear their fair share of the burden of defending peace and freedom around this world.

And now to the leaders of the Communist world, we say: After an era of confrontation, the time has come for an era of negotiation.

We believe this should be an era of peaceful competition, not only in the productivity of our factories but in the quality of our ideas. We extend the hand

的和平竞争时期。我们向所有的人,向俄国人民,向中国人民,向世界各国人民伸出友谊之手。我们为之工作的目标是一个开放的世界、开放的天空、开放的城市、开放的胸怀、开放的思想。

朋友们,在未来8年中,在这个我们即将进入的时期,我认为我们将有争取世界和平的最大机会,但也将面临历史上前所未有的最大的全球性战争的危险。

一个不能在本国维持和平的国家,不会被人相信能在国外维持和平。一个不能在本国得到尊重的总统,也不会在国外得到尊重。一个不能管好本国经济的国家,就不能告诉其他国家如何管好它们的经济。

如果我们要使美国恢复其在国外的威望和曾享有的尊敬,首先应从国内做起——开始这种工作的地方是美利坚合众国。

美国革命过去和现在都是奉献给进步的。但是我国的缔造者们认识到,进步

of friendship to all people, to the Russian people, to the Chinese people, to all people in the world. And we shall work toward the goal of an open world—open skies, open cities, open hearts, open minds.

The next eight years, my friends, this period in which we are entering, I think we will have the greatest opportunity for world peace but also face the greatest danger of world war of any time in our history.

A nation that can't keep the peace at home won't be trusted to keep the peace abroad. A President who isn't treated with respect at home will not be treated with respect abroad. A nation which can't manage its own economy can't tell others how to manage theirs.

If we are to restore prestige and respect for America abroad, the place to begin is at home in the United States of America.

The American Revolution was and is dedicated to progress, but our founders

的首要条件是秩序。

关于进步和秩序之间的关系,现在已经没有争论,因为它们中任何一个若失去对方,本身也就不能存在。

所以,让我们使美国获得良好秩序吧。不过,不是那种压制不同政见并阻挠变革的秩序,而是那种保证人们持有不同政见的权利并为和平变革提供基础的秩序。

如果我们要在这个国家恢复秩序和对法律的尊重,那就首先要做到一点:我们得有一位新的美利坚合众国司法部长。

我向你们保证,我们新的司法部长将按美国总统的指示,发动一场反对国内有组织的罪恶活动的战斗。

我向你们保证,新的美国司法部长将是一名积极的斗士,他将反对在城市中掠夺贫民的放高利贷者和彩票赌博骗子。

recognized that the first requisite of progress is order.

Now, there is no quarrel between progress and order—because neither can exist without the other.

So let us have order in America—not the order that suppresses dissent and discourages change but the order which guarantees the right to dissent and provides the basis for peaceful change.

And if we are to restore order and respect for law in this country there is one place we are going to begin. We are going to have a new Attorney General of the United States of America.

I pledge to you that our new Attorney General will be directed by the President of the United States to launch a war against organized crime in this country.

I pledge to you that the new Attorney General of the United States will be an active belligerent against the loan sharks and the numbers racketeers that rob the urban poor in our cities.

我向你们保证,新的司法部长将开辟一条新的战线,来反对正在腐蚀我国年青一代生活的药丸贩卖者和麻醉品贩卖者。

朋友们,让我今晚所讲的内容清楚地传出这样的信息:那些热衷于在美国社会中进行罪恶和腐蚀活动的人已经接近末日了。犯罪活动这股恶浪不会成为美利坚合众国未来的潮流。

我们将在美国重建免于恐惧的自由,以便美国能在世界上领导重建这项自由的事业。

正像我们今晚承担对秩序的责任一样,让我们对进步也负起责任。

过去5年中,政府接二连三地宣布了帮助失业者的计划、治理城市的计划、救济穷人的计划等等,使我们应接不暇。然而,这些计划给我们带来的却是令人不安的后果,是遍及全国的挫折、暴力和失败。现在,我们的对手还要提出更多类似的

I pledge to you that the new Attorney General will open a new front against the filth peddlers and the narcotics peddlers who are corrupting the lives of the children of this country.

Because, my friends, let this message come through clear from what I say tonight. Time is running out for the merchants of crime and corruption in American society. The wave of crime is not going to be the wave of the future in the United States of America.

We shall re-establish freedom from fear in America so that America can take the lead in re-establishing freedom from fear in the world.

Just as we commit to order tonight, let us commit to progress.

For the past five years we have been deluged by government programs for the unemployed; programs for the cities; programs for the poor. And we have reaped from these programs an ugly harvest of frustration, violence and failure across the land. And now our opponents will be offering more of the same—

计划——再将几十亿美元用于解决就业、住房和福利等问题。我说,现在是停止把几十亿美元扔进已在美利坚合众国失败的计划中去的时候了。

让我们增加美国的财富,以便更慷慨地为老年人、为穷人、为一切不能自助的人提供帮助。

但对那些能够自助的人,我们所需要做的不是增加领取福利救济金的人数,而是将更多的金钱用于工资名册。

对于解决就业和住房问题,应该改变政府现有的一些计划,由政府运用税收和信贷政策去吸引人类历史上争取进步的最重要的工具——美国私人企业参加这场斗争。

让我们建造桥梁,朋友们,建造通向人的尊严的桥梁,以跨越那条将黑色美国同白色美国分隔开来的鸿沟。

more billions for government jobs, government housing, government welfare. I say it is time to quit pouring billions of dollars into programs that have failed in the United States of America.

Let us increase the wealth of America so that we can provide more generously for the aged; and for the needy; and for all those who cannot help themselves.

But for those who are able to help themselves—what we need are not more millions on welfare rolls—but more millions on payrolls in the United States of America.

Instead of government jobs, and government housing, and government welfare, let government use its tax and credit policies to enlist in this battle the greatest engine of progress ever developed in the history of man—American private enterprise.

And let us build bridges, my friends, build bridges to human dignity across that gulf that separates black America from white America.

美国黑人——同美国白人一样——不再需要那些只会使他们长期依赖别人的政府计划。他们不想在国内处于殖民地人民那样的地位。他们需要荣誉、自尊和尊严。但这些只有在取得拥有自己的家庭和公司的平等机会,取得担任经理、管理人员和工人,并参加私人企业的令人振奋的活动的平等机会之后才能实现。

今晚我向你们保证,我们将有提供上述平等机会的新计划。

今晚我们正在创造伟大的历史。

我们不是鸣响全世界都能听到的枪声,我们将在现在还看不到希望的这片土地上点燃千万户人家的希望之灯。

从现在起再过32年,今天活着的美国人中绝大多数将庆祝千年一遇的新年。

从现在起再过8年,在下任总统的第二个任期,我们将庆祝美国革命200周年。

在那个8年后的、光荣的7月4日,我会看到这样一个美国:美国人重新为他们

Black Americans, no more than white Americans, they do not want more government programs which perpetuate dependency. They don't want to be a colony in a nation. They want the pride, and the self-respect, and the dignity that can only come if they have an equal chance to own their own homes, to own their own businesses, to be managers and executives as well as workers, to have apiece of the action in the exciting ventures of private enterprise.

I pledge to you tonight that we shall have new programs which will provide that equal chance.

We make great history tonight.

We do not fire a shot heard around the world but we shall light the lamp of hope in millions of homes across this land in which there is no hope today.

Thirty-two years from now most Americans living today will celebrate a new year that comes once in a thousand years.

Eight years from now, in the second term of the next President, we will celebrate the 200th anniversary of the American Revolution.

This is the kind of a day I see for America on that glorious Fourth—eight years from now. I see a day when Americans are once again proud of their flag.

的国旗感到骄傲,无论在国内或国外,星条旗都将重新作为世界上最伟大的自由和正义的象征而为人尊敬。

我会看到有那么一天:美国总统受到尊敬,他的职务受到尊重,因为他和他的职务值得尊敬和尊重。

我会看到有那么一天:这片土地上的每一个儿童,不论其背景如何,都有机会接受我们的智慧和学校所能提供的最好的教育,都有充分发挥其天赋才智的平等机会。

我会看到有那么一天:美国农村的生活将把人们吸引到农村去,而不是把人们从那里赶走。

我会看到有那么一天:我们在回顾往事时发现,在解决贫民窟、污染和交通问题上,我们已经取得重大突破,而目前这些问题正致命地掐着我们城市的脖子。

我会看到有那么一天:我们的老年公民和几百万其他人可以放心地计划他们

When once again at home and abroad, it is honored as the world's greatest symbol of liberty and justice.

I see a day when the President of the United States is respected and his office is honored because it is worthy of respect and worthy of honor.

I see a day when every child in this land, regardless of his background, has a chance for the best education our wisdom and schools can provide, and an equal chance to go just as high as his talents will take him.

I see a day when life in rural America attracts people to the country, rather than driving them away.

I see a day when we can look back on massive breakthroughs in solving the problems of slums and pollution and traffic which are choking our cities to death.

I see a day when our senior citizens and millions of others can plan for

未来的生活，而不必顾虑政府会使他们手中的美元贬值，来掠夺他们的积蓄。

我会看到有那么一天：我们再次在美国、在世界上获得免于恐惧的自由。我们的国家和全世界都太平无事，地球上每一个人——那些抱有希望、有所追求的人，那些渴望得到自由的人，都把美国看做实现了希望、使梦想成真的光辉榜样，从而寄希望于美国。

同胞们，这就是我要求你们投票支持的事业。这就是我要求你们为之奋斗的事业。在这项事业中，我要求你们不仅为11月份的胜利承担义务，并且进一步为新一届政府承担义务，因为一个人或少数几个领导人就能拯救美国的时代已经过去。如果我们想要成功，今晚就需要全体美国人民的许诺和总动员。

政府可以通过法律；可是，对法律的尊重只能来自虽不掌管法律工作，但将法律放在心头、放在思想上的人民。

the future with the assurance that their government is not going to rob them of their savings by destroying the value of their dollars.

I see a day when we will again have freedom from fear in America and freedom from fear in the world. I see a day when our nation is at peace and the world is at peace and everyone on earth—those who hope, those who aspire, those who crave liberty—will look to America as the shining example of hopes realized and dreams achieved.

My fellow Americans, this is the cause I ask you to vote for. This is the cause I ask you to work for. This is the cause I ask you to commit to—not just for victory in November but beyond that to a new Administration. Because the time when one man or a few leaders could save America is gone. We need tonight nothing less than the total commitment and the total mobilization of the American people if we are to succeed.

Government can pass laws. But respect for law can come only from people who take the law into their hearts and their minds—and not into their hands.

政府可以提供机会;可是,除非人民愿意把握机会,否则机会就毫无意义。

总统可以要求在分裂美国人的种族冲突中实现和解;可是,和解只能来自人民的内心。

美国下一任总统所面对的挑战,在某些方面甚至大于华盛顿或林肯所曾遇到的挑战。因为他所面对的不仅是要在国外,而且是要在国内恢复和平,这在我国历史上是第一次。

没有上帝的帮助,没有你们的帮助,我们必将失败。然而,有了上帝的帮助,有了你们的帮助,我们必将成功。

同胞们,对美国来说,漫长的黑夜即将过去。

现在已经到了我们离开绝望的峡谷,攀上高山的时候,我们即将看到黎明的光辉——美国的新的一天,世界和平与自由的新的曙光。

何百华　译

Government can provide opportunity. But opportunity means nothing unless people are prepared to seize it.

A President can ask for reconciliation in the racial conflict that divides Americans. But reconciliation comes only from the hearts of people.

The next President of the United States will face challenges which in some ways will be greater than those of Washington or Lincoln. Because for the first time in our nation's history, an American President will face not only the problem of restoring peace abroad but of restoring peace at home.

Without God's help and your help, we will surely fail; but with God's help and your help, we shall surely succeed.

My fellow Americans, the long dark night for America is about to end.

The time has come for us to leave the valley of despair and climb the mountain so that we may see the glory of the dawn—a new day for America, and a new dawn for peace and freedom in the world.

为了那个孩子①

理查德·尼克松

1972年11月2日

今天晚上,我在白宫图书馆跟你们说话。这个房间,正如这幢高大建筑物里的其他房间一样,充满了历史的气息。

我经常深夜坐在这里,思索着其他总统曾遭受的危机以及美国的前辈们曾经受的考验。

我试想着我们这一代人之后,坐在这里的总统们将会怎样回顾我们这些岁月。我还考虑到,在这些年里,我能做成什么。

---

①本篇系电视广播演说,发表于大选前夕,充满人情味和富于感染力。

Richard Nixon

November 2, 1972

For That One Child

I am speaking to you tonight from the library of the White House. This room, like all the rooms in this great house, is rich in history.

Often late at night I sit here thinking of the crises other Presidents have known—and of the trials that other generations of Americans have come through.

I think, too, of the Presidents who will be sitting here a generation from now, and how they will look back on these years. And I think of what I want to accomplish in these years.

今天晚上,我想和大家分享一部分我的这些想法。

首先,我想完成世界和平的奠基大业。这样,我们的下一代就能成为本世纪第一代在生活中没有战争,也无须害怕战争的人。

除此以外,我想让美国人——所有的美国人——更清楚地看到,更深刻地体会到,我们这个民族立于历史、立于世界的独特之处是什么。在这个国度中,灵魂和精神是自由的;每一个人都受到尊重;所有的人,个个都有价值,个个都不一样,可以大胆地梦想,并使梦想成真。

我想让所有的美国人都生活得更好——这不仅仅反映在有更好的学校、更多的财富、更清洁的环境、更舒适的房屋以及更吸引人的社区。从精神意义上说,还要有更大程度的满足感、更友善的人际关系、更大的成就感。

我想让每个美国人——所有的美国人——都能焕发出新的热情,追求完美,争取第一,创造第一;达到或超过似乎高不可攀的目标,挖掘出自身未曾意识到的

I would like to share some of those thoughts with you this evening.

Above all, I want to complete the foundations for a world at peace—so that the next generation can be the first in this century to live without war and without the fear of war.

Beyond this, I want Americans—all Americans—to see more clearly and to feel more deeply what it is that makes this Nation of ours unique in history, unique in the world, a nation in which the soul and spirit are free, in which each person is respected, in which the individual human being, each precious, each different, can dare to dream and can live his dreams.

I want progress toward a better life for all Americans—not only in terms of better schools, greater abundance, a cleaner environment, better homes, more attractive communities, but also in a spiritual sense, in terms of greater satisfaction, more kindness in our relations with each other, more fulfillments.

I want each American—all Americans–to find a new zest in the pursuit of excellence, in striving to do their best and to be their best, in learning the supreme satisfaction of setting a seemingly impossible goal, and meeting or surpassing that goal, of finding in themselves that extra reserve of energy or talent

潜在能力、天赋或创造力，并从中获得莫大的满足。

这些就是一个自由的国家里自由的人民的目标。这个国家傲然独立，不靠施舍，不依赖他人，也不因别人的忽冷忽热而忽左忽右。这个国家，人们富有个性，充满了自尊。他们有权利、有能力作出自己的选择，决定自己的生活方向。

这就是为什么我反对无视尊严、无视原则地依赖别人为我们作出决定，规定我们的生活道路。这就是为什么我希望我们复兴个性精神；振兴那种与人民息息相关的政府所富有的勃勃生机与活力；弘扬那种家庭和社区所赋予我们的新的自豪感；增强我们所从事一切工作的责任心，为我们自己负责，也为我们自己尽责，为我们的社区负责，也为我们的社区尽责；因为我们每一个人将通过自己日常生活中的一举一动，决定我们有什么样的社区和国家。

如果齐心合力，我们就能恢复这种精神。那么，4年以后，美国将会带着两个世纪前她初创时的那种使命感，步入她生命中的第三个世纪，更加繁荣昌盛，朝气蓬勃。

or creativity that they had not known was there.

These are goals of a free people, in a free nation, a nation that lives not by handout, not by dependence on others or in hostage to the whims of others, but proud and independent—a nation of individuals with self-respect and with the right and capacity to make their own choices, to chart their own lives.

That is why I want us to turn away from a demeaning, demoralizing dependence on someone else to make our decisions and to guide the course of our lives. That is why I want us to turn toward a renaissance of the individual spirit, toward a new vitality of those governments closest to the people, toward a new pride of place for the family and the community, toward a new sense of responsibility in all that we do, responsibility for ourselves and to ourselves, for our communities and to our communities, knowing that each of us, in every act of his daily life, determines what kind of community and what kind of a country we all will live in.

If, together, we can restore this spirit, then 4 years from now America can enter its third century buoyant and vital and young, with all the purpose that marked its beginning two centuries ago.

下一个4年将决定我们国家开创其第三个世纪的发展方向。我们的方向是什么？是转向国内发展，逃避责任，逃避不仅仅是一个强权大国的责任，而且是一个伟大的人民的责任？而那个伟大的人民生活的国度，正是代表了人类梦中渴望的，并奋斗了数世纪的理想之化身。

我们绝不能逃避责任。如果这样，美国将不再是一个伟大的国家；全世界的自由和平事业将受到致命的危害。

我们的国家之所以是当今伟大、自由的国家，是因为我们的先辈们履行了他们的职责。我们一定要履行我们自己的职责。

我们推进世界和平事业，改善同苏联和中华人民共和国的关系，并不是因为我们自作多情地认为善良的愿望就是一切，也不是因为由于我们不愿打仗，就理所当然地认为其他国家也不愿发动战争。恰恰相反，我们取得了和平的进展，是因

These next 4 years will set the course on which we begin our third century as a nation. What will that course be? Will it have us turning inward, retreating from the responsibilities not only of a great power but of a great people—of a nation that embodies the ideals man has dreamed of and fought for through the centuries?

We cannot retreat from those responsibilities. If we did America would cease to be a great nation, and peace and freedom would be in deadly jeopardy throughout the world.

Ours is a great and a free nation today because past generations of Americans met their responsibilities. And we shall meet ours.

We have made progress toward peace in the world, toward a new relationship with the Soviet Union and the People's Republic of China, not through naive sentimental assumptions that good will is all that matters, or that we can reduce our military strength because we have no intention of making war and we therefore assume other nations would have no such intention. We have achieved progress through peace for precisely the opposite reasons: because we demonstrated that we would not let

为我们不愿在军事上让别国超过,是因为我们根据双方的利弊关系,同他国进行了较量。

历年来,总统候选人总是大肆许诺,当选执政后将推行各种大胆而新奇的方案。今年的总统大选为每个人作出的需要巨额开支的许诺,可谓五花八门,无所不有,也许创下了有史以来的最高纪录。我没有在这次竞选中作过诸如此类的许诺。今天晚上,我也没有这个打算。让我告诉你们为什么。

首先,竞选人历年来许诺的种种狂妄新奇的方案,必须由你们——纳税人——来付款实施。我的竞选对手在这次竞选中所提出的方案,需要增加联邦征税中50%的税额。我认为你们的税额已经过高了。这就是为什么我反对任何会增加你们税额负担的新方案。

其次,太多的竞选承诺不过是形式罢了。我的信条是言必信。我只在有把握时

ourselves be surpassed in military strength and because we bargained with other nations on the basis of their national interest and ours.

It is traditional for a candidate for election to make all sorts of promises about bold new programs he intends to introduce if elected. This year's Presidential campaign has probably established an all-time record for promises of huge new spending programs for just about anything and everything for everybody imaginable. I have not made such promises in this campaign. And I am not going to do so tonight. Let me tell you why.

In the first place, the sort of bold new programs traditionally promised by candidates are all programs that you—the taxpayer—pay for. The programs proposed by our opponents in this campaign would require a So-percent increase in Federal taxes, in your taxes. I think your taxes are already too high. That is why I oppose any new program which would add to your tax burden.

In the second place, too many campaign promises are just that—campaign promises. I believe in keeping the promises I make, and making only those promises I am confident

才许诺。我已经答应将竭尽全力避免征收新税。对于任何违反此项承诺的新方案，我无可承诺。

第三，我自己的立政治国之哲学，不主张把联邦政府新征的美元——你们的美元——作为解决所有社会问题的途径。

我经常说美国之所以强大，并不是政府为人民做了什么，而是人民为自己做了什么。我认为政府应该调动人民的力量，让他们为自己、为社区搞好建设。政府应该广开渠道，激励、支持人民的积极性——而不是在华盛顿指挥一切，扼制这种积极性。

这并不是说联邦政府将在其能够解决问题的各个方面放弃行使其职责。

但这确实意味着联邦政府在经历了40年空前的扩张之后，现在该是矫正这种失衡状态的时候了——把更多的人力、责任和权力下放给各个州和地方，最重要

I can keep. I have promised that I will do all in my power to avoid the need for new taxes. I am not going to promise anything else in the way of new programs that would violate that pledge.

In the third place, my own philosophy of government is not one that looks to new Federal dollars—your dollars—as the solution of every social problem.

I have often said that America became great not because of what government did for people, but because of what people did for themselves. I believe government should free the energies of people to build for themselves and their communities. It should open opportunities, provide incentives, encourage initiative—not stifle initiative by trying to direct everything from Washington.

This does not mean that the Federal Government will abdicate its responsibilities where only it can solve a problem.

It does mean that after 40 years of unprecedented expansion of the Federal Government, the time has come to redress the balance—to shift more people and more responsibility and power back to the States and localities and, most

的是，把它们交还给整个美国人民。

我们没有变弱。美国人民没有变弱。变弱的是政府对人民的信念。我决心恢复政府的这种信念。

我还决心在美国恢复、增强另一种信念。我说的是那种宗教意义上的信念，即道德价值与精神价值，它们从根本上构成了美国经验的一部分。人不能只为自己活着。我们的人格力量、信念力量以及理想力量——所有这些，构成了美国的力量。

当我思考美国意味着什么这一问题时，我想到了广袤的大陆上所包容的一切希望——大都市与小城镇、工厂与农场更加充足的财富，都在无与伦比的程度上被广泛享用；我想到了一种永恒的攻克顽疾、拨乱反正的求索奋斗；我还想到了各种不同年龄、不同信仰、不同种族、不同生活地位的二亿一千万人民大众。

我尤其想到了一个人，一个孩子。那个孩子也许是黑皮肤，也许是黄皮肤，或

important, to the people, all across America.

We have not changed. The American people have not grown weak. What has grown weak is government's faith in people. I am determined to see that faith restored.

I am also determined to see another kind of faith restored and strengthened in America. I speak of the religious faith, the moral and spiritual values that have been so basically a part of our American experience. Man does not live for himself alone, and the strength of our character, the strength of our faith, and the strength of our ideals—these have been the strength of America.

When I think of what America means, I think of all the hope that lies in a vast continent—of great cities and small towns, of factories and farms, of a greater abundance, more widely shared, than the world has ever known, of a constant striving to set right the wrongs that still persist—and I think of 210 million people, of all ages, all persuasions, all races, all stations in life.

More particularly, I think of one person, one child—any child. That child

者是白皮肤；可能很富有，也可能很贫寒；或许是一个男孩，他的家庭在1920年搭坐下等舱来到了这里；或许是一个女孩，她的祖辈在1620年乘五月花号船①来到了这里。那个孩子就是美国。她前面的生活道路还很漫长。她的眼睛里充满了梦想，流泻出每一个美国孩子与生俱有的权利，去充分享受追寻这些梦想的平等机会。

正是为了那个孩子，我需要一个和平的世界，一个能为造就和平所能造就的一切机会。正是为了那个孩子，我需要机会、自由和富裕。正是为了那个孩子，我需要一个公正有序的家园，和一种对他人的权利和情感应有的尊重。

正是为了那个孩子，我想让世人在我们这一代人之后、我们这一世纪之后，作出这样的结论：20世纪70年代的美国有胆有识，忠实地履行了她的职责，迎接了对

---

① 1620年9月，五月花号船载着一批英国清教徒，从英国的德文郡普利茅斯港出发，于同年12月21日到达美国的马萨诸塞州。他们是美国的第一批移民。

may be black or brown or white, rich or poor, a boy whose family came here in steerage in 1920, or a girl whose ancestors came on the Mayflower in 1620. That one child is America, with a life still ahead, with his eyes filled with dreams, and with the birthright of every American child to a full and equal opportunity to pursue those dreams.

It is for that one child that I want a world of peace and a chance to achieve all that peace makes possible. It is for that one child that I want opportunity, and freedom, and abundance. It is for that one child that I want a land of justice, and order, and a decent respect for the rights and the feelings of others.

It is for that one child that I want it said, a generation from now, a century from now, that America in the 1970's had the courage and the vision to meet its responsibilities and to face up to its challenges—to build peace, not merely for

她的挑战——建立和平,不仅仅造福我们这一代,而且造福子孙后代;开发土地,合理支配资源,不仅仅造福我们这一代,而且造福子孙后代;捍卫我们的价值,振兴我们的精神,不仅仅造福我们这一代,而且造福子孙后代。

正是为了那个孩子,我想让下一个4年成为整个美国历史上最辉煌的4年。

这些并不是失之偏颇的党派目标。它们是美国的目标。这就是为什么今天晚上我请求你们去除门户之见,在下周二加入到美国大众选民的行列里去,为代表这些目标的候选人投票。这就是为什么在大选之后,我仍需要你们的支持和协力合作,在下一个4年里,朝着我们的目标努力奋进。

如果我们成功完成了此项任务,那么,那个孩子——我们所有孩子——将可以过上一种人类有史以来比任何时代、任何地方都更有希望、更加辉煌灿烂的生活。

周根骐 译

our generation but for the next generation; to restore the land, to marshal our resources, not merely for our generation but for the next generation; to guard our values and renew our spirit, not merely for our generation but for the next generation.

It is for that one child that I want these next 4 years to be the best 4 years in the whole history of America.

These are not partisan goals. They are America's goals. That is why I ask you tonight, regardless of party, to join the new American majority next Tuesday in voting for candidates who stand for these goals. That is why I ask for your support—after the election—in helping to move forward toward these goals over the next 4 years.

If we succeed in this task, then that one child—all of our children—can look forward to a life more full of hope, promise, than any generation, in any land, in the whole history of mankind.

杰拉尔德·福特 *

1976年8月19日

让我们来改变美国国会

我很荣幸地获得你们的提名,我以自豪和感激之情接受这一提名,并有充分信心为美国人民赢得这一伟大的胜利。我们要在全国每一个州举行决定胜利的竞选活动,从明尼苏达的雪堤,到佐治亚的沙原,我们不会放弃一个州,也不会让出一张

---

* 美国第38任总统(1974—1977),共和党人。1973年10月,副总统阿格纽因涉嫌贪污案辞职,经尼克松提名,他依法填补了这一空缺;上任仅8个月,尼克松总统因水门事件被迫辞职,福特再次依法填补了空缺。本篇节选自他在共和党大会上接受总统候选人提名时发表的演说。

Gerald Ford

August 19, 1976

Let's Change the United States Congress

I am honored by your nomination, and I accept it with pride, with gratitude, and with a total will to win a great victory for the American people. We will wage a winning campaign in every region of this country, from the snowy banks of Minnesota to the sandy plains of Georgia. We concede not

选票。

今晚,我非常自豪地以现任总统的身份出席这次重要会议,自艾森豪威尔向美国人民宣告美国处于和平时期以来,我是第一个出席这类会议的现任总统。

今天晚上,我可以直截了当地告诉你们,我们的国家是殷实的、安全的;我们国家正在走向全面的经济复苏,全体美国人民的生活水准正在提高。

我还要告诉你们,今年,主动权在我们手中。我已经准备好,我渴望在美国人民面前就一些实际问题同吉米·卡特进行面对面的辩论。美国人民有权直接了解我们俩人各自的明确立场。

我非常感激那些为使我赢得共和党提名而始终站在我一边的人们。为了共和党的事业,我奉献了自己整个的成年生活。那些期盼华盛顿有所改变的人们,我很尊重他们的信念。我也盼望有所改变。在多数党长达22年的不幸统治之后,让我们

a single State. We concede not a single vote.

This evening I am proud to stand before this great convention as the first incumbent President since Dwight D. Eisenhower who can tell the American people America is at peace.

Tonight I can tell you straightaway this Nation is sound, this Nation is secure, this Nation is on the march to full economic recovery and a better quality of life for all Americans.

And I will tell you one more thing: This year the issues are on our side. I am ready, I am eager to go before the American people and debate the real issues face to face with Jimmy Carter. The American people have a right to know firsthand exactly where both of us stand.

I am deeply grateful to those who stood with me in winning the nomination of the party whose cause I have served all of my adult life. I respect the convictions of those who want a change in Washington. I want a change, too. After

来改变美国国会。

今晚,我的感激之情已经飞出了这张讲台,我要向远处千千万万朋友们表达这种深情。是他们的信心、他们的努力以及他们无私的支持才使我今天得以站在这里。此时此刻,特别强调他们中的任何一位,都是不公正的,不过,谨让我破例地提一提我的家庭成员——迈克、杰克、史蒂夫和苏珊,尤其是我亲爱的妻子贝蒂。

我们共和党人经历了艰难的斗争,我们不但认为斗争很有好处,还积极参与斗争。不过,今天晚上我们聚集在一起,并不是站在战场上准备宣布停火;相反,我们是把更多的力量集合在训练场上,让大家都准备好,来迎接即将到来的严峻斗争。在此,我要发自肺腑地说,经过几个月的论战以后,现在有里根和我们站在一起,真是感觉很好。①

---

① 指前不久里根曾与他竞争共和党总统候选人提名,现在两人已尽释前嫌,和睦如初。

22 long years of majority misrule, let's change the United States Congress.

My gratitude tonight reaches far beyond this arena to countless friends whose confidence, hard work, and unselfish support have brought me to this moment. It would be unfair to single out anyone, but may I make an exception for my wonderful family—Mike, Jack, Steve, and Susan and especially my dear wife, Betty.

We Republicans have had some tough competition. We not only preach the virtues of competition, we practice them. But tonight we come together not on a battlefield to conclude a cease-fire, but to join forces on a training field that has conditioned us all for the rugged contest ahead. Let me say this from the bottom of my heart: After the scrimmages of the past few months, it really feels good to have Ron Reagan on the same side of the line.

为了壮大我们支持者的阵容，这次大会明智地选择了最能干的美国人中的一位来作为我们的下一任副总统，他就是堪萨斯州的参议员鲍勃·多尔。有了他的帮助，有你们在座各位的帮助，还有千百万美国人民作为后盾，他们向往和平，渴望持久的自由，希望共享美国的繁荣昌盛，他们为美国感到自豪；有了这一切，我们必定会赢得这次大选的胜利。

　　我所讲的胜利，不只是共和党的胜利，而是美国人民的胜利。今晚，你们在家里收听广播，你们是纳税和守法的公民；是你们使我们的制度得以正常运行，也是你们才使得美国发展到今天这个样子，我就是来自于你们中间的一员，我站在你们这一边。

　　过去两年里，我们国家发生了奇妙的事情，7月4日那一天，我们都已经注意到了这一点。经历了多年的混乱和不幸、战争和暴乱、暗杀以及政府高级官员的不道

　　To strengthen our championship lineup, the convention has wisely chosen one of the ablest Americans as our next Vice President, Senator Bob Dole of Kansas. With his help, with your help, with the help of millions of Americans who cherish peace, who want freedom preserved, prosperity shared, and pride in America, we will win this election.

　　I speak not of a Republican victory, but a victory for the American people. You at home listening tonight, you are the people who pay the taxes and obey the laws. You are the people who make our system work. You are the people who make America what it is. It is from your ranks that I come and on your side that I stand.

　　Something wonderful happened to this country of ours the past 2 years. We all came to realize it on the Fourth of July. Together, out of years of turmoil and tragedy, wars and riots, assassinations and wrongdoing in high places, Amer-

德行为,美国人一起重温了1776年的精神。我们再次领会了我们的革命先辈和移民祖先们早期的理想,即自由的人们享有有限的政府和无限的机会。

1976年,我想获得授权,使这种理想变为现实,不过,还需要采纳其他许多非共和党美国人的愿望和意见,才能使这个授权生效,让我有可能完成我的使命。

我一直被称为一个未经选举的总统,一个意外总统。尽管事实上我已经得到国会中绝大多数议员的认可和支持,国会也已经证实我适合担任这个最高职位,不过,我们可能还会听到民主党人那么说的。在既未期盼也未谋求的情况下而当上副总统和总统之后,我对这些高层职位有了一种特殊的感觉。对于我来说,总统和副总统的职位不是我追求的目标,而是我应尽的责任。

因此,今天晚上促使我在这里争取另一个4年任期的,并不是权力和总统职位的诱惑,而是另一种东西,那是每一个勤劳的美国人都能理解的东西,它就是事业

icans recaptured the spirit of 1776. We saw again the pioneer vision of our revolutionary founders and our immigrant ancestors. Their vision was of free men and free women enjoying limited government and unlimited opportunity.

The mandate I want in 1976 is to make this vision a reality, but it will take the voices and the votes of many more Americans who are not Republicans to make that mandate binding and my mission possible.

I have been called an unelected President, an accidental President. We may even hear that again from the other party, despite the fact that I was welcomed and endorsed by an overwhelming majority of their elected representatives in the Congress who certified my fitness to our highest office. Having become Vice President and President without expecting or seeking either, I have a special feeling toward these high offices. To me, the Presidency and the Vice-Presidency were not prizes to be won, but a duty to be done.

So, tonight it is not the power and the glamour of the Presidency that leads me to ask for another 4 years; it is something every hard-working American will

的挑战。这一事业早已开始,却远未完成。

两年前,即在1974年8月9日,我把手放在贝蒂拿着的《圣经》上,作了如同乔治·华盛顿受命时所作的同样的宣誓,那是宪法规定的。我信赖我们的人民,信赖我们的制度,也信赖我自己。当时我说:"同胞们,旷日持久的民族噩梦终于结束了。"

那是我们历史上让人烦恼又令人心碎的时刻。愤怒和怨恨已经上升到相当危险的地步,造成亲朋反目、家庭破裂。我们政治社会的两极分化形成了毫不足取的复仇烈焰。我们的政府制度进入了自阿伯拉罕·林肯作了同样的就职宣誓以来最为僵持的局面。我们的经济在恶性的通货膨胀中挣扎,它使我们很快地跌入到自富兰克林·罗斯福宣誓就职以来最为严重的经济衰退之中。

在那段艰难的日子里,我对我的同胞们说:"我清楚地知道,你们没有投票选我为总统,因此,我请求你们在祈祷中承认我为你们的总统。"

understand—the challenge of a job well begun, but far from finished.

Two years ago, on August 9, 1974, I placed my hand on the Bible, which Betty held, and took the same constitutional oath that was administered to George Washington. I had faith in our people, in our institutions, and in myself. "My fellow Americans," I said, "our long national nightmare is over."

It was an hour in our history that troubled our minds and tore at our hearts. Anger and hatred had risen to dangerous levels, dividing friends and families. The polarization of our political order had aroused unworthy passions of reprisal and revenge. Our governmental system was closer to stalemate than at any time since Abraham Lincoln took the same oath of office. Our economy was in the throes of runaway inflation, taking us headlong into the worst recession since Franklin D. Roosevelt took the same oath.

On that dark day I told my fellow countrymen, "I am acutely aware that you have not elected me as your President by your ballots, so I ask you to confirm me as your President with your prayers."

在白宫的大理石壁炉上刻着约翰·亚当斯的一段祷文,它的结束语是"愿忠诚明智者才可成为白宫的主人"。既然我在那幢具有历史意义的屋子①里工作,我一直努力以这段祷文要求自己。我面临过许多棘手的问题,我也可能犯过错误。但是,总的说来,自1974年8月以来,美国和美国人民都经历了了不起的复苏。的确没有人可以否认这一点。不管控制美国国会的大多数人怎么说,一个简单的事实便是,我们无论在国内还是在国外,都取得了长足的进步。

两年来,我一直站在人民一边,反对国会中渴望拉到选票、挥金如土的多数派。我先后55次否决了奢侈而不明智的立法,其中45次,我使得那些否决生效。那些否决案为美国纳税人省下了巨额的美元。我反对那些权力在手而大肆挥霍税款的人,我同情千千万万微不足道的纳税人。

---

① 指白宫。

On a marble fireplace in the White House is carved a prayer which John Adams wrote. It concludes, "May none but honest and wise men ever rule under this roof." Since I have resided in that historic house, I have tried to live by that prayer. I faced many tough problems. I probably made some mistakes, but on balance, America and Americans have made an incredible comeback since August 1974. Nobody can honestly say otherwise. And the plain truth is that the great progress we have made at home and abroad was in spite of the majority who run the Congress of the United States.

For 2 years I have stood for all the people against a vote-hungry, free-spending congressional majority on Capitol Hill. Fifty-five times I vetoed extravagant and unwise legislation; 45 times I made those vetoes stick. Those vetoes have saved American taxpayers billions and billions of dollars. I am against the big tax spender and for the little taxpayer.

我曾经提议一项永久性的减税,同时削减经费开支,目的是刺激经济的发展,以减轻身负重压的中等收入纳税人的负担。你们个人的免税额应该从750美元提高到1000美元。民主党的政纲谈到税改问题,但有个很大的问题,那就是他们控制的国会并不付诸行动。

我提出根据法院指令,对上学儿童的汽车接送问题要实行宪法的限制。民主党的政纲承认,汽车接送应该是最后一个手段,可是问题同样在于,他们控制的国会按兵不动。

我还提出大范围修改刑法,以便对犯罪和非法吸毒进行严厉的制裁。对于美国用于控制犯罪的费用高达900亿美元这一点,民主党也感到痛惜,但问题仍然是,他们把持的国会没有行动。

民主党政纲大谈强有力的防卫。在这方面存在的问题恰恰相反——他们控制的

I called for a permanent tax cut, coupled with spending reductions, to stimulate the economy and relieve hard-pressed, middle-income taxpayers. Your personal exemption must be raised from $750 to $1,000. The other party's platform talks about tax reform, but there is one big problem—their own Congress won't act.

I called for reasonable constitutional restrictions on court-ordered busing of schoolchildren, but the other party's platform concedes that busing should be a last resort. But there is the same problem–their own Congress won't act.

I called for a major overhaul of criminal laws to crack down on crime and illegal drugs. The other party's platform deplores America's $90 billion cost of crime. There is the problem again—heir own Congress won't act.

The other party's platform talks about a strong defense. Now, here is the

国会的确有所行动。在过去的10年里,他们从我们的国防需求中砍去500亿美元。

朋友们,问题不在华盛顿,问题出在他们控制的国会。

你们知道,美国总统并不是一个魔术师,只要挥舞魔杖或签署文件,便可以即刻停止一场战争,扭转经济衰退,或消灭官僚主义。美国宪法规定总统掌握大权,但是,所有的权力全部来自于美国人民,是美国人民授权给他的。

这就是为什么今天晚上我要求助于美国人民的原因。我不仅请求你们的祈祷,还要请求你们的鼎力支持,请求得到你们的意见和赞同。

我带着两年的政绩来到你们面前,那是未经你们授权的;我向你们保证,我愿在你们的授权之下,在下一个4年里做出更好的政绩来。

正如艾尔·史密斯州长过去经常说的:"让我们看一看记载。"两年前,通货膨胀率达12%,销售业不景气,工厂倒闭,每周都有成千上万的人被解雇;对未来的

other side of the problem—their own Congress did act. They slashed $50 billion from our national defense needs in the last 10 years.

My friends, Washington is not the problem; their Congress is the problem.

You know, the President of the United States is not a magician who can wave a wand or sign a paper that will instantly end a war, cure a recession, or make bureaucracy disappear. A President has immense powers under the Constitution, but all of them ultimately come from the American people and their mandate to him.

That is why, tonight, I turn to the American people and ask not only for your prayers but also for your strength and your support, for your voice, and for your vote.

I come before you with a 2-year record of performance without your mandate. I offer you a 4-year pledge of greater performance with your mandate.

As Governor Al Smith used to say, "Let's look at the record." Two years ago inflation was 12 percent. Sales were off. Plants were shut down. Thousands were

恐惧遏制了经济的发展，也威胁着千百万个家庭。

让我们再看一看1974年8月以来的情况。通货膨胀率已降至6%，工资总额在上升，利润也在提高；生产上去了，又刺激了消费。自从经济衰退状况得到改观以来，差不多有400万美国人找到了新的工作或是回到了原来的工作岗位。今年是美国历史上男女就业人数最多的一年。我们重新恢复了信心，并正在大踏步地从全面的经济复苏走向稳定的繁荣。

两年前，美国正处于从东南亚撤军的困境之中。10年来，民主党控制的历届国会削弱了我们的全球防御，并威胁着我们的战略形势。以色列和阿拉伯国家之间不断加剧的紧张局势，看来不可避免地将导致一场新的战争。全世界都拭目以待地想知道下一步美国将怎么做。正处于一片内乱中的我们，那时是否有这份意愿，有这个精力和统一意志去追求自由呢？

being laid off every week. Fear of the future was throttling down our economy and threatening millions of families.

Let's look at the record since August 1974. Inflation has been cut in half. Payrolls are up. Profits are up. Production is up. Purchases are up. Since the recession was turned around, almost 4 million of our fellow Americans have found new jobs or got their old jobs back. This year more men and women have jobs than ever before in the history of the United States. Confidence has returned, and we are in the full surge of sound recovery to steady prosperity.

Two years ago America was mired in withdrawal from Southeast Asia. A decade of Congresses had shortchanged our global defenses and threatened our strategic posture. Mounting tension between Israel and the Arab nations made another war seem inevitable. The whole world watched and wondered where America was going. Did we in our domestic turmoil have the will, the stamina, and the unity to stand up for freedom?

再看一看两年前8月份以来的记载吧。今天,美国正处于和平时期,并在争取全球的和平。今晚,没有一个美国人在地球上任何一个地方与别人处于交战状态。

我们同西欧及日本在军事上和经济上的联系比以往任何时候都更加紧密。我们同东欧、苏联以及中国的关系是稳固的、警醒的、前景看好的。我所制订的政策使得太平洋地区、非洲和拉丁美洲地区的人民得以稳步地向前发展。信赖美国的以色列和埃及已经走出了历史性的一步,这将使整个中东问题有望得到最终的公正的解决。

如今,美国凭借实力以保持和平的政策得到了全世界的尊重,美国又一次成为自由世界的充满自信的领头人。没有人对于我们为和平所作出的贡献表示怀疑,然而,也没有人应当怀疑,当我们的根本利益面临危险的时候,我们会使用武力,我们会这样做的。

Look at the record since August, 2 years ago. Today America is at peace and seeks peace for all nations. Not a single American is at war anywhere on the face of this Earth tonight.

Our ties with Western Europe and Japan, economic as well as military, were never stronger. Our relations with Eastern Europe, the Soviet Union, and mainland China are firm, vigilant, and forward looking. Policies I have initiated offer sound progress for the peoples of the Pacific, Africa, and Latin America. Israel and Egypt, both trusting the United States, have taken an historic step that promises an eventual just settlement for the whole Middle East.

The world now respects America´s policy of peace through strength. The United States is again the confident leader of the free world. Nobody questions our dedication to peace, but nobody doubts our willingness to use our strength when our vital interests are at stake, and we will.

我呼吁建立现代化的强大的陆军、海军、空军和海军陆战队,以保持美国的长久安全。强大的军事实力总是和平的最佳保障。不过,美国的实力从来都不只是停留在军队上,这种实力还体现在我们的公民和国家领导人之间的相互承诺上,无论是在最高标准的伦理道德观方面,还是在我们国家目前正在经历的精神重建之中,都体现了这种实力。

两年前,人民对最高层官员的信心两度被打碎,而这些官员的权力无一例外全是由人民所授予的。美国人不再相信他们选出的领袖们的诺言,同时也失去了一部分对自己的信心。

还是让我们再一次回顾一下1974年8月以来的情况吧。从一开始,我的政府一直是公正的、坦率的、透明度很高的。当我整个的社会生活和私人生活因接替副总统的职务而接受审查时,我重申了我的终生信条:事实是一种凝聚剂,它使整个政

I called for an up-to-date, powerful Army, Navy, Air Force, and Marines that will keep America secure for decades. A strong military posture is always the best insurance for peace. But America's strength has never rested on arms alone. It is rooted in our mutual commitment of our citizens and leaders in the highest standards of ethics and morality and in the spiritual renewal which our Nation is undergoing right now.

Two years ago people's confidence in their highest officials, to whom they had overwhelmingly entrusted power, had twice been shattered. Losing faith in the word of their elected leaders, Americans lost some of their own faith in themselves.

Again, let's look at the record since August 1974. From the start my administration has been open, candid, forthright. While my entire public and private life was under searching examination for the Vice-Presidency, I reaffirmed my lifelong conviction that truth is the glue that holds government together—not

府凝为一体，当然不只是政府，还有文明本身。我一直要求政府职能部门中的每一个人都保持诚实、正派、为人正直。众议院和参议院也有同样的责任。

美国人民是不会同意国会中存在双重标准的。那些制定我们今天的法律的人，不应该贬低我们重要的立法机关的声誉。这个机关中曾产生过一批伟人：丹尼尔·韦伯斯特、亨利·克莱、山姆·雷伯恩以及罗伯特·A.塔夫脱。无论在首都，还是在州府，抑或是在市政府，个人的道德始终应该符合公众的希望。

1974年8月至1976年8月之间，有记载表明我们正稳步向前发展，走向繁荣、和平，并深孚众望。我的经历是一种发展进步的经历，而不是碌碌无为；我的经历是具体的记载，而不是阿谀逢迎；我的经历是一种业绩，而不是空头许诺。这是一种我自豪地感到要继续下去的经历，也是美国人民——无论是民主党、独立派、还是共和党——在11月2日都会予以支持的经历。

only government but civilization itself. I have demanded honesty, decency, and personal integrity from everybody in the executive branch of the Government. The House and Senate have the same duty.

The American people will not accept a double standard in the United States Congress. Those who make our laws today must not debase the reputation of our great legislative bodies that have given us such giants as Daniel Webster, Henry Clay, Sam Rayburn, and Robert A. Taft. Whether in the Nation's Capital, the State capital, or city hall, private morality and public trust must go together.

From August of 1974 to August of 1976, the record shows steady progress upward toward prosperity, peace, and public trust. My record is one of progress, not platitudes. My record is one of specifics, not smiles. My record is one of performance, not promises. It is a record I am proud to run on. It is a record the American people–Democrats, Independents, and Republicans alike–will support on November 2.

我向你们保证,在以后的4年里,我们将沿着已经开创的道路坚定地走下去。不过,我无意躺在功劳簿上停滞不前,我们将进一步解决通货膨胀问题,我们将继续努力去除官僚作风的痼疾,并纠正这种不良行为。我们将提交一个到1978年为止的平衡预算。我们将致力于提高工作、娱乐、家庭及社区的生活质量。我们不会放弃城市建设,我们将支持各种类型的能保证街道安全、营造健康环境以及恢复社区特色的城建项目。我们要把孩子的教育问题交由他们的父母及当地学校当局来负责。

我们会确保林肯的政党仍然是主张同等权利的政党。我们要制订一种人人平等的纳税办法,这种办法对家庭、个体农场以及个体经营都保持其一致性。

我们要保证社会保险制度的完整性,改善对老年人的医疗照顾办法,使年长的公民能有健康的身体,能享受他们辛苦得来的幸福。我们没有理由让他们因为要获得健康而走向破产。

For the next 4 years I pledge to you that I will hold to the steady course we have begun. But I have no intention of standing on the record alone. We will continue winning the fight against inflation. We will go on reducing the dead weight and impudence of bureaucracy. We will submit a balanced budget by 1978. We will improve the quality of life at work, at play, and in our homes and in our neighborhoods. We will not abandon our cities. We will encourage urban programs which assure safety in the streets, create healthy environments, and restore neighborhood pride. We will return control of our children's education to parents and local school authorities.

We will make sure that the party of Lincoln remains the party of equal rights.We will create a tax structure that is fair for all our citizens, one that preserves the continuity of the family home, the family farm, and the family business.

We will ensure the integrity of the social security system and improve Medicare so that our older citizens can enjoy the health and the happiness that they have earned. There is no reason they should have to go broke just to get well.

我们要使这个富裕的国家切实关心那些不太走运的人，务必要怀着同情心，以得体的举止去满足他们的各种需求。我们要紧缩政府开支，并控制其增长，使那些需要养家糊口的人以及小企业主能增加一些实际收入。

我们要营造一种经济环境，让每一个愿意工作的人都能得到一份有意义的工作，让所有的美国人都过上像样的生活。我们要确保所有的年轻人比我们这一代人有更好的出路，能接受良好的教育，能有一份他们引以为豪的职业。

我们要推行一项农业政策，保证让所有的农民享有公平的市场价格，这项政策将刺激生产的全面发展，致使出口盛况空前，人人得到温饱。我们绝不会把美国农民的收成拿到国际外交上去作抵押，也不会制订贸易禁令。

在出现动荡的地方，尤其在中东地区，我们要继续发挥强有力的指导作用，去争取和平、正义和经济发展。我们要通过耐心的谈判和可靠的军事协议，来建立一

We will make sure that this rich Nation does not neglect citizens who are less fortunate, but provides for their needs with compassion and with dignity. We will reduce the growth and the cost of government and allow individual breadwinners and businesses to keep more of the money that they earn.

We will create a climate in which our economy will provide a meaningful job for everyone who wants to work and a decent standard of life for all Americans. We will ensure that all of our young people have a better chance in life than we had, an education they can use, and a career they can be proud of.

We will carry out a farm policy that assures a fair market price for the farmer, encourages full production, leads to record exports, and eases the hunger within the human family. We will never use the bounty of America's farmers as a pawn in international diplomacy. There will be no embargoes.

We will continue our strong leadership to bring peace, justice, and economic progress where there is turmoil, especially in the Middle East. We will build

个更安全更公正的世界,这些谈判和军事协议可以减少发生危险争端以及恐怖的热核战争的可能性。在我就任总统期间,我们不会回到那条导致冲突、把文明化为乌有的道路上去。

我们要建设一个让人民不仅在物质上而且在精神上都感到富有的美国,一个让人民不仅为自己也为民族和国家感到自豪的美国。

我们要靠实干,而不是靠许诺;要靠经验,而不是靠权术;要靠实际的发展,而不是靠那些在遥远的将来才会隐隐约约昭示出来的神秘计划。

美国人民是明智的,比我们的对手想象的还要明智。他们知道谁要为每一个竞选承诺付出代价。他们并不害怕事实,我们要把事实告诉他们。

我们的竞选从头到尾都是可靠的,它肯定是可以信赖的。我们要斗争到底,赢得胜利。当然,我们已经看到了一些民意测验,听到一些评论家评论我们的政党已

---

a safer and saner world through patient negotiations and dependable arms agreements which reduce the danger of conflict and horror of thermonuclear war. While I am President, we will not return to a collision course that could reduce civilization to ashes.

We will build an America where people feel rich in spirit as well as in worldly goods. We will build an America where people feel proud about themselves and about their country.

We will build on performance, not promises; experience, not expediency; real progress instead of mysterious plans to be revealed in some dim and distant future.

The American people are wise, wiser than our opponents think. They know who pays for every campaign promise. They are not afraid of the truth. We will tell them the truth.

From start to finish, our campaign will be credible; it will be responsible. We will come out fighting, and we will win. Yes, we have all seen the polls

经毫无生机。我以前就听到过这种论调,哈里·杜鲁门也听到过。我来告诉你们我的想法,真正起作用的民意测验,只是在11月2日美国人民要去的那些投票站。

此时此刻,我预计美国人民那天晚上将会说:"杰里①,你干得好!继续干吧!"

当我想到千家万户坐在家里的电视机前观看这个重要会议的时候,我无法说出他们中哪些是共和党人,哪些是民主党人,哪些是独立派。我无法看见他们的肤色,也不了解他们的信仰,我只知道他们都是美国人。

我看见那些热爱自己的丈夫、热爱自己的妻子和孩子的美国人。我看见的美国人,他们热爱自己的国家,热爱她的过去和将来。我看见的美国人,他们勤奋工作,但是,为了使孩子们、使自己的国家享有自由,他们愿意牺牲经努力奋斗而得来的一切。

①杰拉尔德·福特的昵称。

---

and the pundits who say our party is dead. I have heard that before. So did Harry Truman. I will tell you what I think. The only polls that count are the polls the American people go to on November 2.

And right now, I predict that the American people are going to say that night, "Jerry, you have done a good job, keep right on doing it."

As I try in my imagination to look into the homes where families are watching the end of this great convention, I can't tell which faces are Republicans, which are Democrats, and which are Independents. I cannot see their color or their creed. I see only Americans.

I see Americans who love their husbands, their wives, and their children. I see Americans who love their country for what it has been and what it must become. I see Americans who work hard, but who are willing to sacrifice all they have worked for to keep their children and their country free.

我看见美国人在默默地祈祷,他们祈祷国与国之间和平共处,祈祷人与人之间相安无事。我们的确喜欢我们的邻国,我们也已经原谅了那些曾经侵犯过我们的人。

我看见了崭新的一代人,他们知道什么是对的,也很了解他们自己。这一代人决心维护自己的理想和环境,维护我们的国家,乃至全世界。

同胞们,我喜爱我所看见的一切。对这个伟大国家的未来,我没有一丝一毫的担心。当我们一起朝前迈进的时候,我再次承诺我前面已经承诺过的:拥护宪法;行公义事,如同上帝指示我何为善;为美国竭尽我的一切所能。

上帝助我,我不会让你们失望。

包 涵 译

I see Americans who in their own quiet way pray for peace among nations and peace among themselves. We do love our neighbors, and we do forgive those who have trespassed against us.

I see a new generation that knows what is right and knows itself, a generation determined to preserve its ideals, its environment, our Nation, and the world.

My fellow Americans, I like what I see. I have no fear for the future of this great country. And as we go forward together, I promise you once more what I promised before: to uphold the Constitution, to do what is right as God gives me to see the right, and to do the very best that I can for America.

God helping me, I won't let you down.

我们即将拥有的美国

吉米·卡特 *

1976 年 7 月 15 日

我叫吉米·卡特,我正在竞选总统。

从我第一次说这些话以来,已经过了很长时间,在走遍我们伟大祖国各地后,我来到这里接受你们的提名。

1976年的政治局面将与往年不同。它可能成为一个令人鼓

---

* 美国第 39 任总统(1977—1981),民主党人。本篇是他在民主党代表大会上接受总统候选人提名时发表的演讲。在水门事件和一系列政界丑闻的冲击下,美国人普遍感到震惊和失望,卡特及时抓住这种心态,围绕如何恢复对政府的信任的主题展开了竞选活动。

Jimmy Carter

July 15, 1976

The America That We Will Have

My name is Jimmy Carter, and I'm running for President.

It's been a long time since I said those words the first time, and now I've come here after seeing our great country to accept your nomination.

Nineteen seventy-six will not be a year of politics as usual.

舞、充满希望的年份。它将是人们所关注,并冷静而清醒地重新评价我国的性质和目标的一年——选民的行为已经使专家们感到迷惑不解的一年。我向你们保证,1976年将是我们把这个国家的政府交还这个国家的人民的年份。

美国充满了新的气息。我们曾被国外的一场悲剧性战争与国内的丑闻和背弃诺言的行径所动摇。我们的人民正在寻找新的声音、新的观念和新的领导人。

政府有其局限性,不能解决我们所有的问题,尽管如此,我们美国人仍不接受这样一种看法:我们必须甘于失败并容忍庸人的作为,或忍受次等质量的生活。因为我相信:我们能够安然度过这个困难时刻,且比以往更加坚强。像军队经过战斗一样,我们经受了火的锤炼——我们受到了训练,受到了教育。

在持久而简单的道德价值观的指引下,我们已成为既无幻想的唯心主义者,又仍然牢记国家和社会、正义和自由这些古老理想的唯物主义者。

It can be a year of inspiration and hope, and it will be a year of concern, of quiet and sober reassessment of our nation's character and purpose. It has already been a year when voters have confounded the experts. And I guarantee you that it will be the year when we give the government of this country back to the people of this country.

There is a new mood in America. We have been shaken by a tragic war abroad and by scandals and broken promises at home. Our people are searching for new voices and new ideas and new leaders.

Although government has its limits and cannot solve all our problems, we Americans reject the view that we must be reconciled to failures and mediocrity, or to an inferior quality of life. For I believe that we can come through this time of trouble stronger than ever. Like troops who have been in combat, we have been tempered in the fire; we have been disciplined, and we have been educated.

Guided by lasting and simple moral values, we have emerged idealists without illusions, realists who still know the old dreams of justice and liberty, of country and of community.

但是,近年来,我们的国家看到了领导人的失职。我们受到了伤害,我们的理想破灭了。我们看到一堵越来越高的墙把我们和政府分隔开来了。

我们失去了历史上把我们的人民和我们的政府结合起来的一些宝贵东西。我们觉得道德上的堕落已经削弱了我们的国家,它已因缺乏目标和价值观而受到严重的损害。同时,我们觉得公职人员已不再相信我们。

我们的国家漫无目的地漂流为时已久。我们没有领导的情况为时已久。我们的政府分裂、陷入僵局的情况为时已久。我们受制于否决权的情况为时已久。在一届疲惫乏力、陈腐过时的政府手里,我们吃足了苦头,它没有新的观念,没有朝气和活力,没有眼光,没有美国人民对它的信心。现在人们有一种担心:我们最好的年月已经过去。但我对你们说,我们国家的最佳时期还在前头。

我们国家经受了一段时期的苦难,现在该是进行医治的时候了。

But in recent years our nation has seen a failure of leadership. We have been hurt, and we have been disillusioned. We have seen a wall go up that separates us from our own government.

We have lost some precious things that historically have bound our people and our government together. We feel that moral decay has weakened our country, that it is crippled by a lack of goals and values, and that our public officials have lost faith in us.

We have been a nation adrift too long. We have been without leadership too long. We have had divided and deadlocked government too long. We have been governed by veto too long. We have suffered enough at the hands of a tired and worn-out administration without new ideas, without youth or vitality, without vision and without the confidence of the American people. There is a fear that our best years are behind us. But I say to you that our nation's best is still ahead.

Our country has lived through a time of torment. It is now a time for healing.

那些只管作出决定,犯错误后从来不必作出说明,不会因不公正行为而感到痛苦的政治、经济实权人物,使许多人不得不忍受痛苦。在失业问题严重时,他们从来不需要加入求职的队伍。在混乱而令人迷惑的福利制度造成匮乏贫困时,他们从来不必为食物、衣着或一席栖身之地发愁。当公立学校因纠纷、争斗而闹分裂,教学质量下降时,他们的子女就去上专设的私立学校。当官僚机构人事臃肿混乱时,权势人物总能发现并占据具有特殊影响和权利的合适职务。不公平的税务制度适应了他们的要求。在严格控制下进行的秘密活动总是阻碍着改革。

我们不能互相欺骗。为使自己长期保持实力而形成的龌龊的权钱勾结已经屡有所闻,普通公民当然是被拒之门外不得与闻的。

国家所犯的每一次严重错误,美国人民都是被排除于有关过程之外的。如果我们的政府能够反映美国人民的明智判断、对事理的正确认识和高尚的道德品

Too many have had to suffer at the hands of a political economic elite who have shaped decisions and never had to account for mistakes or to suffer from injustice. When unemployment prevails, they never stand in line looking for a job. When deprivation results from a confused and bewildering welfare system, they never do without food or clothing or a place to sleep. When the public schools are inferior or torn by strife, their children go to exclusive private schools. And when the bureaucracy is bloated and confused, the powerful always manage to discover and occupy niches of special influence and privilege. An unfair tax structure serves their needs. And tight secrecy always seems to prevent reform.

All of us must be careful not to cheat each other. Too often unholy, selfperpetuating alliances have been formed between money and politics, and the average citizen has been held at arm's length.

Each time our nation has made a serious mistake the American people have been excluded from the process. The tragedy of Vietnam and Cambodia, the disgrace of Watergate, and the embarrassment of the CIA revelations could have

质,那么越南和柬埔寨的悲剧、水门事件的耻辱和中央情报局泄密的难堪局面,都是可以避免的。

现在是重新审视我们自己的政府的时候了,应该暴露那些秘密活动,揭露那些院外活动集团成员施加于人的无正当理由的压力,消除浪费现象,使文职官员摆脱冗杂的官僚主义公事,提供严格的管理,并且时刻牢记在任何市镇或城市,市长、州长和总统所代表的都是同样的选民。

作为州长,我每天得同复杂、混乱、重叠而且导致浪费的联邦官僚主义公事打交道。作为总统,我要你们帮助我为我们的国家建立一个有能力的、节约的、目的明确并且易于管理的政府。我承认这不容易,但我若当选,就一定要做到,你们可以信赖这样的政府! 我们必须加强政府,使它最紧密地接近人民。企业、工会、农业、教育、科学等部门和政府不应孤立地奋斗,而应朝着共同的目标和共有的机会

been avoided if our government had simply reflected the sound judgement and good common sense and the high moral character of the American people.

It is time for us to take a new look at our own government, to strip away the secrecy, to expose the unwarranted pressure of lobbyists, to eliminate waste, to release our civil servants from bureaucratic chaos, to provide tough management, and always to remember that in any town or city the mayor, the governor, and the President represent exactly the same constituents.

As a governor, I had to deal each day with the complicated and confused and overlapping and wasteful federal government bureaucracy. As President, I want you to help me evolve an efficient, economical, purposeful, and manageable government for our nation. Now, I recognize the difficulty, but if I'm elected, it's going to be done. And you can depend on it! We must strengthen the government closest to the people. Business, labor, agriculture, education, science, and government should not struggle in isolation from one another but should be able to strive toward

努力。我们的资金应该主要投向人民,而不是投向建筑物和武器。必须以尊敬、热情的态度和爱心,对待贫穷、年老、体弱和受苦的人们。

今年我已经多次谈到过爱心的问题。对任何一个政府的检验不是看它如何受到权势人物的欢迎,而是看它如何诚实而公平地对待那些必须依靠它的人。

现在是对所得税制度进行全面改革的时候了。我还要对你们说,那种税制是人类的一个耻辱。我这一辈子多次听到了税务改革的承诺,但从未真正实现。在你们的帮助下我们最终将使它实现,你们可以信赖新的税制。

这里是一些对我们国家真正有好处的事情。现在是全面进行选民登记的时候了。

现在是在全国范围内对全体人民实施全面保健计划的时候了。

现在是真正结束种族和性别歧视的时候了,办法是让那些受歧视之苦的人充分参与政府的决策过程。我若当选,他们将进入政府工作。

---

mutual goals and shared opportunities. We should make major investments in people and not in buildings and weapons. The poor, the aged, the weak, the afflicted must be treated with respect and compassion and with love.

I have spoken a lot of times this year about love. The test of any government is not how popular it is with the powerful but how honestly and fairly it deals with those who must depend on it.

It is time for a complete overhaul of our income tax system. I still tell you: It is a disgrace to the human race. All my life I have heard promises about tax reform, but it never quite happens. With your help, we are finally going to make it happen. And you can depend on it.

Here is something that can really help our country: It is time for universal voter registration.

It is time for a nationwide comprehensive health program for all our people.

It is time to guarantee an end to discrimination because of race or sex by full involvement in the decision making process of government by those who know what it is to suffer from discrimination. And they'll be in the government if I am elected.

现在是执行法律的时候了。除非我们有一个秩序井然的社会,否则我们就不能教育孩子,不能在人民中间创造和谐相处的生活,不能保全人的基本自由。现在,犯罪行为和缺乏公道对于那些无力保护自己的人尤为残酷。任何人触犯刑律都应迅速逮捕和审判,并应受到公正而量刑标准一致的惩罚。

现在是政府领导人和地位最低的公民同样尊重法律的时候了,这样才能永远结束双重审判标准。我看不出有任何理由让大人物中的坏蛋逍遥法外,而将穷苦人关进监狱。

政府的一项简单而应有的功能,就是使人们易于为善,而难于作恶。

作为一名工程师、设计者和商人,我清楚地懂得,以提高生产力和满足需要的工资为基础的、强有力的自由企业制对我们国家的价值。我们民主党人相信竞争优于管制。我们打算把对消费者的有力保护,与政府对自由经济制度的最低干预

It is time for the law to be enforced. We cannot educate children, we cannot create harmony among our people, we cannot preserve basic human freedom unless we have an orderly society. Crime and lack of justice are especially cruel to those who are least able to protect themselves. Swift arrest and trial, fair and uniform punishment, should be expected by anyone who would break our laws.

It is time for our government leaders to respect the law no less than the humblest citizen, so that we can end once and for all a double standard of justice. I see no reason why big-shot crooks should go free and the poor ones go to jail.

A simple and a proper function of government is just to make it easy for us to do good and difficult for us to do wrong.

As an engineer, a planner, a businessman, I see clearly the value to our nation of a strong system of free enterprise based on increase productivity and adequate wages. We Democrats believe that competition is better than regulation, and we intend to combine strong safeguards for consumers with minimal intrusion

这两个方面结合起来。

我认为任何一个有工作能力的人都应该工作——都应该有工作的机会。只要我们还有八九百万美国人找不到工作,我们就无法结束急速加剧的通货膨胀,我们就绝不会有平衡的预算——平衡的预算是我决心要实现的。如果一种经济制度认为失业是有价值或有好处的,它必将彻底失败。我们不能以使人失业的办法来抑制通货膨胀。

任何一位总统的首要职责都是保证国家的安全——保证我们不受攻击或讹诈的自由,保证我们拥有与盟国一起维持和平的能力。

但是和平并不仅仅意味着没有战争。和平是旨在消灭国际恐怖主义的行动。和平是保护人权的不懈努力。和平是力量与善意相结合的表现。我们将为和平祈祷,为和平奋斗,以期最终能为所有国家永远消除核破坏的威胁。

of government in our free economic system.

I believe that anyone who is able to work ought to work—and ought to have a chance to work. We will never have an end to the inflationary spiral, we will never have a balanced budget—which I am determined to see—as long as we have eight or nine million Americans out of work who cannot find a job. Any system of economics is bankrupt if it sees either value or virtue in unemployment. We simply cannot check inflation by keeping people out of work.

The foremost responsibility of any President, above all else, is to guarantee the security of our nation—a guarantee of freedom from the threat of successful attack or blackmail, and the ability with our allies to maintain peace.

But peace is not the mere absence of war. Peace is action to stamp out international terrorism. Peace is the unceasing effort to preserve human rights. Peace is a combined demonstration of strength and good will. We will pray for peace and we will work for peace, until we have removed from all nations for all time the threat of nuclear destruction.

对于我们的朋友和盟国，我要说：使我们在为民主共同作出贡献的过程中团结起来的东西，要比有时在经济或政治问题上使我们分裂开来的东西重要得多。

　　对于努力摆脱贫困的国家，我要说：美国理解你们的追求，并且向你们伸出援助之手。

　　对于那些想与我们进行竞争的国家，我要说：我们既不害怕竞争，也不认为竞争会妨碍我们之间更为广泛的合作。

　　对于所有的人，我要说：经过二百多年之后，美国在它对自由与平等所承担的义务中依旧信心十足，充满活力，而且我们将永远保持这种信心和活力。

　　我们能够拥有这样的美国：它将使经济需要与我们建立一种可以自豪地传之后代的环境的愿望统一起来。

　　我们能够拥有这样的美国：它将向我的孩子、你们的孩子和每一个孩子提供质量优异的教育。

To our friends and allies I say that what unites us through our common dedication to democracy is much more important than that which occasionally divides us on economics or politics.

To the nations that seek to lift themselves from poverty I say that America shares your aspirations and extends its hand to you.

To those nation-states that wish to compete with us I say that we neither fear competition nor see it as an obstacle to wider cooperation.

To all people I say that after two hundred years America still remains confident and youthful in its commitment to freedom and equality, and we always will be.

We can have an America that has reconciled its economic needs with its desire for an environment that we can pass on with pride to the next generation.

We can have an America that provides excellence in education to my child and your child and every child.

我们能够拥有这样的美国：它支持我们的种族多样性、宗教多样性、文化多样性，并引以为豪，因为它知道，使我们成为伟大的国家并继续保持这种地位的那些力量、朝气和创造性就来源于这种多元传统。

　　我们能够拥有这样的美国：它不是压制或监视人民，而是尊重人民的尊严、隐私和不受干扰的权利。

　　我们能够拥有这样的美国：在这里，自由与平等不会发生矛盾，而是互相支持；在这里，我国早期领袖们的理想将在我们的时代全面实现。

　　我们能够拥有这样的美国：它将运用学生的理想主义、护士或社会工作者的热情、农民的坚定性、教师的智慧、商界领袖的务实精神、年老公民的经验和劳动者的希望，为我们全体人民建设更美好生活。

　　我们能够拥有这样的美国，我们即将拥有这样的美国！

We can have an America that encourages and takes pride in our ethnic diversity, our religious diversity, our cultural diversity—knowing that out of this pluralistic heritage has come the strength and the vitality and the creativity that has made us great and will keep us great.

We can have an American government that does not oppress or spy on its own people but respects our dignity and our privacy and our right to be let alone.

We can have an America where freedom, on the one hand, and equality, on the other hand, are mutually supportive and not in conflict, and where the dreams of our nation's first leaders are fully realized in our own day and age.

And we can have an America which harnesses the idealism of the student, the compassion of a nurse or the social worker, the determination of a farmer, the wisdom of a teacher, the practicality of the business leader, the experience of the senior citizen, and the hope of a laborer to build a better life for us all.

And we can have it, and we're going to have it!

我将看到美国团结起来,重新前进。这是一个多样性的、朝气蓬勃和宽容大度的国家,带着自豪和信心进入我们的第三个世纪——一个实践着我国宪法的崇高原则、符合我国人民的庄重举止的美国。

这才是我们所要求的美国。这就是我们即将拥有的美国。

这次大会以后,我们将阔步前进。我们也许会有意见分歧,但仍团结一致,因为我们都冷静地下定了决心,要使我国家恢复豁达、进取、慷慨的精神风貌,我们都准备好投身于国家的伟大事业。作为兄弟姐妹,我们的心将由于把我们自己称为美国人而重新充满豪情。

秦文勇　译

I see an America on the move again, united, a diverse and vital and tolerant nation, entering our third century with pride and confidence, an America that lives up to the majesty of our Constitution and the simple decency of our people.

This is the America we want. This is the America that we will have.

We will go forward from this convention with some differences of opinion perhaps, but nevertheless united in a calm determination to make our country large and driving and generous in spirit once again, ready to embark on great national deeds. And once again, as brothers and sisters, our hearts will swell with pride to call ourselves Americans.

本次竞选运动的主要问题

罗纳德·里根 *

1980年7月17日

我深刻地意识到你们的信任所赋予我的责任,因而我接受你们的提名,参加美利坚合众国总统的竞选。我以深深的感激之情接受你们的提名,并愿借此机会代表我们大家感谢底特律和密歇根的人民对我们的热情接待。同时,我感谢你们真挚

---

* 美国第40任总统(1981—1989),共和党人。做过电视节目主持人和演员,曾任加州州长。1980年击败卡特上台后,实行减税以振兴经济,增加军费以"重振国威"。本篇是他在密歇根州底特律市共和党大会上接受总统候选人提名时的演说,严厉抨击卡特执政带来了"灾难",提出了许多振兴美国的措施,其中包括承诺在3年内把所得税率降低30%,从而深深打动了选民。

Ronald Reagan

July 17, 1980

The Major Issue of This Campaign

With a deep awareness of the responsibility conferred by your trust, I accept your nomination for the presidency of the United States. I do so with deep gratitude, and I think also I might interject on behalf of all of us, our thanks to Detroit and the people of Michigan and to this city for the warm hospitality they have shown. And I thank you for your

地支持我推荐乔治·布什为副总统候选人。

今晚,我为我们的党感到非常自豪。这次大会向全美国展示了一个持有积极的计划以解决我国各种问题的统一的党;一个愿意同全国一切持有同样价值观的人达成新的共识的党,这些价值观体现于下面这几个词:家庭、工作、邻里、和平和自由。

我知道我们曾有过这样那样的争执,可那只涉及实现目标的方法。在目标上没有争论。作为总统,我将与50个州长建立旨在鼓励他们消除对妇女的歧视的一种联系。我将密切注视联邦法律,以保证它们的实施,并在必要时增加某些法规。

在我国历史上,美国人从来没有像现在这样不得不面对着危及我们生存的3种威胁,其中任何一种都能毁掉我们。我们面对着逐渐走向崩溃的经济、已被削弱的国防和建立在供应不足基础上的能源政策。

wholehearted response to my recommendation in regard to George Bush as a candidate for vice president.

I am very proud of our party tonight. This convention has shown to all America a party united, with positive programs for solving the nation's problems; a party ready to build a new consensus with all those across the land who share a community of values embodied in these words: family, work, neighborhood, peace and freedom.

I know we have had a quarrel or two, but only as to the method of attaining a goal. There was no argument about the goal. As president, I will establish a liaison with the 50 governors to encourage them to eliminate, where it exists, discrimination against women. I will monitor federal laws to insure their implementation and to add statutes if they are needed.

Never before in our history have Americans been called upon to face three grave threats to our very existence, any one of which could destroy us. We face a disintegrating economy, a weakened defense and an energy policy based on the sharing of scarcity.

本次竞选运动的主要问题是，民主党领导人——在白宫的和在国会的——对于落在我们身上的这种前所未有的灾难，负有直接的政治、个人和道义责任。他们告诉我们说，他们已经最大限度地做了力所能及的事情。他们说美国已经有过众所周知的全盛时期，我们的国家已经达到了顶点。他们期望你们对孩子们说：美国人民不再抱有妥善处理他们各种问题的意愿；未来将要求人们作出牺牲，却给予人们极少的机遇。

同胞们，我完全反对这种看法。美国人是创造了地球上最高生活水平的最慷慨的人民，他们不会接受如下的观念：我们只有通过使自己后退，才能为别人创建一个更好的世界。那些认为我们只能那样做的人无权领导这个国家。

我不会站在一旁眼看这个伟大的国家在庸人领导下毁灭自己，那些庸人身不由己地从一个危机漂向另一个危机，逐渐损害了我国的意志和目标。我们聚集在

The major issue of this campaign is the direct political, personal and moral responsibility of Democratic Party leadership—in the White House and in Congress—for this unprecedented calamity which has befallen us. They tell us they have done the most that humanly could be done. They say that the United States has had its day in the sun; that our nation has passed its zenith. They expect you to tell your children that the American people no longer have the will to cope with their problems; that the future will be one of sacrifice and few opportunities.

My fellow citizens, I utterly reject that view. The American people, the most generous on earth, who created the highest standard of living, are not going to accept the notion that we can only make a better world for others by moving backwards ourselves. Those who believe we can have no business leading the nation.

I will not stand by and watch this great country destroy itself under mediocre leadership that drifts from one crisis to the next, eroding our national will and purpose. We have come together here because the American people deserve

这里,因为美国人民应该从他们委以国家最高职务的人那里得到更好的东西,我们决心起来为此努力。

首先,我们必须克服现政府所搞的那一套:以通货膨胀、高失业率、经济衰退、飞涨的税款和赤字开支为原料,以能源危机为调味品,烹制出一份新的、完全无法消化的经济炖杂烩。那是一种使全国人民倒胃口的经济炖杂烩。

我们的问题不是抽象的经济理论,而是有血有肉的问题,是给人们带来痛苦、损害他们的道德品质的问题。人民不应由于政府把错误归罪于他们而进一步受到侮辱。我们之所以有通货膨胀问题不是——如卡特先生所说的那样——因为我们生活得太好了。

一个坚决拒绝量入为出,并已在前几天对我们说本年赤字将达600亿美元的政府首脑,竟敢伸出手指来谴责一直努力避免亏损而又未获成功的企业和工会。

---

better from those to whom they entrust our nation's highest offices, and we stand united in our resolve to do something about it.

First, we must overcome something the present administration has cooked up: a new and altogether indigestible economic stew, one part inflation, one part high unemployment, one part recession, one part runaway taxes, one party deficit spending and seasoned by an energy crisis. It's an economic stew that has turned the national stomach.

Ours are not problems of abstract economic theory. Those are problems of flesh and blood; problems that cause pain and destroy the moral fiber of real people who should not suffer the further indignity of being told by the government that it is all somehow their fault. We do not have inflation because—as Mr. Carter says—we have lived too well.

The head of a government which has utterly refused to live within its means and which has, in the last few days, told us that this year's deficit will be $60 billion, dares to point the finger of blame at business and labor, both of which have been engaged in a losing struggle just trying to stay even.

他告诉我们,高额税款是对我们有利的,那似乎是说,政府花费我们的钱不会造成通货膨胀,而当我们花费时就会引起通货膨胀了。

那些造成我国历史上最严重的能源短缺的人要我们节约一些,以便用光石油、汽油和天然气的时刻稍迟一些到来。节约当然是可取的,我们绝不应该浪费能源。但是节约不是满足能源需求的唯一办法。

美国必须设法提供更多的能源。共和党解决经济问题的方案是以发展生产力为基础的。

在我们的地下和海岸线附近储藏着大量石油和天然气,却未被开采。因为现政府似乎相信,美国人民宁愿忍受更多的规定、税款和限制,而不愿拥有更多的能源。

煤炭含有巨大的潜能。在严格保证安全的操作规程下生产的核能也是如此。

High taxes, we are told, are somehow good for us, as if, when government spends our money it isn't inflationary, but when we spend it, it is.

Those who preside over the worst energy shortage in our history tell us to use less, so that we will run out of oil, gasoline, and natural gas a little more slowly. Conservation is desirable, of course, for we must not waste energy. But conservation is not the sole answer to our energy needs.

America must get to work producing more energy. The Republican program for solving economic problems is based on growth and productivity.

Large amounts of oil and natural gas lay beneath our land and off our shores, untouched because the present administration seems to believe the American people would rather see more regulation, taxes and controls than more energy.

Coal offers great potential. So does nuclear energy produced under rigorous

它可以为几千家工厂、几百万个职位和家庭供应电力。利用此类能源的计划绝不能为极少数反对经济增长的人所挫败,他们的阻挠活动常常能在管理机构中获得注意和支持。

请不要误会,我们不会允许我国人民的安全和我们的环境受到损害,但须重申:我国人民在经济上的繁荣兴旺,也是组成我们环境的一个基本部分。

我们的问题是严重而长期的。然而,我们从那些高居领导职位的人那里听到的全都是一些同样的、听厌了的提议,要求政府更多地徒劳无益的空忙、瞎搞和更多的控制——所有这些都是导致我们目前这种状况的根本缘由。

我们必须有清晰的眼光,辨明什么是非常重要的事和什么是仅属可取的事,其次必须有勇气将政府重新置于控制之下,使它能为人民所接受。

非常重要的工作是我们既要使经济增长保持前进的势头,又要使帮助社会上

safety standards. It could supply electricity for thousands of industries and millions of jobs and homes. It must not be thwarted by a tiny minority opposed to economic growth which often finds friendly ears in regulatory agencies for its obstructionist campaigns.

Make no mistake. We will not permit the safety of our people or our environment heritage to be jeopardized, but we are going to reaffirm that the economic prosperity of our people is a fundamental part of our environment.

Our problems are both acute and chronic, yet all we hear from those in positions of leadership are the same tired proposals for more government tinkering, more meddling and more control—all of which led us to this state in the first place.

We must have the clarity of vision to see the difference between what is essential and what is merely desirable, and then the courage to bring our government back under control and make it acceptable to the people.

It is essential that we maintain both the forward momentum of economic growth and the strength of the safety net beneath those in society who need

需要帮助的人的安全网保持力量。我们还认为,保持社会保障制度各个方面的公正性是非常重要的。

除了这些非常重要的事项之外,我认为联邦政府显然已发展得过于臃肿。现在是让政府节食消肿的时候了。因此,我成为总统后的第一个举措将是立即彻底冻结联邦雇用任何人员。然后,从企业、工会和其他方面召集最优秀的人才,来对政府各部、局和依靠联邦拨款的机构进行仔细的审查。我们也要寻求在各级政府中工作的许多富有献身精神的、勤奋工作的雇员的帮助和意见,他们像其他人一样要求一个有效率的政府。我知道,许多人由于在工作中看到那种失败和正在失败的政策已引起混乱和浪费而心灰意冷了。

工作和家庭在我们的生活中处于中心地位,是我们作为自由人民所享有的尊严的基础。如果我们夺走人们的劳动所得,或夺走他们的工作,我们就使他们失去

help. We also believe it is essential that the integrity of all aspects of Social Security are preserved.

Beyond these essentials, I believe it is clear our federal government is overgrown and overweight. Indeed, it is time for our government to go on a diet. Therefore, my first act as chief executive will be to impose an immediate and thorough freeze on federal hiring. Then, we are going to enlist the very best minds from business, labor and whatever quarter to conduct a detailed review of every department, bureau and agency that lives by federal appropriations. We are also going to enlist the help and ideas of many dedicated and hard working government employees at all levels who want a more efficient government as much as the rest of us do. I know that many are demoralized by the confusion and waste they confront in their work as a result of failed and failing policies.

Work and family are at the center of our lives; the foundation of our dignity as a free people. When we deprive people of what they have earned, or

了尊严,并且破坏了他们的家庭。除非有工作,否则我们就不能供养家庭;除非人们既有钱也有信心进行投资,否则我们就不能提供就业机会。

这些概念来源于这样的经济制度:它在200多年间帮助我们掌握了一大片土地,为我们的人民创造出从前做梦也想不到的繁荣,而且为世界上其他地方数以百万计的人提供了衣食。如果我们的政府不再忽视这个经济制度所赖以建立的基本价值观,不再辜负那些使这个制度运作下去的美国工人的信任和美好意愿,那么将来它必将继续为我们服务。

美国人民现正承担着我国历史上和平时期最沉重的税款——根据现行法律,明年1月的税款负担将更沉重。税款使我们自己不胜负担,造成了经济上的枯竭和滞胀,破坏了人们储蓄、投资和生产的能力和动机。

必须制止这种情况。我们必须制止这种财政上的自我毁灭,以使我们的经济

take away their jobs, we destroy their dignity and undermine their families. We cannot support our families unless there are jobs; and we cannot have jobs unless people have both money to invest and the faith to invest it.

There are concepts that stem from an economic system that for more than 200 years has helped us master a continent, create a previously undreamed of prosperity for our people and has fed millions of others around the globe. That system will continue to serve us in the future if our government will stop ignoring the basic values on which it was built and stop betraying the trust and good will of the American workers who keep it going.

The American people are carrying the heaviest peacetime tax burden in our nation's history—and it will grow even heavier, under present law, next January. We are taxing ourselves into economic exhaustion and stagnation, crushing our ability and incentive to save, invest and produce.

This must stop. We must halt this fiscal self-destruction and restore sanity

制度恢复正常。

长期以来我一直主张：在3年内把所得税率降低30%。这种分阶段减税办法将首先在1981年对分期付款的初付款项减税10%，这是共和党人、国会和我都已提出的主张。

对于减轻美国人民的沉重负担来说，分阶段降低税率还只是一个开始，我们不应止步于此。

在我总统任期内的每一财政年度，在经济状况和预算所列重点事项允许的范围内，我将努力做得更多。这中间包括改进企业折旧税，以便刺激投资，更换工厂和设备，使更多美国人重新得到工作，使我们国家在世界商业中重新具有竞争力。我们还将按国民生产总值的一定百分比来降低政府开支。

对于那些缺乏技能的人，我们将设法帮助他们学到技能。对于那些没有就业

---

to our economic system.

I have long advocated a 30 percent reduction in income tax rates over a period of three years. This phased tax reduction would begin with a 10 percent "down payment" tax cut in 1981, which the Republicans and Congress and I have already proposed.

A phased reduction of tax rates would go a long way toward easing the heavy burden on the American people. But, we should not stop here.

Within the context of economic conditions and appropriate budget priorities during each fiscal year of my presidency, I would strive to go further. This would include improvement in business depreciation taxes so we can stimulate investment in order to get plants and equipment replaced, put more Americans back to work and put our nation back on the road to being competitive in world commerce. We will also work to reduce the cost of government as a percentage of our gross national product.

For those without skills, we'll find a way to help them get skills. For those without job opportunities, we'll stimulate new opportunities, particularly in

机会的人,我们将——特别是在他们所住的贫民区——促成新的就业机会。对于那些放弃了希望的人,我们将使他们恢复希望,欢迎他们加入使美国恢复伟大形象的全国性运动中来!

当我们将目光从国内转向国外事务时,我们看到了现政府政绩中同样令人不安的一页。

——一支苏联战斗队在古巴进行训练工作,离我们的海岸仅90英里。

——一支苏联侵略军占领了阿富汗,进一步威胁着我们在中东的重要利益。

——美国国防力量处于几十年来的最低点,而苏联用于战略武器和常规武器的支出都大大超过了我们。

——我们的欧洲盟国紧张地注视着来自东方的越来越大的威胁,希望我国出面领导它们,却失望了。

the inner cities where they live. For those who have abandoned hope, we'll restore hope and we'll welcome them into a great national crusade to make America great again!

When we move from domestic affairs and cast our eyes abroad, we see an equally sorry chapter on the record of the present administration.

—As Soviet combat brigade trains in Cuba, just 90 miles from our shores.

—A Soviet army of invasion occupies Afghanistan, further threatening our vital interests in the Middle East.

—America's defense strength is at its lowest ebb in a generation, while the Soviet Union is vastly outspending us in both strategic and conventional arms.

—Our European allies, looking nervously at the growing menace from the East, turn to us for leadership and fail to find it.

——更加不可思议的是,50多个美国同胞在国外被一个独裁国家扣为人质已超过8个月①,使我们遭到了全世界的嘲笑。

大大小小的敌手检验着我们的意志,并竭力动摇我们的决心。但我们在应该展示力量的时候却表现出了软弱,在形势要求我们坚定沉着时却表现出了优柔寡断。

在我们所追求的全部目标中,第一位的,最重要的是建立持久的世界和平。我们必须始终不渝地准备以诚意进行谈判,愿意遵循任何能够缓和紧张局势并推进和平可能性的合理途径。但是让我们的朋友和对我们不怀好意的人都注意:美国对本国公民和世界人民都负有责任,绝不允许那些意在破坏自由的人来左右地球上人类未来的生活道路。我愿把我的当选视为证明我们已经重下决心保持世界和

---

① 指1979年11月美国驻伊朗使馆人员被扣为人质。

And, incredibly more than 50 of our fellow Americans have been held captive for over eight months by a dictatorial foreign power that holds us up to ridicule before the world.

Adversaries large and small test our will and seek to confound our resolve, but we are given weakness when we need strength; vacillation when the times demand firmness.

Of all the objectives we seek, first and foremost is the establishment of lasting world peace. We must always stand ready to negotiate in good faith, ready to pursue any reasonable avenue that holds forth the promise of lessening tensions and furthering the prospects of peace. But let our friends and those who may wish us ill take Note: the United States has an obligation to its citizens and to the people of the world never to let those who would destroy freedom dictate the future course of human life on this planet. I would regard my election as proof that we have renewed our resolve to preserve world peace and

平与自由。这个国家将重新强大起来,足以做到这一点。

今晚,让我们把自己奉献给使美国重新振兴起来的事业。我要求你们不但信任我,而且信任你们的价值观——我们的价值观——使我负责实践这些价值观。我要求你们信任那个不分任何种族、宗教、社会、政治、地区或经济界限的美国精神;这种精神曾使从世界各地来到这里寻求自由的千百万移民的内心充满热情。

有人说那种精神已不复存在。但我在全国大小城市和农村中都看到了它,触摸到了它。美国精神仍然存在,如果你我都愿去做该做的事,实实在在地去做那些刺激经济、提高生产力、使美国重返工作的事,它就会迸发出强大的活力。

我承认我有点害怕提出我即将提出的事情——我更怕不提出这事——那就是我们应在一个默默祷告的时刻开始我们联合起来进行的战斗。愿上帝保佑美国。

钟维尧　译

---

freedom. This nation will once again be strong enough to do that.

Tonight, let us dedicate ourselves to renewing the American compact. I ask you not simply to "Trust me," but to trust your values—our values—and to hold me responsible for living up to them. I ask you to trust that American spirit which knows no ethnic, religious, social, political, regional, or economic boundaries; the spirit that burned with zeal in the hearts of millions of immigrants from every corner of the Earth who came here in search of freedom.

Some say that spirit no longer exists. But I have seen it—I have felt it—all across the land; in the big cities, the small towns and in rural America. The American spirit is still there, ready to blaze into life if you and I are willing to do what has to be done; the practical, down-to-earth things that will stimulate our economy, increase productivity and put America back to work.

I'll confess that I've been a little afraid to suggest what I'm going to suggest—I'm more afraid not to—that we begin our crusade joined together in a moment of silent prayer. God bless America.

罗纳德·里根

1984 年 11 月 3 日

美国的未来掌握在你们的手中①

再过3天,本次竞选就要结束了。美国的未来掌握在你们手中。当你们在家中或邻舍与家人和朋友谈论这次选举时,有一件事我想大家都能够取得一致:我们都想投票支持什么,而不是反对什么。我们投票是为了一个更美好的美国,一个人民团结的更加强大的国家,一个充满希望和新机会的和平的未来,一个心想事成的未来,一个因为美国行、美国人也行的未来。

① 在 1984 年大选前夕,里根总统利用每周一次的广播演说的机会,充分施展演说才华,罗列政绩,竭力粉饰其鹰派外表,并不失时机地嘲讽对手。

Ronald Reagan

November 3, 1984

America's Future Will Be in Your Hands

In 3 days this election campaign will be over, and America's future will be in your hands. As you discuss the election with family and friends in your homes and neighborhoods, I think there's one thing we can all agree on. We all want to vote for something, not against something. We want to vote for a better America, for a stronger country with our people pulling together; a future of peace, filled with hope and new opportunity, a future where our progress is limited only by our own dreams and determination and where Americans are working because America is working.

因此,在我看来,要问的问题似乎非常简单明确:哪一方的政绩和建议会带来更好的机会,使你们和你们的家庭享有美好、成功的未来?我们的对手不会多花时间谈论他们的政绩,这是可以理解的。他们的政绩不言而喻。

在入主白宫和控制了国会两院4年之后,他们留下的是在国内外更加虚弱的美国。他们想让我们忘却他们的遗产:在国内是退而求其次,是两位数的通货膨胀,是创纪录的税收和利率;在国外则是动荡加剧,和平屡遭威胁。如果他们不是那么固执地把那帖令人厌恶的苦药继续强加于人的话,我倒愿意忘却那份纪录。

至于他们的新建议,与老建议的不同之处仅有一点:许诺更多了。他们将花费更多的钱,把你们的税款提得更高,高达每户1890美元,超过了每月150美元。

现在,我的竞选对手急切地想要你们相信,他的巨额增税建议不会有损于你们的家庭。这就是他在电视宣传上所说的。这种电视宣传的可信度,同他把自己打

So, it seems to me the question to be asked is a straightforward one: Which team's record and proposals stand a better chance to enable you and your families to enjoy a strong and successful future? Well, our opponents don't spend much time speaking about their record. And that's understandable. Their record speaks for itself.

After 4 years of controlling the White House and both Houses of Congress, they left America weaker, both at home and abroad. They would have us forget their legacy of an America second-best, double-digit inflation, record taxes and interest rates at home; growing instability and threats to peace abroad. I'd be willing to forget that record, too, if they weren't so bound and determined to give us more of that medicine that made us sick.

As for their new proposals, they differ from their old ones in only one respect: They've promised more. They will spend more, and they will raise your taxes much higher, the equivalent of $1,890 per household, more than $150 per month.

Now, my opponent wants very badly to make you believe his enormous tax increase proposal won't hurt your families. That's what his commercials say.

扮成一个支持强大国防的热心人的宣传一模一样。他站在航空母舰的甲板上,却投票反对建造;站在F-14战斗机旁,却投票反对购置;站在美国士兵身边,却反对增加其薪饷。

我们的对手决意恢复超过以往的税收和开支。如果他们再度控制政府,那么美国人在回顾我们的任期时,就会把它视为在日益恶化的通货膨胀和衰退的无涯荒漠中一晃而过的繁荣绿洲。

是的,他们用心可谓良苦,但是,仅有良苦用心是不够的。过去他们的政策造成了美国的衰退,今天他们会使我们再度衰弱,而且将来还会使我们进一步衰弱。

美国能够做得更好,而且还能好上加好。事实是,美国正在做得更好。我们的美国梦是让雄鹰翱翔,而他们的美国梦将把我们带回雄鹰铩羽的年代,这就是分歧的焦点。

And those commercials are every bit as believable as the ones he ran portraying himself as a person committed to a strong national defense, standing on the deck of a carrier, even though he voted against them, with F-14 fighters, which he also voted against, and beside American enlisted men, whose salary increases he opposed.

Our opponents are determined to bring back even more big taxing and spending than before. And if they regain control of this government, Americans may look back on our term as one brief oasis of prosperity in an endless desert of worsening inflation and recession.

Yes, their intentions are good. But good intentions aren't good enough. Their policies made America weak before. They would make us weak again today, and even weaker still in the future.

America can do better, much better. And the fact is, America is doing better. The principal difference is, our vision for America will let the eagle soar. Theirs will return us to the days of the sore eagle.

我们仍然面对诸多重大问题,但是我们今天的经济比4年前更强大了,因为我们已削减了税率,抑制了通货膨胀,降低了利率,还创造了600万个新职位。美国更加安全了,因为我们正在重建我们的国防和联盟,以实力来确保和平。

今天,美国的发展正引导世界跨入复兴的时代,这有助于建立一个更安全、更繁荣的世界。世人对美国的尊敬和信任又开始增加了。与4年前不同,美国今天摆出威慑的态势,而苏联则裹足不前,这一切也有助于建立一个更加安全的世界和更美好的未来。

我们已取得了良好的开端,但这仅仅是开端而已。我们要进一步降低税率,为每个美国人创造更多的工作和机会,不让任何人落伍。不让任何人落伍意味着我们必须继续努力,使衰老的产业现代化,重建我们的内地城市和美国的贫困地区,这样,每一个想要工作的美国人才都能找到一份工作。

We still face great problems, but today our economy is stronger than 4 years ago because we've cut your tax rates, brought inflation and interest rates down, and created 6 million new jobs. And America is more secure, because we're rebuilding our defenses and our alliances to ensure peace through strength.

Today the United States expansion is leading the world into recovery, and that contributes to a safer, more prosperous world. Respect for America and confidence in America are rising again. And unlike 4 years ago, the United States is deterring, the Soviets aren't advancing, and all this, too, contributes to a safer world and a better future.

We've made a good start, but it's only a start. We want to lower your tax rates further to create more jobs and opportunities for every American with nobody left behind. And nobody left behind means we must continue our efforts to modernize our older industries and to rebuild our inner cities and distressed areas of America, so every American who wants a job can find a job.

我们提出企业振兴立法,以鼓励贫困地区的实业发展并创造工作机会。但是从第一天起,我们的企业振兴提案就被国会领导层当作要挟的砝码。也正是这些人,他们似乎还期望美国黑人和西班牙裔美国人,会以整齐步伐紧跟民主党走呢。

我向所有希望有机会开始攀登经济阶梯的人保证,我们一定会建设更加美好的生活:如果你们给予我们支持,我们绝不会把你们的选票视为理所当然。

我相信美国人正以新的力量、信心、精神和团结走到一起来了。我从心底里感谢你们给了我在过去 4 年中为你们服务的荣誉。我敦促你们星期二都去投票,并希望你们投我们团队的票,投我们整个团体的票。这样我们就能够取得更大的进步,为你们大家创建一个充满机会的、强大而安全的未来。

下周再见,谢谢! 愿上帝保佑你们!

钟维尧　译

We've sponsored enterprise zone legislation, to encourage business development and creation of jobs in distressed areas. But from day one, our enterprise zone proposal has been held hostage by the House leadership, the very people who act as if they expect black and Hispanic Americans to march in lockstep with the Democratic Party.

I can assure all of you who want the opportunity to begin climbing the economic ladder, to build a better life: If you give us your support, we will never take your votes for granted.

I believe Americans are coming together with new strength, confidence, spirit, and unity. From the bottom of my heart, I thank you for allowing me the honor of serving you these past 4 years. I urge you to vote on Tuesday, and I hope you'll cast your votes for our team, our entire team, so we can make even greater progress in building a strong, secure future of opportunity for all of you.

Until next week, thanks for listening. God bless you.

使美国变得更安全、更强大

乔治·H.布什*

1992年8月20日

我十分自豪、十分荣幸地接受美国总统候选人提名。

4年以前,我谈到了使命——对我这一生、对我们国家的使命。我谈到了一件紧迫的使命——保卫我们的安全并促进实现

---

①美国第41任总统(1989—1993),共和党人。1988年和民主党总统候选人杜卡基斯对垒,最终获胜。本篇是他在共和党代表大会上再度接受总统候选人提名时发表的演说。他在大力宣扬自己在内政和外交上取得的成就的同时,煞费苦心地试图让选民们注意克林顿的年轻稚嫩。即使如此,他还是不敌打着变革旗号的民主党人克林顿,未能实现连任。

George H. Bush
August 20, 1992

To Make America Safer and Stronger

I am proud to receive and I am honored to accept your nomination for President of the United States.

Four years ago, I spoke about missions for my life and for our country. I spoke of one urgent mission, defending our

我们在国外的目标。

我的对手们说我在对外政策上花费了过多时间。似乎为应付核战争而进行演习、让学童们躲藏在课桌下的举动所反映的形势是无足轻重的。我看到了使我们的孩子们免除核战争噩梦的可能性,我也使他们免除了那种噩梦。

在过去4年中,呼吸到自由这种新鲜空气的人数之多在整个人类历史上是空前的。我看到了帮助他们的机会,我也实际帮助了他们。

就上述两方面而言,当时出现的,不是一年,也不是10年,而是整个人类历史上难遇的良机。我为我们的孩子和子孙抓住了那些机会,对此我毫不感到愧悔。

现在,苏联熊可能一去不复返了,但是树林中仍有狼。在伊拉克领袖萨达姆·侯赛因进犯科威特时,我们看清了这一点。当时的中东可能变成触发一场核战争的地区——我们的能源供应成为扣在他们手里的抵押品。所以我们那时的做法是

security and promoting the American ideal abroad.

My opponents say I spend too much time on foreign policy, as if it didn't matter that schoolchildren once hid under their desks in drills to prepare for nuclear war. I saw the chance to rid our children's dreams of the nuclear nightmare, and I did.

Over the past 4 years, more people have breathed the fresh air of freedom than in all of human history. I saw a chance to help, and I did.

These were the two defining opportunities not of a year, not of a decade, but of an entire span of human history. I seized those opportunities for our kids and our grandkids, and I make no apologies for that.

Now, the Soviet bear may be gone, but there are still wolves in the woods. We saw that when Saddam Hussein invaded Kuwait. The Mideast might have become a nuclear powder keg, our energy supplies held hostage. So we did

正确的、必要的。我们清除了一种威胁,解放了一国人民,并将一个暴君禁闭在他自己的国家。

看看阿肯色州国民警卫队的领导人,那位想成为三军总司令的人是怎样做的?在我咬断枪弹时,他在咬自己的指甲。在国会投票支持我以后两天,我的竞选对手说话表态了。我引用他的原话:"如果赞成票和反对票的票数很接近,我想我会投票支持多数人的意见的。但是,我也同意少数人提出的论点。"在我听来,他的方针可以用他乘坐公共汽车旅行时所见到的一块道路标志牌来概括:天雨路滑,小心驾驶。

注意,这是严重的问题。请想一想民主党最后一次控制宾夕法尼亚大街两头时①,外交政策的种种失误所造成的影响:加油站上的长队;谷物禁运;被蒙住双眼

---

① "大街两头"指白宫和国会,它们都位于首都华盛顿宾夕法尼亚大街。

what was right and what was necessary. We destroyed a threat, freed a people, and locked a tyrant in the prison of his own country.

What about the leader of the Arkansas National Guard, the man who hopes to be Commander in Chief? Well, I bit the bullet, and he bit his nails. Two days after Congress followed my lead, my opponent said this, and I quote directly: "I guess I would have voted with the majority if it was a close vote. But I agree with the arguments the minority made." Now, sounds to me like his policy can be summed up by a road sign he's probably seen on his bus tour, "Slippery When Wet."

Look, this is serious business. Think about the impact of our foreign policy failures the last time the Democrats controlled both ends of Pennsylvania Av-

的美国人质。

在未来4年中,我们的外交政策还将遇到更多像科威特那样的挑战。我们必须抵制恐怖主义者和侵略者;必须控制并销毁危险的武器。争取自由的斗争远未结束。我还希望成为第一位访问自由的、民主的古巴的总统。

在面对这种种挑战时,谁来领导世界?不是我的竞选对手。他在接受总统候选人提名时发表的演说中,只用了65秒钟来告诉我们他对世界的看法。

那时他说——我再次引用他的原话,我要做到公平、确凿有据——美国正到处受到"嘲笑"。好,把这告诉世界各国人民吧,在他们心目中,美国依然代表着一种理想。把这告诉世界各地的领袖人物吧,在他们心目中,美国仍是值得尊敬的。被人嘲笑?把这告诉曾经投身于"沙漠风暴"的男男女女吧。

近来你们从报纸上读到了一些东西,因此,这里让我离开正题插入几句话。这

enue: gas lines, grain embargoes, American hostages blindfolded.

There will be more foreign policy challenges like Kuwait in the next 4 years, terrorists and aggressors to stand up to, dangerous weapons to be controlled and destroyed. Freedom's fight is not finished. I look forward to being the first President to visit a free, democratic Cuba.

Who will lead the world in the face of these challenges? Not my opponent. In his acceptance speech he devoted just 65 seconds to telling us about the world.

Then he said that America was, and I quote again—I want to be fair and factual—I quote, being "ridiculed" everywhere. Well, tell that to the people around the world, for whom America is still a dream. Tell that to leaders around the world, from whom America commands respect. Ridiculed? Tell that to the men and women of Desert Storm.

Let me just make an aside comment here because of what you've been

是一个政治问题比较突出的年份,但是世界上存在着不少危险。你们可以确信,我绝不会让政治干扰外交方面的决策。暂且不管选举结果如何,凡是美利坚合众国国家安全所要求的事,我都会全力以赴地去做。这是我发自内心的保证。

这次选举涉及了变革问题。这没有什么异乎寻常,因为美国革命是永远不会结束的。今天,变革的步伐正在加快。我们面对着新的机会和新的挑战。问题在于你们相信谁能使变革产生效益,有利于你们。

我的竞选对手说美国是一个正处于衰落中的国家。关于我们的经济,他说美国的排名在德国之下,正降到接近不发达的斯里兰卡。

不要轻信任何人,尤其不要轻信一个正在竞选总统的人告诉你美国已是一个二等国家。

也许他没有听说我们仍然是世界上最大的经济强国。以各国销往境外的产品

reading in the paper. This is a political year, but there's a lot of danger in the world. You can be sure I will never let politics interfere with a foreign policy decision. Forget the election; I will do right, what is right for the national security of the United States of America, and that is a pledge from my heart.

This election is about change. But that's not unusual, because the American revolution is never ending. Today, the pace of change is accelerating. We face new opportunities and new challenges. The question is: Who do you trust to make change work for you?

My opponent says America is a nation in decline. Of our economy, he says we are somewhere on the list beneath Germany, heading south toward Sri Lanka.

Well, don't let anyone tell you that America is second-rate, especially somebody running for President.

Maybe he hasn't heard that we are still the world's largest economy. No other nation sells more outside its borders. The Germans, the British, the

而言,没有任何国家及得上我们。德国人、英国人、日本人都赶不上你们,赶不上美国工人和美国农民的生产力。我的竞选对手不愿提到这些。他不会提醒你们:利率是20年来最低的,数以百万计的美国人改善了他们家庭的经济情况。你们也不会听他谈到通货膨胀——这个掠夺中层阶级的盗贼已被关进了最为牢固的监狱。

我将继续努力,以提高个人收入免税额,并通过削减资产收益税来创造更多的就业机会。这会特别有助于小型工商企业。你们知道,小型企业创造的就业机会可以占全部就业机会的三分之二。但我的竞选对手对小型企业的计划显然只顾眼前,因而是危险的。除了课征新的所得税以外,他的计划还将开征一种新的工资发放总额税和另一种新税,以支付政府接管医疗保健工作和进行培训工作所需的费用。而这些还只是个开始。

我认为小型企业需要从税款负担、管制条例和诉讼案件中解脱出来。

Japanese can't touch the productivity of you, the American worker and the American farmer. My opponent won't mention that. He won't remind you that interest rates are the lowest they've been in 20 years, and millions of Americans have refinanced their homes. You just won't hear that inflation, the thief of the middle class, has been locked in a maximum security prison.

I will also continue to fight to increase the personal exemption and to create jobs by winning a cut in capital gains taxes. That will especially help small businesses. You know, they create—small businesses—they create two-thirds of the new jobs in America. But my opponent's plan for small business is clear, present, and dangerous. Beside new income taxes, his plan will lead to a new payroll tax to pay for a Government takeover of health care and another new tax to pay for training. That is just the beginning.

I believe that small business needs relief from taxation, regulation, and litigation.

我看到在我国的城镇街坊中正出现一种情况：能言善辩的律师忙得不可开交,医生们却不敢开业行医。某些父母不愿帮助子女参加少年棒球俱乐部的活动。我们应该减少互相争执、诉讼,我们应该更多地互相关心、帮助。

为加速我们的经济发展,为使孩子们准备好进入下一个世纪,还有其他一些事需要我们去做。我们必须对研究工作和培训工人的工作采取新的鼓励措施。小型企业需要资本和贷款。国防工业部门的工人需要新的职位。我有一个计划,将为每一个美国人提供他负担得起的医疗保健;通过减少笔墨官司和法律诉讼来控制开支;加强对最穷困者的照顾、救济。

我们不需要我的竞选对手所提出的由政府大规模接管医疗保健工作的计划,那会对医疗保健实行配给供应,不给你选择医生的权利。

关于我们的学校,我的竞选对手和我都要求改变孩子们学习的方式。他只要

I see something happening in our towns and in our neighborhoods. Sharp lawyers are running wild. Doctors are afraid to practice medicine, and some moms and pops won't even coach Little League any more. We must sue each other less and care for each other more.

There are other things we need to do to get our economy up to speed, prepare our kids for the next century. We must have new incentives for research and new training for workers. Small businesses need capital and credit, and defense workers need new jobs. I have a plan to provide affordable health care for every American, controlling costs by cutting paperwork and lawsuits and expanding coverage to the poorest of the poor.

We do not need my opponent's plan for a massive Government takeover of health care, which would ration care and deny you the right to choose a doctor.

What about our schools? My opponent and I both want to change the way our kids learn. He wants to change our schools a little bit, and I want to

求对学校进行很少的变革,而我却要求进行很多变革。以家长究竟能否为孩子们选择最好的学校这件事为例。我的竞选对手说,只要学校是由政府管理的,就没有什么问题。我却说每个家长和儿童都应该能够选择学校——在公立的、私立的、宗教的学校中进行选择。

所以,对于解决我们的问题,大家面前有着明确的选择。我们是不是求助于其他国家正在扔掉的那种官僚主义的破毯子? 或者,把人民为他们自己而加强国家安全时所需要的自由和激励交给他们?

我正在奋斗的目标有:对美国产品开放的市场;更低的政府开支;减税;小型企业的机会;司法和医疗保健改革;职业培训;建立在竞争基础上的、为进入21世纪做准备的新型学校。

当然,我们必须进行变革,可是有些价值观是永远不会过时的。我相信团聚在一起的家庭,相信父亲应该和家人一起住在家里。我深刻地相信每一个个人,不论

---

change them a lot. Take the issue of whether parents should be able to choose the best school for their kids. My opponent says that's okay, as long as the school is run by government. And I say every parent and child should have a real choice of schools, public, private, or religious.

So we have a clear choice to fix our problems. Do we turn to the tattered blanket of bureaucracy that other nations are tossing away? Or do we give our people the freedom and incentives to build security for themselves?

Here's what I'm fighting for: Open markets for American products; lower Government spending; tax relief; opportunities for small business; legal and health reform; job training; and new schools built on competition, ready for the 21st century.

Sure we must change, but some values are timeless. I believe in families that stick together, fathers who stick around. I happen to believe very deeply in the worth of each individual human being, born or unborn. I believe in teaching

已出生的或尚未出生的,都是有价值的。我相信对孩子们进行明辨是非的教育,教育他们尊重辛勤的劳动,并爱护邻居。我相信只要上帝在我们心中有特殊的地位,那么美国在上帝的心中也永远有特殊的地位。也许正因为如此,我始终相信爱国精神不只是一种观点,而具有更多的内涵。

我知道今天美国人是忧虑不安的。在我们的厨房餐桌旁,常可听到焦虑的谈话。但是我从我站着的这个地方所看到的,不是美国的日落,而是美国的日出。

我们有整整一代人为世界的变化作出了牺牲,这些变化终于到来,随后将在我们美国人的餐桌上传递盛满繁荣兴旺的甜酒。

对此我们做好准备了吗?我知道我们已做好准备。我在国内旅行时,遇到了退伍军人,他们曾在坦克的回转炮塔旁工作,现在却操纵着高技术经济的键盘。我看到,具有美国人了不起的创新能力的教师们,正为一个新的世纪将一种新的学习方法传授给学生。我遇到了按紧张繁忙的日程表干着双份工作的家长,他们仍然

our kids the difference between what's wrong and what's right, teaching them respect for hard work and to love their neighbors. I believe that America will always have a special place in God's heart, as long as He has a special place in ours. Maybe that's why I've always believed that patriotism is not just another point of view.

Now, I know that Americans are uneasy today. There is anxious talk around our kitchen tables. But from where I stand, I see not America's sunset but a sunrise.

The world changes for which we've sacrificed for a generation have finally come to pass, and with them a rare and unprecedented opportunity to pass the sweet cup of prosperity around our American table.

Are we up to it? I know we are. As I travel our land, I meet veterans who once worked the turrets of a tank and can now master the keyboards of high-tech economy. I see teachers blessed with the incredible American capacity for innovation who are teaching our children a new way to learn for a new century.

在寻找新方法来教育孩子懂得古老的价值观,以便孩子们能在混乱动荡的世界里保持沉着冷静。

我为正在美国进行着的事情感到鼓舞,不是为那些宣称对政府抱有新的热情的人,而是为那些对人的潜力抱有不变的、持久的信心的人感到振奋。美国永远是旭日东升的国家。

今晚我求助于永不屈服的、不朽的、不可否认的美国精神。我请求你们考虑:既然全世界都在走我们的路,我们为什么要回过头去走他们的路呢?

我所要求于你们的不仅是对我的计划的支持,而是承诺——通过使一个经受了40多年变化的机构振作起来的办法——重建我们的国家,使它重新焕发光彩。

今晚我对你们说,请和我一起参加为收获我们的世界性胜利果实而进行的运动——去赢得和平——为我国全体人民而使美国变得更为安全、更为强大。

王建华 译

I meet parents, some working two jobs with hectic schedules, who still find new ways to teach old values to steady their kids in a turbulent world.

I take heart from what is happening in America, not from those who profess a new passion for government but from those with an old and enduring faith in the human potential. America is the land where the sun is always peeking over the horizon.

Tonight I appeal to that unyielding, undying, undeniable American spirit. I ask you to consider, now that the entire world is moving our way, why would we want to go back their way?

I ask not just for your support for my agenda but for your commitment to renew and rebuild our Nation by shaking up the one institution that has withstood change for over four decades.

Well, tonight I say to you: Join me in our new crusade, to reap the rewards of our global victory, to win the peace, so that we may make America safer and stronger for all our people.

在得克萨斯州休斯敦"1992胜利庆功宴"上的讲话①

乔治·H.布什

1992年10月8日

今夜属于我们整个团队，属于我们值得自豪的共和党。正如各位可以想象的，最近我并不愿过多引用民意调查结果。但是罗伯特提醒了我一些事，我不禁想起昨晚刚出来的结果。此项统计并不是美国有线新闻网、美国广播公司、盖洛普民意调查或者《华尔街日报》做出的，而是一份儿童杂志《每周读者》

①离大选还有25天，老布什在演说中力图表现出对获胜的极大信心，并嘲讽对手克林顿提出的稚嫩的改革措施，然而最终他未能获得连任。

George H. Bush

October 8, 1992

Remarks at a Victory '92 Dinner in Houston, Texas

This evening is for our entire ticket, from top to bottom, the proud Republican team. As you can imagine, I'm not in the habit much lately of quoting polls. But Rob reminded me of something; I couldn't help but notice that new poll that came out just last night. It wasn't CNN or ABC or Gallup or the *Wall Street Journal*; it was that little kids' magazine, *Weekly*

的统计。他们对全美60万儿童做了民意调查,结果表明39%的孩子希望比尔·克林顿当选总统,而56%的孩子希望是乔治·布什。

你们不要以为过去几个月的压力已经使我冲昏了头脑,认为我想从第四代中寻求安慰——[笑声]请听我一言。《每周读者》的统计结果在历来的总统选举预测中的准确度都不低,自1956年以来就没有错过。但今年是公认的古怪之年,是我记得的政坛中最为奇怪的一年,我可不想让任何偶然之事发生。所以当民主党在下周或接下来几天离开华盛顿的时候,我会让鲍勃·多尔、鲍勃·米歇尔和所有其他共和党人偷偷上国会山①通过第28条修正案,把选举年龄降低到5岁。让克林顿州长带着他的萨克斯管去卡拉OK拉票吧,[笑声]我们将让他在"芝麻街"②心碎。

①国会大厦位于国会山上,是美国联邦的最高立法机构。
②美国著名的电视节目,主要是给学龄前儿童关于数字和字母的启蒙教育。

Reader. They polled over 600,000 kids across America: 39 percent wanted Bill Clinton for President and 56 percent wanted George Bush.

Before you think that the pressure of the past few months has gone to my head and that I'm seeking solace in fourth graders —[laughter]—let me point out something. *Weekly Reader* is not a bad thermometer of what happens in elections. That particular poll hasn't been wrong since 1956. But this is admittedly a weird year, the strangest year I can ever remember in politics, and I don't want to leave anything to chance. So when the Democrats leave Washington next week, or in the next few days, I'm asking Bob Dole, Bob Michel, and all the other Republicans to sneak up to Capitol Hill and pass the 28th amendment, lowering the voting age to 5-year-olds. Let Governor Clinton take his saxophone and go after the MTV vote —[laughter]—we'll tear him apart on "Sesame Street."

但是说真的,忘了暂时的民调结果吧,忘了那些数字吧。我们将会赢得这次竞选,我们将会继续领导这个国家四年。让我告诉你们我如此自信的三个原因吧。

首先是我们过去的执政记录。今年我们听到许多关于美国出了问题的言论,但是请别对我们帮助全人类赢得的重大胜利视而不见。

当我为这个星期天的辩论做准备的时候,我的思绪回到了12年前的另一场辩论。我想那是里根总统在克里夫兰,哦,是吉米·卡特和当时的挑战者罗纳德·里根之间的一场辩论。在卡特总统的总结陈词中,他发自内心地谈到了曾经与女儿艾米的一段对话,艾米曾说对核武器的控制是人类所面临的最大问题。有的人笑了,而我没有笑,里根总统也没有笑。

卡特总统和许多好心人当时大力提倡冻结核武器。还记得该运动吗?但是我和里根总统竭尽全力为和平政策而战。12年之后,遍布世界各个角落超过数十亿

But seriously, forget the polls. Forget the pundits. We are going to win this election. And we're going to lead this Nation for 4 more years. And let me tell you three reasons why I remain so confident.

The first is our record. We've heard a lot of talk this year about what's wrong with America. But let's not lose sight of the grand victory that we have helped win for all humanity.

As I study for the debate this Sunday, my thoughts went back to another debate 12 years ago. I believe it was in Cleveland with President Reagan, between Jimmy Carter and then-challenger Ronald Reagan. In his closing statement, President Carter, speaking from the heart, talked about how he'd had a conversation with his daughter, Amy, in which she said that the control of nuclear weapons was the greatest problem facing mankind. Some laughed. I didn't, and nor did President Reagan.

Well, President Carter and many well-meaning people advocated at that point a nuclear freeze. Remember the freeze movement? But President Reagan and I fought for a policy of peace through strength. And 12 years later, over a billion

的人第一次呼吸到了自由的空气。今夜,数百万的美国儿童站了出来,他们没有提到他们的芭比娃娃;他们想到的不是核武器,而是甜美的可以让他们感到满足的和平之梦。那很重要吗? 是的,你们知道那很重要。

我们将会赢得胜利的第二个原因是我们的思想观念对于美国的中产阶级是有意义的。

克林顿州长喜欢引用一个又一个的统计数字,引用种种可以诋毁美国的数字,称所有事情都是那么的糟糕。但是我们的问题从来都没有被放在全球经济发展放缓的大环境中加以考虑。直到现在,直到过去的几天,人们才真正开始考虑我们的解决方案。

克林顿州长总喜欢说他自己是"一个与众不同的民主党人"。不过,在我看来

people in every corner of the globe have taken their first breath of freedom. Tonight, as millions of American kids pull back the covers and shut off their talking Barbie dolls, they think not of nuclear weapons, but of the sweet and satisfying dreams of peace. Does that matter? You bet it does.

The second reason we'll win is because our ideas make sense to middle class Americans.

Governor Clinton likes to quote statistic after statistic, all kind of tearing down America, pointing out how bad everything is. But our problems are never put in the context of a global slowdown. Only now, only in the past few days, have people really started to compare our solutions.

Governor Clinton likes to say that he's, quote, "a different kind of Democrat," unquote. Well, to me there's nothing different about $150 billion in new taxes,

他似乎没有什么不同。1500亿美元的新税收啊,比迈克·杜卡基思[1]和华特·蒙代尔[2]加起来的还多。他的这种做法无异于一边做着空头承诺,一边却从劳动人民的口袋中搜刮铜板。6月,克林顿州长提出了一项高达2200亿美元的新政府开支,他称之为"投资"。他说话时的语气就好比医生对你说:"这针一点都不疼"。

我以为那可以满足克林顿州长的胃口,但是那似乎只是饭前的开胃品。我们做了一个小小的计算。自6月的那天开始,克林顿州长至少又承诺了一个2000亿美元的"投资"。而这些才仅仅是我们能够明码标价的,每天在他的新承诺里就有十亿美元的投资。克林顿州长因此获得了一个新绰号:十亿比尔。但是谁来兑现克林顿的这些票据呢?还不是那些老角色——中产阶级,他们得去付这笔账。

---

[1] 来自马萨诸塞州的州长,1988年民主党的总统候选人。
[2] 在竞选1984年总统时,被里根压倒性击败。

---

more than Michael Dukakis and Walter Mondale combined. There's nothing different about making pie-in-the-sky promises with one hand while pulling dollars out of working people's wallets with the other. In June, Governor Clinton proposed $220 billion in new Government spending. And he called it "investment." And he used that same tone that doctors use when they say, this shot won't hurt you one bit.

I thought that would satisfy Governor Clinton's appetite, but it turned out to be just an hors d'oeuvre. We did a little calculating. Since that day in June, Governor Clinton has promised at least another $200 billion, quote, "in investments." Those are just the ones we've been able to put a price tag on, a billion dollars in new promises every single day. And so Governor Clinton has earned a new nickname, Billion Dollar Bill. But who is going to pay Bill's bills? The same people who always pay, the middle class. They're going to do it.

几个星期前,美国企业经济学人协会比较了克林顿州长的每天十亿美元的支出计划和我精减政府规模、缴纳较低税款的促进增长的政策。绝大多数人认为,如按照我们的计划实施,通货膨胀和利率将会降低,预算赤字也将减少。

克林顿州长这星期曾说过一句话:他站在"历史的正确一边"。不过我恐怕他的经验不足已经暴露出来了。从马那瓜湖①到莫斯科,历史已经开始摒弃税收、规章以及中央调控,开始摒弃那些挥霍国家财富的政府计划制定人,而那些创造它的人们,无论男女,开始走上了历史舞台。哦,不,克林顿州长,历史站在我们这边,这也是为什么我们将在25天后创造历史的原因。

我相信第三个原因,我真的相信这个原因会使我们赢得胜利,用一个词来表示,那就是信任。我们在这场竞选活动中用了大部分时间来谈论经济和国民政策,

---

①位于尼加拉瓜西部。

A couple of weeks ago, the National Association of Business Economists compared Governor Clinton's billion-dollar-a-day spending plan with my progrowth policies of smaller Government and lower taxes. And the vast majority said that under our plan, under my plan, inflation would be lower, interest rates would be lower, and the budget deficit would be smaller.

Governor Clinton said this week that his side is, quote, "on the right side of history." But I fear his inexperience is showing. From Managua to Moscow, history is moving away from taxes and regulation and central control. History is casting aside the Government planner, who spends the wealth of nations, and lifting up the men and women who create it. No, Governor Clinton, history is on our side, and that's why we will make history in 25 days.

I believe the third reason—I really believe this one—one reason we will win, in a word, is trust. We've spent most of the time in this campaign talking

确实我们也应该这样做,因为这是我们今天所面临的最为重要的问题。但是,我们得知道,当我们选出一位美国总统的时候,也是我们选出一个在任何时刻都可能要作出艰难决定的人,他可能要把另一个人的年轻儿女,或是要把美国人民送上战场。

我在1989年和随后的"沙漠风暴"①中不得不作出这样的决定。受我们委托作出这些决定的总统,必须具备高尚的人格,为人诚实正直。昨晚我在上拉里·金②的节目时,被问到一些站在我对手立场上的问题。在此让我重复一下我的观点,因为它让我感受颇深:我的对手写过他曾在伦敦发动了一场反对越南战争的游行示威。对我来说,我简直不能理解,当我们的孩子在半个地球之外的地方阵亡时,某

---

① 1991年1月17日晨,以美国为首的多国部队开始向伊拉克发起代号为"沙漠风暴"的军事打击。
② 美国电视主持界的教父级人物,CNN王牌主持。

about economic and domestic policy, as well as we should, because those are the most important problems facing us today. We should remember, however, that when we elect a President of the United States, we're electing someone who at any time may have to deal with the awesome decision of sending someone else's young son or daughter, America's men and women, into battle.

I had to make that decision in 1989, and then again in Desert Storm. The President we entrust with these decisions must have character, honesty, and integrity. Last night on the Larry King show, I was asked about some issues in my opponent's background. Let me repeat the point I made, because I feel so strongly about it: My opponent has written that he once mobilized demonstrations in London against the Vietnam war. I simply for the life of me cannot understand how someone can go to London, another country, and mobilize demon-

些人怎么可以到伦敦,到另一个国家去发动反对美国的这样一次游行示威。

这并不再是爱国主义的问题。在国内你可以到处示威。我和芭芭拉①从白宫一眼望出去,就像朗姆和南希以前那样,每天外面总有一些人,可能是在抗议或者提出异议、行使他们的权利。那是属于美国社会的一部分。但我不能理解,当我们那些从贫民窟募征来的可怜孩子们在遥远的国土阵亡时,有人竟然在外国发动示威游行。你可以说我思想陈腐,跟不上时代,但那对我来说没有任何意义。

我想美国人民会敬重一个有经验、有人格魅力、有能力作出艰难决定的人。我希望这意味着他们将会在11月3日为我投上一票。

人们都说,朋友就是一个知道你的一切但却仍然喜欢你的人。不过今夜我要告诉你们,朋友还是一个在你落后的时候能够站在你的身边,帮助你赶上前去的

---

① 芭芭拉·布什,乔治·赫伯特·布什总统的妻子。

strations against the United States of America when our kids are dying halfway around the world.

The issue here isn't patriotism. You can demonstrate all you want here at home. Barbara and I look out, as Ron and Nancy did, out of the White House, and there's somebody out there every single day, properly protesting or raising objections, exercising their rights. That's part of America. But I can't understand someone mobilizing demonstrations in a foreign county when poor kids, drafted out of the ghettos, are dying in a faraway land. You can call me old-fashioned, but that just does not make sense to me.

I think the American people respect experience and character and proven ability to make a tough decision. I hope that means that they will vote for me on November 3d.

It has been said that a friend is someone who knows everything there is to know about you and likes you anyway. And, tonight, I would add that the definition of a friend is someone who stands by your side while you're behind, so

人。我和芭芭拉所幸有数以千计的朋友,今晚你们使我们感动万分。当我们对你们所有人表达衷心感谢时,我还要提醒你们,我们的奋斗并不仅仅只是为了赢得一场竞选;我们的奋斗是为了振兴美国,使国内和平能与我们对世界和平作出的贡献相匹配。

今晚你们给了我力量、激情和自信,可以在剩下的25天里继续把我们的想法告诉美国人民。是你们把我送到圣路易斯,怀着满腔热血,准备为那场辩论而战斗!

侯佳嘉 译

that you can pull ahead. Barbara and I are blessed with thousands of friends, and you have touched our hearts tonight. As we say a hearty thanks to all of you, I remind you that our struggle is to more than win an election; our struggle is to renew America so that we can match the peace we have achieved in the world with that peace of mind here at home.

Tonight, you have given me the strength and the passion and the inner confidence to take our ideas to the American people for 25 more days. You're sending me into St. Louis for that debate with a full head of steam.

新的誓约

比尔·克林顿 *

1992 年 7 月 16 日

今晚我要同你们谈一谈我对未来的希望、对美国人民的信心和我们一起努力所能建立起来的那种国家的看法。

我们民主党的政纲中有一句话说明了一切:"集中体现美国最重要的家庭政策、城市政策、劳动政策、少数民族政策和外

---

* 美国第 42 任总统(1993—2000),民主党人。第二次世界大战后出生的第一位总统,也是 20 世纪最后一位美国总统。他是一位滔滔不绝的演说家,本篇是他 1992 年在纽约民主党代表大会上接受总统候选人提名时发表的演说。他以"中产阶级"的名义接受了提名,并志在必得地宣布:"现在是美国进行变革的时候了。"

Bill Clinton

July 16, 1992

The New Covenant

Tonight I want to talk with you about my hope for the future, my faith in the American people, and my vision of the kind of country we can build together.

One sentence in the Platform we built says it all. The most important family policy, urban policy, labor policy, minority policy, and foreign policy America can have is an expanding

交政策的是一种提供高工资、要求高技能不断发展的企业家经济。"

因此,我以所有承担工作、缴纳税款、抚育孩子、遵守纪律的人的名义,以组成我国被遗忘的中产阶级的勤勉的美国人的名义,接受你们提名我为美国总统候选人。

我就是中产阶级的儿子。我若当选为总统,你们就不再会被人遗忘了。

我要给那些贪得无厌、一心保持现状的人传递一条信息:你们得意的时代来了,又去了。现在是在美国进行变革的时候了。

现在有1000万美国人失业,还有几千万美国人比以前干得更多却挣得更少。现任总统说,在经济复苏之前,失业者队伍常会略有扩大。但是,在经济能够真正恢复以前,失业者的队伍只会增加一个人。总统先生,你就是那个人。

这次选举是要让权力回到你们的手中,是要让政府回到你们的身旁。这次选举是要把人民放在首位。

entrepreneurial economy of high-wage, high-skilled jobs.

And so, in the name of all those who do the work and pay the taxes, raise the kids, and play by the rules, in the name of the hardworking Americans who make up our forgotten middle class, I proudly accept your nomination for President of the United States.

I am a product of that middle class, and when I am President, you will be forgotten no more.

I have news for the forces of greed and the defenders of the status quo: Your time has come and gone. Its time for a change in America.

Tonight 10 million of our fellow Americans are out of work, tens of millions more work harder for lower pay. The incumbent President says that unemployment always goes up a little before a recovery begins, but unemployment only has to go up by one more person before a real recovery can begin. And Mr. President, you are that man.

This election is about putting power back in your hands and putting government back on your side. It's about putting people first.

我希望，在美国，"家庭价值观"存在于我们的行动中，而不只是表现于我们的言谈上。那样的美国应该包括所有的家庭，每一个传统的家庭，每一个不同辈分的人组成的大家庭，每一个双亲家庭，每一个单亲家庭，和每一个领养孩子的家庭。总之，每一个家庭。

对于我国那些不愿支付子女赡养费而遗弃子女的父亲，我要严肃地说：对你们的子女负起责任来吧，否则我们就要强迫你负起这种责任。因为不能由政府养育儿童，那是父母的责任，你们应该养育子女。

对于那些缺少父爱或母爱而艰难生活、成长的美国儿童，我要说：我理解你们的感情。但你们同样是受到重视的。

你们与美国休戚相关。绝不允许任何人对你们说：你们不能按照自己的愿望长大成才。如果有些政治家使你们觉得你们不属于他们那个大家庭，那就走过来

I want an America where family values live in our actions, not just in our speeches. An America that includes every family. Every traditional family and every extended family. Every two parent family. Every single-parent family. And every foster family. Every family.

I do want to say something to the fathers in this country who have chosen to abandon their children by neglecting their child support: Take responsibility for your children or we will force you to do so. Because governments don't raise children; parents do. And you should.

And I want to say something to every child in America tonight who is out there trying to grow up without a father or a mother: I know how you feel. You are special too.

You matter to America. And don't you ever let anybody tell you can't become whatever you want to be. And if other politicians make you feel like you are not

加入我们的大家庭。

12年来各种失误中最让我气愤的是，政府已经脱离了我们的价值观，而政治家们却还在大肆渲染这些价值观。我对此感到厌烦之至。

从小受到的教育使我相信，美国梦应该建立在有报酬的辛勤工作的基础上。但是我们却看到，华盛顿的那些人把这条美国伦理标准颠倒了过去。

长期以来，那些照章办事、恪守信仰的人受到了不公正的苛刻待遇，而那些走捷径、占便宜的人却无功受禄。

人们比以往任何时候都更辛苦地工作，因而更少陪伴孩子们，晚间和周末都在工作，没法出席家长教师联谊会，没时间陪孩子参加少年棒球俱乐部或童子军的活动。可是他们的收入却在下降，税款负担却在加重。医疗保健、住房和教育等各种费用正走向高峰。

part of their family, come on and be part of ours.

The thing that makes me angriest about what has gone wrong in the last 12 years is that our government has lost touch with our values, while our politicians continue to shout about them. I'm tired of it!

I was raised to believe the American Dream was built on rewarding hard work. But we have seen the folks of Washington turn the American ethic on its head.

For too long those who play by the rules and keep the faith have gotten the shaft, and those who cut corners and cut deals have been rewarded.

People are working harder than ever, spending less time with their children, working nights and weekends at their jobs instead of going to PTA and Little League or Scouts. And their incomes are still going down. Their taxes are still going up. And the costs of health care, housing and education are going through the roof.

同时，越来越多的优秀人才，尽管一周工作40个小时，也难免陷入贫困。

我们的人民要求变革，但是政府阻挠变革。它受到了各种有特权的、私人的利益的劫持、胁迫。它已经忘记在这里实际付账的是谁。它正从你们手里拿走更多的钱，却回报得更少。我们必须抛弃华盛顿那种思想僵死的政治，让人民得到他们应该得到的那种政府——为他们工作的政府。

总统应该是推动进步事业的强大力量。此时此刻，我能理解林肯总统在内战中当麦克莱伦将军不愿进攻时心中的感受。他当时对麦克莱伦说："如果您不打算挥师进攻，我可以借用一下您的军队吗？"

现在，我要对乔治·布什说，如果您不想用您的权力来帮助美国，那就靠边站吧。我来这样做。

我们的国家正在落后，总统无法摆脱一种已经失败的经济理论。从里根和布

Meanwhile, more and more of our best people are falling into poverty even though they work 40 hours a week.

Our people are pleading for change, but government is in the way. It has been hijacked by privileged private interests. It has forgotten who really pays the bills around here. It has taken more of your money and given you less in return. We have got to go beyond the brain-dead politics in Washington and give our people the kind of government they deserve, a government that works for them.

A President ought to be a powerful force for progress. But right now I know how President Lincoln felt when General McClellan wouldn't attack in the Civil War. He asked him, "If you're not going to use your army, may I borrow it?"

And so I say: George Bush, if you won't use our power to help America, step aside. I will.

Our country is falling behind. The President is caught in the grip of a failed

什掌权以来，我们在工资方面已从世界第一位下降为第13位。

4年以前，总统候选人布什说，美国是个特别的地方，不仅仅是"联合国名单上从阿尔巴尼亚到津巴布韦的另一个令人感到愉快的国家"。现在，在布什总统的治理下，美国经济正徘徊于德国和斯里兰卡之间。

总统先生，对多数美国人来说，生活已比你就职前严酷、艰难得多了。

我们国家落后得太多、太快了，以致几个月前，日本首相说他的确对美国感到"同情"。当我成为你们的总统时，世界各国将不再以怜悯的眼光轻视我们，而是重新以尊重的态度看待我们。

我手中虽无包治一切的良方，但我知道原来的办法行不通。滴入式经济学①确

---

① 滴入式经济学认为，政府与其将财政津贴直接用于福利事业或公共建设，不如将财政津贴交由大企业陆续流入小企业和消费者之手更能促进经济增长。

---

economic theory. We have gone from first to 13th in the world in wages since Ronald Reagan and Bush have been in office.

Four years ago, candidate Bush said, "America is a special place, not just another pleasant country somewhere on the UN Roll Call between Albania and Zimbabwe." Now under President Bush, America has an unpleasant economy struck somewhere between Germany and Sri Lanka.

And for most Americans, Mr. President, life's a lot less kind and a lot less gentle than it was before your administration took office.

Our country has fallen so far so fast that just a few months ago the Japanese prime minister actually said he felt sympathy for the United States. Sympathy. When I am your President, the rest of the world will not look down on us with pity but up to us with respect again.

Now, I don't have all the answers, but I do know the old ways don't work.

实已经失败。大型行政管理机构,无论是官方的或私人的,都已失去了作用。

这就是我们为什么需要一个新型政府——一个为人民提供更多的使用权力的机会,却为特定集团成员提供更少津贴的政府;一个为年轻人提供更多可供选择的学校,为老年人和残疾人提供更多可选择的长期医疗保健的政府;一个规模比较小、而效率比较高的政府;一个努力增加机会而不扩大官僚机构的政府,因为它懂得,就业机会必须来自生机勃勃、极其重要的自由贸易制。

我把这种新的政府管理方法叫作新誓约——在人民和他们的政府之间的一种庄重的协议,其基础不仅在于我们每一个人都能从国家取得东西,而且在于我们全体都必须给予国家东西。

我们给人民提供建立在原有的价值观基础上的新选择。我们提供机会。我们要求责任心。我们将重新建立一个美国社会。我们提供的机会既不是保守主义的,

Trickledown economics has sure failed. And big bureaucracies, both private and public, they've failed too.

That's why we need a new approach to government, a government that offers more empowerment and less entitlement. More choices for young people in the schools they attend. And more choices for the elderly and for people with disabilities and the long-term care they receive. A government that is leaner, not meaner; a government that expands opportunity, not bureaucracy; a government that understands that jobs must come from growth in a vibrant and vital system of free enterprise.

I call this approach the New Covenant, a solemn agreement between the people and their government based not simply on what each of us can take but what all of us must give to our Nation.

We offer our people a new choice based on old values. We offer opportunity. We demand responsibility. We will build an American community again.

也不是自由主义的。在许多方面,它甚至不能以共和党的主张或民主党的主张来衡量。它是全新的、不同一般的。它必将发挥作用。

我再说一遍:没有理想,美国必亡。我们的新誓约有着什么样的理想呢?那就是:

——一个在几十种新行业中有着几百万个就业机会、满怀信心地向着21世纪前进的美国。它将对企业家和商界人士说:我们将给予你们前所未有的鼓励和机会,让你们提高工作人员的技能,并在新的世界经济格局中为美国人创造就业机会和美国财富。但是你们必须完成分内工作,你们必须负起责任来。这就是新誓约的要求。

——一个再次将大学大门向速记员和炼钢工人的子女敞开的美国。我们将说:人人都可以借钱上大学,但是人人都必须完成分内工作。你们所借的钱必须归

The choice we offer is not conservative or liberal. In many ways, it is not even Republican or Democratic. It is different. It is new. And it will work.

And so I say again: Where there is no vision, America will perish. What is the vision of our New Covenant?

An America with millions of new jobs and dozens of new industries, moving confidently toward the 21st century. An America that says to entrepreneurs and businesspeople: We will give you more incentives and more opportunity than ever before to develop the skills of your workers and to create American jobs and American wealth in the new global economy. But you must do your part, you must be responsible. That's what this New Covenant is all about.

An America in which the doors of colleges are thrown open once again to the sons and daughters of stenographers and steelworkers. We will say: Everybody can borrow money to go to college. But you must do your part. You must

还——用你们的工资,或者,最好是返回家乡,为你们的社区服务。请想一想,几千万精力充沛的年轻人通过各种方式为国家服务的情景吧:他们或维持街道的治安,或给孩子们上课,或护理病人,或照看老年人和残疾人,或帮助年轻人摆脱毒品、摆脱帮派,他们将使我们大家看到新的希望和无限的可能性。这就是新誓约的要求。

——一个视医疗保健为权利,而不是特殊待遇的美国。我们对全体人民说:你们的政府终于有勇气去打击那些借医疗保健牟取暴利的人了,它将使每一个家庭都负担得起医疗保健。但是你们必须完成分内工作:采取预防保健、产前保健、儿童免疫措施;挽救生命、节省金钱、从令人心碎的遭遇中挽救家庭。这就是新誓约的要求。

——一个使中层阶级的收入而不是使中层阶级的税款负担上升的美国。一个

pay it back, from your paychecks or, better yet, by going back home and serving your communities. Just think of it. Think of it. Millions of energetic young men and women serving their country by policing the streets or teaching the children or caring for the sick. Or working with the elderly and people with disabilities. Or helping young people to stay off drugs and out of gangs, giving us all a sense of new hope and limitless possibilities. That's what this New Covenant is all about.

An America in which health care is a right, not a privilege , in which we say to all of our people: Your government has the courage finally to take on the health care profiteers and make health care affordable for every family. But you must do your part. Preventive care, prenatal care, childhood immunization-saving lives, saving money, saving families from heartbreak. That's what the New Covenant is all about.

An America in which middle-class incomes, not middle-class taxes, are

要求年收益超过20万美元的少数富人缴纳应付税款的美国。一个不对富人巧取豪夺,但也不对中层阶级横征暴敛的美国。责任从上层开始。这就是新誓约的要求。

——一个使我们所熟悉的那种福利救济办法得以结束的美国。我们将对那些依赖救济的人说:你们将有也应有机会得到训练和教育,得到儿童保育和医疗保险,以解放你们自己。但到你们能工作时,你们就必须工作,因为救济应该是第二位的,它不是一种生活道路。这就是新誓约的要求。

——一个有着世界上最强的国防力量,必要时准备并愿意使用武力的美国。一个在保存和保护环境的全球性努力中站在最前列,并且促进全球发展的美国。一个在从东欧到南美的地区内,在我们这个半球的海地和古巴,捍卫自由和民主事业的美国。

冷战的结束使我们得以减少军费开支,而仍保持世界上最强大的防御力量。

going up. An America, yes, in which the wealthiest few, those making over $200,000 a year, are asked to pay their fair share. An America in which the rich are not soaked, but the middle class is not drowned, either. Responsibility starts at the top. That's what the New Covenant is all about.

An America where we end welfare as we know it. We will say to those on welfare: You will have, and you deserve, the opportunity, through training and education, through child care and medical coverage, to liberate yourself. But then, when you can, you must work, because welfare should be a second chance, not a way of life. That's what the New Covenant is all about.

An America with the world's strongest defense, ready and willing to use force when necessary, the forefront of the global effort to preserve and protect our common environment—and promoting global growth. An America that champions the cause of freedom and democracy from Eastern Europe to Southern Africa—and in our own hemispheres, in Haiti and Cuba.

The end of the Cold War permits us to reduce defense spending while still maintaining the strongest defense in the world, but we must plow back every dollar

但是，我们必须把削减下来的军事费用中的每一个美元都投资于国内，为美国人增加就业机会。我清楚地知道世界需要一个强大的美国，但我们也懂得力量的积聚开始于本国。

但是新誓约涉及的不仅是你们和你们家庭的机会和责任。它也涉及我们共有的这个社会。

今晚你们中的每一个人都深切地知道，美国的分裂太严重了。现在是医治美国的时候了。

我们必须对每一个美国人说：抛弃那种使我们不辨是非、不明事理的成见吧。我们是一个互相依赖的整体。我们中所有的人都需要别人，也为别人所需要。我们不能抛弃或遗忘任何一个人。然而，尽管我们中多数人都做得很对，但长期以来政治家们却说美国的问题就出在我们身上。我们被政治家贬称为"他们"。

of defense cuts into building American jobs right here at home. I know well that the world needs a strong America, but we have learned that strength begins at home.

But the New Covenant is about more than opportunities and responsibilities for you and your families. It's also about our common community.

Tonight every one of you knows deep in your heart that we are too divided. It is time to heal America.

And so we must say to every American: Look beyond the stereotypes that blind us. We need each other—all of us—we need each other. We don't have a person to waste, and yet for too long politicians have told the most of us that are doing all right that what's really wrong with America is the rest of us—them.

少数民族成员是"他们",自由主义者是"他们",穷人是"他们",无家可归者是"他们",残疾人是"他们",同性恋者是"他们",我们几乎达到了把自己也称为"他们"的地步。他们,他们,他们。

但是,这是美国。这里没有"他们",只有我们。

这是我们的国家,她在上帝的佑护下不可分割,人人都享有自由和公正。

这就是我们对国家效忠的誓言,这就是新誓约的要求。

总之,新誓约所要求的只是使我们大家都重新成为美国人——新时期中的老式美国人。机会,责任,社会。在我们齐心协力为这些奋斗时,美国就将阔步前进。

秦文勇　译

Them, the minorities. Them, the liberals. Them, the poor. Them, the homeless. Them, the people with disabilities. Them, the gays. We've gotten to where we've nearly them'ed ourselves to death. Them, and them, and them.

But this is America. There is no them. There is only us.

One nation, under God, indivisible, with liberty and justice for all.

That is our Pledge of Allegiance, and that's what the New Covenant is all about.

In the end, my fellow Americans, this New Covenant simply asks us all to be Americans again—old-fashioned Americans for a new time. Opportunity, responsibility, community. When we pull together, America will pull ahead.

机会共享,责任共担①

比尔·克林顿

1996年11月2日

早上好。在下周二即将投票之前,我想谈谈我认为对于我国来说至关重要的问题。许多人把选举当作分裂我们的机会。但是,我相信,此次选举将使我们团结在一起,共同前进。当我们齐聚一处,找到共同的立场,作为一个国家,我们将更为强大,战无不胜。

---

① 本篇系广播演说,志在连任的克林顿总统提出了"机会共享,责任共担"这一口号。

Bill Clinton

November 2, 1996

Opportunity for All and Responsibility from All

Good morning. Today I want to talk about something I believe is particularly important to our Nation as we prepare to vote on Tuesday. Many people treat elections as opportunities to divide us. But I believe this election can unite us to go forward together. When we come together to find common ground, we are stronger as a nation and there is no challenge we can't meet.

5年前我宣布参选总统,那时全国上下深受挫折。失业率居高不下,财政赤字失去控制,新的就业机会匮乏,我们的价值观似乎遭到了全面质疑。很多人认为,我们的问题到了难以解决的地步:高涨的犯罪率将打垮我们;依赖社会福利的破落家庭将永远摆脱不了被救济的命运;恐惧和仇恨将在不同背景、不同信仰的美国人之间筑起永远无法逾越的鸿沟。华盛顿陷入了互相谴责的游戏和政治纷争中,无法或不愿采取任何行动。我当时认为,该是停止互相谴责、开始研究怎么办的时候了。

我的计划很简单:拒绝旧的标签、虚伪的争辩和分裂的政治。取而代之的是,巩固美国的基本信条:机会共享,责任共担,为所有美国人建立一个强大的国家。这是副总统戈尔和我在过去4年竭尽全力去实现的目标。

关于预算问题,分裂的旧政治要求我们在平衡预算和履行对人民和未来所承

Just over 5 years ago, I announced my candidacy for President. It was a time of deep and widespread frustration in America. Unemployment was high. The deficit was out of control. New jobs were scarce. Our values seemed under assault from every direction. And to many it seemed our problems were unsolvable: Rising crime would overwhelm us; broken families trapped on welfare would never break free from the cycle of dependence; fear and hatred would force a permanent wedge between Americans of different backgrounds and beliefs. Washington, caught up in blame games and tangled in politics, was unable or unwilling to act. I believed it was time to stop asking who's to blame and start asking, what are we going to do about it?

I had a simple strategy: Reject old labels, false debates, and divisive politics. Instead, strengthen America's basic bargain: opportunity for all Americans, responsibility from all Americans, and a stronger community of all Americans. That's how Vice President Gore and I have tried to approach everything we've done for the last 4 years.

When it came to the budget, the old politics of division demanded a choice between balancing the budget and living up to the obligations we owe to one

担的责任之间作出选择。我们说不能这样选择,我们必须两者兼顾。我们必须平衡预算,以保持经济强劲增长;同时,我们也必须确保医疗保险制度、公共医疗补助制度、教育和环境。

4年来,我们减少了63%的财政赤字,达到了15年以来的最低点。与此同时,我们保障我们父辈和祖父辈们的健康,为我们的孩子投资教育,为子孙后代保护我们的环境。美国创造了1070万个就业机会和400万位房产业主。失业率降低到5.2%,家庭年平均收入在两年内就增加了1600美元。

现在我们就必须完成这一工作,在继续保护我们的价值观的同时,平衡预算。我的平衡预算计划将在2000年消灭财政赤字,同时,我们将加强医疗保险制度、公共医疗补助制度,扩大教育投资和保护环境,以此来保护我们的价值观。

关于打击犯罪问题,分裂的旧政治要求我们在更多警力、严厉处罚与高效防

another and to our future. We said, that's no choice; we have to do both. We have to balance the budget to keep our economy growing strong, and we have to protect Medicare, Medicaid, education, and the environment.

We've cut the deficit for 4 years in a row by 63 percent, to its lowest level in 15 years. But we protected the health of our parents and grandparents, we invested in the education of our children, and we protected our environment for future generations. Together America has created 10.7 million new jobs and 4 million new homeowners. Unemployment is at 5.2 percent, and the average family income has risen $1,600 in just 2 years.

Now we have to finish the job and balance the budget while we continue to protect our values. My balanced budget plan eliminates the deficit by 2002, while protecting our values by strengthening Medicare and Medicaid, expanding our investments in education, protecting our environment.

When it came to fighting crime, the old politics of division demanded a choice between more police and tough penalties, or effective prevention and fewer

范、减少街道枪击事件之间作出选择。我们认为,我们既需要更多的警力和更严厉的处罚,也需要高效的防范和减少街道枪击事件。因此,我们正在向街面投入10万名新警力。我们通过了《三击出局法案》①,对大毒枭和袭警者处以死刑。我们限制攻击性武器的泛滥,通过了《布雷迪法案》②,为争取安全和远离毒品的校园而努力。

两周前,联邦调查局报告称,犯罪率连续4年下降至10年以来的最低点。现在,我们有更多的事情要做,从而在未来4年继续保持犯罪率的下降。我们必须完成向街面投入10万警力,将目标锁定暴力团伙,控制住那些唯一目标是射穿警察防弹背心的子弹。

---

① 《三击出局法案》是美国1994年提出的反犯罪政策,刑事法律中的累犯制度。
② 《布雷迪法案》是1994年生效的美国枪支管理法,以在里根总统遇刺中受害的新闻发言人吉姆·布雷迪的名字命名。

guns on the street. We said we need more police and tougher penalties, but we also need effective prevention and fewer guns on the street. So we're putting 100,000 new police officers on the street. We passed "three strikes and you're out" and the death penalty for drug kingpins and cop killers. We banned assault weapons, passed the Brady bill, and fought for safe and drug-free schools.

Two weeks ago, the FBI reported that crime had dropped 4 years in a row to a 10-year low. Now we have more to do to keep crime dropping for 4 more years. We have to finish putting 100,000 police on the street, target violent gangs, ban bullets whose only purpose is to pierce the bulletproof vests of police officers.

关于福利制度改革问题，分裂的旧政治要求我们在一方面是严格的时间限制和工作需求，另一方面是孩子的抚育和为迁居者创造工作之间作出选择。我们认为，我们需要严格的时间限制和工作需求，因为福利制度是第二次机会，而不是一种生活方式。但是，我们同样需要一起来创造就业机会，因为如果我们期盼工作，就必须保证提供工作机会。

　　今天，依赖救济的人数比我执政之初减少了将近200万。今年8月，我签署了将永远改变福利制度的历史性的改革法令[①]。现在我们有职责充分利用这次机会，带领数百万家庭从依赖福利制度走向工作岗位。在未来4年，我计划推动100多万人摆脱救济，走向工作岗位。

[①]《个人责任和工作机会协调法案》，又称《福利改革法案》。意在探索由联邦向州、由政府向私人的分权，以更为市场化的道路，以企业家精神来对福利制度进行全方位的改革。

　　When it came to welfare reform, the old politics of division demanded a choice between strict time limits and work requirements, on the one hand, and child care and creating jobs for people to move, on the other hand. We said, we need time limits and work requirements because welfare is supposed to be a second chance, not a way of life. But we also need to work together to create jobs, because if we expect work we have to make sure people have a chance to work.

　　Well, today there are nearly 2 million fewer people on welfare than there were the day I took office. In August, I signed historic welfare reform legislation that would change the welfare system forever. Now we have a responsibility to make the most of this opportunity to lift millions of families from welfare to work. And I have a plan to move a million more people from welfare to work over the next 4 years.

关于美国社会,分裂的旧政治毫无可取之处。它不是引导人们为了共同的信仰而团结起来,而是在我们之间制造隔阂,利用我们的恐惧。我们必须让这一幕不再上演。

不幸的是,在大选进入尾声之际,一些人企图利用上述问题谋取政治利益。我要告诉他们,我们早已预见了此结果。分裂政治只能产生分裂和僵局。而寻求共同的立场,则会产生解决办法、进步发展和无愧于我们过去的未来。

因此,不管你们是属于林肯一派还是杰斐逊一派,不管你们是中立派还是无党派,记住,你们中的大多数属于美国。我们都处于这一社会中。我们共同进退。因此,让我们搭起一座足够宽、足够结实的桥梁,一起走向21世纪美国的灿烂明天。

张衡 译　王建华 校

When it came to our American community, the old politics of division was at its worst. Instead of bringing people together around common values, the old politics of division tried to drive wedges between us, to take advantage of our fears. We must never let that happen again.

Unfortunately, here at the end of the election, some people are tempted to take advantage of these issues for political advantage. I say to them, we've seen the results of this before. The politics of division yields only division and gridlock. The search for common ground yields solutions and progress and a future worthy of our past.

So whether you belong to the party of Lincoln, the party of Jefferson, whether you're independent or unaffiliated, remember that most of all you belong to the community of America. We are all in this together. We will rise or fall together. So let us build a bridge together, wide enough and strong enough to carry all of us into the bright future that is America in the 21st century.

开创一个有责任心的时代

乔治·W. 布什 *

2000年8月3日

我接受你们的提名,谢谢你们给了我这份荣誉。我们团结起来,就能恢复美国的目标。

在这里,在费城,开国元勋们首次提出了那个目标。本杰明·富兰克林出席了那次会议,还有托马斯·杰斐逊,当然,还有

---

* 美国第43任总统(2001—),共和党人。21世纪美国第一位总统,又称"小布什"。本篇是他在费城接受共和党代表大会提名时发表的演说。他将矛头对准了克林顿政府,称:"这届政府有过机会,但他们没有很好地进行领导,我们来领导吧。"他呼吁美国公民行动起来,共同开创一个"充满责任心的时代"。

George W. Bush

August 3, 2000

Ushering in an Era of Responsibility

I accept your nomination. Thank you for this honor. Together, we will renew America's purpose.

Our founders first defined that purpose here in Philadelphia. Ben Franklin was here. Thomas Jefferson. And, of

乔治·华盛顿——他的朋友们都叫他"乔治·W"①。

迪克·切尼②站在我的旁边,我感到很自豪。他为人正直,判断力强,他已经证明,为公众服务是一项崇高的事业。一个具有如此品格的人将接替艾尔·戈尔出任美国的副总统,这是美国的骄傲。

今晚,我特别要感谢我的家人。

无论我在一生中做成了哪些大事,我请求劳拉嫁给我,是我迄今为止所做的最杰出的决定。

对我们的两个女儿,芭芭拉和詹纳,我要说,我爱你们,并为你们感到骄傲。今年秋天,你们上了大学以后,别在外面待得太晚,常给老爸发一封电子邮件,好吗?

---

① 小布什的绰号也叫"乔治·W"。
② 迪科·切尼(1941—),小布什的竞选搭档,曾任美国国防部长。

---

course, George Washington—or, as his friends called him, "George W."

I am proud to have Dick Cheney at my side. He is a man of integrity and sound judgment, who has proven that public service can be noble service. America will be proud to have a leader of such character to succeed Al Gore as Vice President of the United States.

I am especially grateful tonight to my family.

No matter what else I do in life, asking Laura to marry me was the best decision I ever made.

To our daughters, Barbara and Jenna, we love you, we're proud of you, and as you head off to college this fall, don't stay out too late, and e-mail your old dad once in a while, will you?

对母亲,我要说,您的每个孩子都爱你,我也爱你。

在我成长的过程中,母亲给了我爱和忠告,而我给了她满头白发。我还要感谢父亲——他是我所知道的最体面的人。一位慈祥的老人竟然如此坚强,我在一生中常常对此感到诧异。爸,我想让您知道,做您的儿子是多么骄傲。

我父亲是伟大的一代人的最后一位总统。那一代美国人轰炸了海滩,解放了集中营,把我们从灾难中拯救出来。

有些人再也没有回来。

而回来的人把战斗勋章锁进了抽屉,投入了工作,以英勇的气概构筑了高速公路,盖起了大学、郊区和工厂,建成了伟大的城市和联盟——为美国世纪奠定了坚实的基础。

现在,作为这些成就的继承者,我们面临着一个问题。

And mother, everyone loves you and so do I.

Growing up, she gave me love and lots of advice. I gave her white hair. And I want to thank my father—the most decent man I have ever known. All my life I have been amazed that a gentle soul could be so strong. And Dad, I want you to know how proud I am to be your son.

My father was the last president of a great generation. A generation of Americans who stormed beaches, liberated concentration camps and delivered us from evil.

Some never came home.

Those who did put their medals in drawers, went to work, and built on a heroic scale highways and universities, suburbs and factories, great cities and grand alliances—the strong foundations of an American Century.

Now the question comes to the sons and daughters of this achievement.

我们被赋予怎样的使命？

在我国历史上，这是一个令人赞叹的时刻。繁荣带来的希望从未像现在这样诱人。但是，富足时代就像危急时刻一样，都是对美利坚性格的考验。

繁荣可以是我们手中的一件工具——由此出发，把我们的国家建设得更美好。反过来，繁荣也可以是我国制度上的一剂毒药——消磨我们的紧迫感、同情心和责任心。

我们的机遇太美好了，我们的生命太短促了，所以，我们不能虚度光阴。

所以，今晚我们对全国立下誓言：

我们会抓住这个充满希望的时刻。

我们会利用这个好机会，实现崇高的目标。

我们将着手解决一系列难题，解除我国安全和健康退休保障所面临的威胁，

What is asked of us?

This is a remarkable moment in the life of our nation. Never has the promise of prosperity been so vivid. But times of plenty, like times of crisis, are tests of American character.

Prosperity can be a tool in our hands—used to build and better our country. Or it can be a drug in our system—dulling our sense of urgency, of empathy, of duty.

Our opportunities are too great, our lives too short, to waste this moment.

So tonight we vow to our nation:

We will seize this moment of American promise.

We will use these good times for great goals.

We will confront the hard issues—threats to our national security, threats

绝不让当今时代的挑战演变成留给孩子们的危机。

我们还要把繁荣的希望,带到这个国家的每一个被遗忘的角落。

给每一个男人和女人一次成功的机会,给每一个孩子一次学习的机会,给每一个家庭一次过上尊严和充满希望的生活的机会。

克林顿和戈尔政府轻轻松松地虚度了整整8年的繁荣时光。

而最不费力的路总是下坡路。

但美国之路却是一条上升的路。

这个国家敢作敢为,体面而高尚,准备迎接变革。

现任总统代表了最有潜能的一代人。他们群英荟萃,才华横溢,技艺高超。但是,结果怎么样呢?他作了那么多许诺,却没有达到任何重大的目标。

10多年前,冷战的坚冰消融了,在里根总统和布什总统的领导下,冷战的高墙

to our health and retirement security—before the challenges of our time become crises for our children.

And we will extend the promise of prosperity to every forgotten corner of this country.

To every man and woman, a chance to succeed. To every child, a chance to learn. To every family, a chance to live with dignity and hope.

For eight years, the Clinton/Gore administration has coasted through prosperity.

And the path of least resistance is always downhill.

But America's way is the rising road.

This nation is daring and decent and ready for change.

Our current president embodied the potential of a generation. So many talents. So much charm. Such great skill. But, in the end, to what end? So much promise, to no great purpose.

Little more than a decade ago, the Cold War thawed and, with the leadership

倒塌了。

然而,克林顿和戈尔政府不但没有抓住机会,反而浪费了机会。我们看到,美国的国力在不断削弱,美国的影响力忽大忽小,很不稳定。

我们军队的战斗力不强,士气低落。

假如目前的这位总司令发出战斗号令,至少会有整整两个师的人会说:长官,我们还没准备好呢。

这届政府有过机会,但他们没有很好地进行领导。我们来领导吧。

这一代人有机会接受美国历史上最好的教育,但我们却未能让每一个人分享这个机会。在我们为穷人开办的学校中,10个四年级学生中竟有7个看不懂简单的儿童读物。

而这届政府却仍然因循守旧,不思变革,把成千上万的年轻人困于学校,那里

of Presidents Reagan and Bush, that wall came down.

But instead of seizing this moment, the Clinton/Gore administration has squandered it. We have seen a steady erosion of American power and an unsteady exercise of American influence.

Our military is low on parts, pay and morale.

If called on by the commander-in-chief today, two entire divisions of the Army would have to report: Not ready for duty, sir.

This administration had its moment. They had their chance. They have not led. We will.

This generation was given the gift of the best education in American history. Yet we do not share that gift with everyone. Seven of ten fourth-graders in our highest poverty schools cannot read a simple children's book.

And still this administration continues on the same old path with the same

的暴力活动如家常便饭,而学习的风气却很淡漠。

这届政府有过机会,但他们没有很好地进行领导。我们来领导吧。

美国有强大的经济和足够的盈余。我们有公共资源和公众的意志——甚至有过超越两党分歧的机遇——可以用来加强社会保障体系,并改善医疗保健制度。

但是,在上述需求不断增长的8年间,这届政府却无所作为。

这届政府有过机会,但他们没有很好地进行领导。我们来领导吧。

我们这一代人有机会重新确立某些基本的价值观念——我们已经成长起来,不会未老先衰。

但在需要领导的时刻降临时,这届政府却没有教育好我们的孩子,反而使他们的幻想破灭了。

这届政府有过机会,但他们没有很好地进行领导。我们来领导吧。

---

old programs—while millions are trapped in schools where violence is common and learning is rare.

This administration had its chance. They have not led. We will.

America has a strong economy and a surplus. We have the public resources and the public will—even the bipartisan opportunities—to strengthen Social Security and repair Medicare.

But this administration—during eight years of increasing need—did nothing.

They had their moment. They have not led. We will.

Our generation has a chance to reclaim some essential values—to show we have grown up before we grow old.

But when the moment for leadership came, this administration did not teach our children, it disillusioned them.

They had their chance. They have not led. We will.

现在,他们又来请求大家再给他们一次机会。

我们的回答是什么呢?

这次不给他们任何机会。

今年不给他们任何机会。

现在不是给他们第三次机会①的时候,现在是迎接新开端的时候。这个国家里正在崛起的一代人有着伟大的抱负。

伟大的抱负不随股市的涨落而起伏,它不是用金钱买得到的。

伟大产生于战胜了挑战的美利坚性格和勇气。

当纽约的刘易斯·莫里斯即将在《独立宣言》上签字时,他的哥哥奉劝他考虑后果,说如果签字,就将失去所有的家产。

---

①指民主党人通过选举,已经两次入主白宫。

And now they come asking for another chance.

Our answer?

Not this time.

Not this year.

This is not a time for third chances, it is a time for new beginnings. The rising generations of this country have our own appointment with greatness.

It does not rise or fall with the stock market. It cannot be bought with our wealth.

Greatness is found when American character and American courage overcome American challenges.

When Lewis Morris of New York was about to sign the *Declaration of Independence*, his brother advised against it, warning he would lose all his property.

莫里斯是一个性格直率的开国元老,他说:"让后果滚蛋吧,把笔递给我!"多么铿锵有力的美国雄辩!

我们在第二次世界大战中听到了这个声音。在盟军预定发动进攻的那天早晨,艾森豪威尔告诉伞兵部队别担心,而一个战士回答说:"将军,我们才不担心呢。现在轮到希特勒担心了。"

我们在民权运动中听到了这个声音。那时,勇敢的人们没有说"我们将进行斗争",或者"让我们走着瞧",而是说"我们将克服"①。

一个美国总统必须能唤起那种性格。

今晚,在这个大厅里,让我们下定决心,我们的党不应当是裹足不前的党,而应当是改革创新的党。

---

① 这是美国民权运动中一首著名歌曲的名称,表达了以马丁·路德·金为首的民权运动者立誓克服一切困难,并通过和平手段来争取民权的信念。

Morris, a plain-spoken Founder, responded "Damn the consequences, give me the pen." That is the eloquence of American action.

We heard it during World War II, when General Eisenhower told paratroopers on D-Day morning not to worry—and one replied, "We're not worried, General. It's Hitler's turn to worry now."

We heard it in the civil rights movement, when brave men and women did not say "We shall cope," or "We shall see." They said "We shall overcome."

An American president must call upon that character.

Tonight, in this hall, we resolve to be, not the party of repose, but the party of reform.

我们将为美国历史写下新的篇章,而不仅仅是增添脚注。

我们将用自己的双手,为父亲们和母亲们留下的遗产添砖加瓦,使这个国家比以前更伟大。

我们知道,要担当起领导的责任,就需要迎接种种考验,因为各种难题已经错综复杂地交织在一起。

我们将加强社会保障和医疗保健制度,这样做既是为了当今最伟大的一代人,也是为了我们的子孙后代。

医疗保健制度不仅仅满足了老年人的需要,它还反映了我们社会的价值观。

我们会把它建立在坚实的财政基础上,并且使每一个需要用药的老年人都能买得到药和买得起药。

至于青年工人们,我们将让你们作出选择——从你们的工资税中拨出一部

We will write, not footnotes, but chapters in the American story.

We will add the work of our hands to the inheritance of our fathers and mothers—and leave this nation greater than we found it.

We know the tests of leadership. The issues are joined.

We will strengthen Social Security and Medicare for the greatest generation, and for generations to come.

Medicare does more than meet the needs of our elderly, it reflects the values of our society.

We will set it on firm financial ground, and make prescription drugs available and affordable for every senior who needs them.

For younger workers, we will give you the option—your choice—to put a

分，注入稳健而负责的投资计划。

这意味着，你们的钱将产生更大的收益，三四十年以后，这笔钱将能帮助你们安心退休，也可以传给你们的子女。

这笔钱既然存在你们的名下，存在你们的账户中，它就不仅是一个计划，而是你们的财产。

现在是给予美国工人不会被任何政客夺走保障和独立的时候了。

在教育方面，太多的美国儿童被毫无标准地圈进学校——只根据他们的年龄，而不顾他们的知识水平，被胡乱地塞到各个年级。

这是一种歧视，一种显而易见的歧视，是由于期望值太低而导致的一种偏见。

我国应当像对待其他形式的歧视一样来对待它，应当结束这一局面。

说到儿童教育，不能把一个地方的标准套用到所有地区，因此，当地人民应当

part of your payroll taxes into sound, responsible investments.

This will mean a higher return on your money, and, over 30 or 40 years, a nest egg to help your retirement, or pass along to your children.

When this money is in your name, in your account, it's not just a program, it's your property.

Now is the time to give American workers security and independence that no politician can ever take away.

On education. Too many American children are segregated into schools without standards, shuffled from grade-to-grade because of their age, regardless of their knowledge.

This is discrimination, pure and simple—the soft bigotry of low expectations.

And our nation should treat it like other forms of discrimination. We should end it.

One size does not fit all when it comes to educating our children, so local

管理当地的学校。

而那些花费你们税款的人应当负起责任。

当一个校区接受了联邦拨款来教育贫苦儿童时,我们期待学生们能学有长进。如果做不到这一点,家长应当用这笔钱另作选择。

现在是重视幼童学习计划,教育所有的儿童能读会写,振兴美国公立学校的声望的时候了。对领导层的另一个考验是减税问题。

现在的各种税额占我国经济的百分之一。我国曾经有过如此高的税额,但有着很好的理由,因为我们投入了第二次世界大战。

今天,我国的高税额导致了盈余。有人说,不断增加的联邦盈余,意味着华盛顿有更多的钱可用。

遗憾的是,这些人把话说反了。

people should control local schools.

And those who spend your tax dollars must be held accountable.

When a school district receives federal funds to teach poor children, we expect them to learn. And if they don't, parents should get the money to make a different choice.

Now is the time to make Head Start an early learning program, teach all our children to read, and renew the promise of America's public schools. Another test of leadership is tax relief.

The last time taxes were this high as a percentage of our economy, there was a good reason—We were fighting World War II.

Today, our high taxes fund a surplus. Some say that growing federal surplus means Washington has more money to spend.

But they've got it backwards.

盈余并不属于政府。盈余属于人民。

我要借此机会,在税法问题上提倡常识和恢复公平。

我会根据原则来处理这件事。

从原则上说,每一户家庭、每一个农场主和小业主,都应当可以自由地把毕生财富传给所爱的人。

所以,我们将废除死亡税。

从原则上说,没有任何一个美国人必须把自己的三分之一收入交给联邦政府。

所以,我们将为所有的美国人减税。

从原则上说,最需要帮助的人应当得到最大的帮助。

所以,我们将把最低税率从15%降到10%,并把儿童的纳税津贴翻一番。

现在是改革税制,让纳税人共享盈余的时候了。

The surplus is not the government's money. The surplus is the people's money.

I will use this moment of opportunity to bring common sense and fairness to the tax code.

And I will act on principle.

On principle every family, every farmer and small businessperson, should be free to pass on their life's work to those they love.

So we will abolish the death tax.

On principle no one in America should have to pay more than a third of their income to the federal government.

So we will reduce tax rates for everyone, in every bracket.

On principle those in the greatest need should receive the greatest help.

So we will lower the bottom rate from 15 percent to 10 percent and double the child tax credit.

Now is the time to reform the tax code and share some of the surplus with the people who pay the bills.

世界需要美国的力量和领导,而美国武装部队需要更好的装备、更好的训练和更多的钱。

我们将赋予美国军队保卫和平的手段,我们还将赠给他们一件礼物——一位尊重军人并受军人尊重的总司令。

经过越南战争锤炼的一代人,必须牢记越南战争的教训。

当美国在世界上使用武力时,必须是为了正义的事业,有着明确的目标和必胜的把握。

我将努力减少世界上的核武器和由核武器造成的紧张局势——发挥美国的影响力,为世界带来几十年的和平。

我的政府将尽早部署导弹防御体系,以防我国遭到进攻和讹诈。

现在不是维护过时的条约的时候,而是保卫美国人民的时候。

The world needs America's strength and leadership, and America's armed forces need better equipment, better training, and better pay.

We will give our military the means to keep the peace, and we will give it one thing more—a commander-in-chief who respects our men and women in uniform, and a commander-in-chief who earns their respect.

A generation shaped by Vietnam must remember the lessons of Vietnam.

When America uses force in the world, the cause must be just, the goal must be clear, and the victory must be overwhelming.

I will work to reduce nuclear weapons and nuclear tension in the world—to turn these years of influence into decades of peace.

And, at the earliest possible date, my administration will deploy missile defenses to guard against attack and blackmail.

Now is the time, not to defend outdated treaties, but to defend the American people.

繁荣时期是检验一个政府有没有眼光的时期,而我们的国家今天需要的正是眼光。这是一个事实,或者,用我的对手的话来说,是"冒险计划"。他把我今晚谈到的每一项计划,统统称作"冒险计划",而且他重复了一遍又一遍。

这就是他想传递的全部信息——在政治上设置路障,在哲学上禁止通行。

如果我的对手当年参与了制定登月行动,那可能是一个"冒险的火箭计划"。

如果爱迪生在试验灯泡时,我的对手在场,那就是一个"冒险的反对蜡烛计划"。

如果因特网发明时他在场……我理解,他其实的确在场。

他现在领导着曾经由富兰克林·罗斯福领导的党,但他所能提供的唯一的东西就是惧怕。①

---

① 美国第 32 任总统富兰克林·罗斯福在上任时适逢经济危机,为鼓动民心,他在就职时说:"我们唯一不得不畏惧的东西就是畏惧。"

A time of prosperity is a test of vision. And our nation today needs vision. That is a fact, or as my opponent might call it, a "risky truth scheme." Every one of the proposals I've talked about tonight, he has called a "risky scheme," over and over again.

It is the sum of his message—the politics of the roadblock, the philosophy of the stop sign.

If my opponent had been there at the moon launch, it would have been a "risky rocket scheme."

If he'd been there when Edison was testing the light bulb, it would have been a "risky anti-candle scheme."

And if he'd been there when the Internet was invented well. I understand he actually was there for that.

He now leads the party of Franklin Delano Roosevelt. But the only thing he has to offer is fear itself.

那种观点是很典型的,华盛顿的许多人都持这种观点——总是在灯火快熄灭时才看见出路。

但是,我来自不同的地方,这使我成为一个不同的领导人。在中原腹地,在得克萨斯州,在我成长的地方,当地的格言是"天无止境",我们对此深信不疑。

人们有无穷的精力,有一个基本的信念,那就是:只要努力工作,任何人都能成功,而每一个人都应该得到一次机会。

我们需要一位领导人,来抓住这个新世纪所提供的种种机会——我们有新的药物来治疗疾病,我们有令人惊异的技术来推动我国经济的发展和保持和平。

但是,我们的新经济切不可忘记老传统,切不可忘记为人类尊严而进行的斗争尚未完成。

在这里,我们面临着一个挑战,这是一个对我国的宗旨和立国前提的挑战。

That outlook is typical of many in Washington—always seeing the tunnel at the end of the light.

But I come from a different place, and it has made me a different leader. In Midland, Texas, where I grew up, the town motto was "the sky is the limit", and we believed it.

There was a restless energy, a basic conviction that, with hard work, anybody could succeed, and everybody deserved a chance.

And we need a leader to seize the opportunities of this new century—the new cures of medicine, the amazing technologies that will drive our economy and keep the peace.

But our new economy must never forget the old, unfinished struggle for human dignity.

And here we face a challenge to the very heart and founding premise of our nation.

几年前，我参观了得克萨斯州的一个青少年管教所，与那里的少年犯进行了交谈。他们是一些愤怒而惆怅的孩子，都犯有成年人的罪行。

然而，当我直视他们的眼睛，我明白了，他们还只是一些孩子。

在谈话结束时，一个大约15岁的孩子举手问我，这个问题至今仍然萦绕在我的脑际："你对我怎么看？"

他似乎是在问我，就像许多仍在苦苦挣扎的美国人一样，"我有没有希望？我有没有机会？"或者说得直率些，"你，一个西装笔挺的白人，真的关心我的遭遇吗？"

一个微弱的声音，但说出了许多人的心里话。单亲母亲含辛茹苦地抚养自己的孩子，支付租金。移民们在一个新世界里开始了艰苦的生活。失去父爱的孩子们聚到一起，从流氓团伙那里似乎找到了友谊，毒品似乎给了他们暂时的安宁，性交似乎是属于他们的权利。但是，我们的国家也应该是他们的。

A couple of years ago, I visited a juvenile jail in Texas, and talked with a group of young inmates. They were angry, wary kids. All had committed grownup crimes.

Yet when I looked in their eyes, I realized some of them were still little boys.

Toward the end of conversation, one young man, about 15, raised his hand and asked a haunting question: "What do you think of me?"

He seemed to be asking, like many Americans who struggle, "Is there hope for me? Do I have a chance?" And, frankly, "Do you, a white man in a suit, really care what happens to me?"

A small voice, but it speaks for so many. Single moms struggling to feed the kids and pay the rent. Immigrants starting a hard life in a new world. Children without fathers in neighborhoods where gangs seem like friendship, where drugs promise peace, and where sex, sadly, seems like the closest thing to belonging. We are their country, too.

我们每一个人都应该分享国家的希望,否则,大家都会失去希望。

如果管教所里的那个孩子认为,他已经不能自拔和毫无希望——如果他认为他的生命已经失去了价值,而其他人的生命对他来说也毫无价值——那么,我们都将失去一切。

如果不治理这些问题,它们就将在我国内部筑起高墙。在墙的一边,是财富、技术、教育和雄心;在墙的另一边,则是贫困、监狱、毒瘾和失望。

美国同胞们,我们必须推倒那堵高墙。

庞大的政府不是解决问题的答案;取代官僚制的方法不是冷漠无情。

这需要我们把保守主义价值和保守主义观念注入为公正和机会而进行的激烈斗争中去。

这就是我所说的有同情心的保守主义。在这个基础上,我们将治理我们的国家。

And each of us must share in its promise, or that promise is diminished for all.

If that boy in jail believes he is trapped and worthless and hopeless—if he believes his life has no value, then other lives have no value to him—and we are ALL diminished.

When these problems aren't confronted, it builds a wall within our nation. On one side are wealth and technology, education and ambition. On the other side of the wall are poverty and prison, addiction and despair.

And, my fellow Americans, we must tear down that wall.

Big government is not the answer. But the alternative to bureaucracy is not indifference.

It is to put conservative values and conservative ideas into the thick of the fight for justice and opportunity.

This is what I mean by compassionate conservatism. And on this ground we will govern our nation.

我们将给予低收入美国人课税津贴,使他们能购买所需的和应得的个人健康保险。

我们将改革目前的住宅租赁计划,帮助成千上万低收入家庭安居乐业,找回尊严。

然后,我们将采取更大胆的福利改革,支持贫民收容所、食品救济站和妇婴急救中心等组织所开展的英勇工作——他们正在改造社区,一个街区又一个街区地进行改造,一个人又一个人地进行改造。

从现在算起的100年以后,人们在回忆今天的时代时,它不应该是一个物质富裕而思想贫乏的时代。

相反,我们应该开创一个充满责任心的时代。

我们这一代人向极限进行了挑战,从某种程度上说,我国已从中获益。

We will give low-income Americans tax credits to buy the private health insurance they need and deserve.

We will transform today's housing rental program to help hundreds of thousands of low-income families find stability and dignity in a home of their own.

And, in the next bold step of welfare reform, we will support the heroic work of homeless shelters and hospices, food pantries and crisis pregnancy centers—people reclaiming their communities block-by-block and heart-by-heart.

A hundred years from now, this must not be remembered as an age rich in possessions and poor in ideals.

Instead, we must usher in an era of responsibility.

My generation tested limits—and our country, in some ways, is better for it.

妇女现在已经得到了更平等的对待。我们在种族问题上也取得了稳妥的进步,如果说进步得还太慢。我们正在学会保护周围的自然界。我们会把这些进步继续下去,我们绝不走回头路。

我们曾经迷路,但我们正在回到正确的道路上。

我们已经发现,"我们是什么人"比"我们拥有什么财产"更重要。我们知道,我们必须恢复我们的价值观,以振兴我们的国家。

这正是美国开国元勋们的理想。

他们从来不认为,我国的伟大在于财富的增加和军队的推进,相反,他们认为,我国的伟大在于细微的关爱行动、勇气和自我否定。

他们最崇高的希望,正如罗伯特·弗罗斯特①所说,是要"用好的品格占领大地"。

---

① 美国诗人,善用传统诗歌和口语表达现代感情,多次获普利策奖。著有《白桦》《修墙》和诗集《山间》等。

Women are now treated more equally. Racial progress has been steady, if still too slow. We are learning to protect the natural world around us. We will continue this progress, and we will not turn back.

At times, we lost our way. But we are coming home.

We have discovered that who we are is more important than what we have. And we know we must renew our values to restore our country.

This is the vision of America's founders.

They never saw our nation's greatness in rising wealth or advancing armies, but in small, unnumbered acts of caring and courage and self-denial.

Their highest hope, as Robert Frost described it, was "to occupy the land with character."

13代人以后,那仍然是我们的目标——用好的品格占领大地。

在一个负责任的时代,我们每个人都有重要的任务——只有我们才能完成这些任务。

我们每个人都有责任爱护和指导自己的孩子,并帮助有急需的邻居。

犹太教堂、天主教堂和清真寺不仅有责任崇拜神灵,而且有责任提供服务。

公司有责任公平对待工人,并使空气和水保持清新。

我国的领导人有责任处理难题,而不是将难题推给别人。

要把这个国家引导到负责任的时代,一位总统本身必须有责任心。

所以,当我把手按在圣经上时,我会发誓,不仅要坚持我国的法律,而且要坚持总统办公室的荣誉和尊严。帮助我吧,上帝!

我认为,总统职位——美国政府的最终决策者——是为崇高目标而设定的。

And that, 13 generations later, is still our goal—to occupy the land with character.

In a responsibility era, each of us has important tasks—work that only we can do.

Each of us is responsible to love and guide our children, and help a neighbor in need.

Synagogues, churches and mosques are responsible not only to worship but to serve.

Corporations are responsible to treat their workers fairly, and leave the air and waters clean.

Our nation's leaders are responsible to confront problems, not pass them on to others.

And to lead this nation to a responsibility era, a president himself must be responsible.

And so, when I put my hand on the Bible, I will swear to not only uphold the laws of our land, I will swear to uphold the honor and dignity of the office to which I have been elected, so help me God.

I believe the presidency—the final point of decision in the American government—was made for great purposes.

这个职位，需要把林肯的良知、西奥多·罗斯福的精力、哈里·杜鲁门的诚信和罗纳德·里根的乐观综合起来。

对我来说，争取获得这一职位并非毕生的野心，但它确实是毕生一次的机会。

我将最大限度地发挥这一职位的作用。我相信，通过谨慎和必胜的信念，而不是通过选票，才能作出伟大的决定。

我不需要先给你们号脉，才能知道自己的想法。我不会在每个转折关头都要重新包装自己。我不是披着从别人那里借来的衣服参加竞选的。我一旦采取行动，你们就会知道我采取行动的原因；我一旦开口说话，你们就会知道我心里在想些什么。

我相信宽容，并非不顾自己的信念，恰恰是因为信念。

我相信上帝，它召唤我们热爱邻居，而不是评判邻居。

It is the office of Lincoln's conscience and Teddy Roosevelt's energy and Harry Truman's integrity and Ronald Reagan's optimism.

For me, gaining this office is not the ambition of a lifetime, but it IS the opportunity of a lifetime.

And I will make the most of it. I believe great decisions are made with care, made with conviction, not made with polls.

I do not need to take your pulse before I know my own mind. I do not reinvent myself at every turn. I am not running in borrowed clothes. When I act, you will know my reasons. When I speak, you will know my heart.

I believe in tolerance, not in spite of my faith, but because of it.

I believe in a God who calls us, not to judge our neighbors, but to love them.

我相信慈悲,因为我看到了慈悲;我相信和平,因为我感受到了和平;我相信宽恕,因为我需要宽恕。

我相信,真正的领导是一种添砖加瓦、而不是四分五裂的过程。我不会攻击这个国家的任何一部分,因为我想要领导整个国家。

我相信这将是一次艰难的竞选,直到最后一刻。

他们的作战系统已经就绪,并已经开动起来,而我们也已经严阵以待。他们的攻击将是残酷的,但他们将遭到回击。我们这一方是轻车熟路,而他们那一方却面临着许多新问题。

如今,我们的党是一个思想活跃和致力于创新的党,一个理想主义和充满包容精神的党,一个怀有简单而宏大的希望的党。

同胞们,我们可以重新开始。经历了所有的喧嚷、所有的丑闻、所有的痛苦和

I believe in grace, because I have seen it ... In peace, because I have felt it ... In forgiveness, because I have needed it.

I believe true leadership is a process of addition, not an act of division. I will not attack a part of this country, because I want to lead the whole of it.

And I believe this will be a tough race, down to the wire.

Their war room is up and running, but we are ready. Their attacks will be relentless, but they will be answered. We are facing something familiar, but they are facing something new.

We are now the party of ideas and innovation, the party of idealism and inclusion, the party of a simple and powerful hope.

My fellow citizens, we can begin again. After all of the shouting, and all

信念破灭之后,我们可以重新开始。

人们等得太久了,但现在不用等多久了。

一个欣欣向荣的民族已经准备好振兴自己的目标,并为崇高的目的而团结起来,不用等多久了。

我国必须重新燃起我与那个失足少年谈到过的希望,不用等多久了。

我国已经做好准备,迎接高标准和新领袖,不用等多久了。

一个失去思想光芒的时代,正在让位于一个有责任心的时代,不用等多久了。

我知道,面前的任务是多么艰巨。

我知道,总统办公室是把荣耀变为祝福的地方。

但是,我热切地希望开始前面的工作。

我相信,美国已经准备好迎接新开端。

---

of the scandal. After all of the bitterness and broken faith. We can begin again.

The wait has been long, but it won't be long now.

A prosperous nation is ready to renew its purpose and unite behind great goals ... and it won't be long now.

Our nation must renew the hopes of that boy I talked with in jail, and so many like him, and it won't be long now.

Our country is ready for high standards and new leaders, and it won't be long now.

An era of tarnished ideals is giving way to a responsibility era, and it won't be long now.

I know how serious the task is before me.

I know the presidency is an office that turns pride into prayer.

But I am eager to start on the work ahead.

And I believe America is ready for a new beginning.

朋友们，在埃尔帕索有一位艺术家汤姆·李①，他说出了我对我们伟大国家的感受。

他说，他和他的夫人"住在山的东边"。

那是太阳升起的一边，而不是太阳落下的一边。

那是看见新的一天正在到来的一边，而不是目送今日正在逝去的一边。

美国位于太阳升起的一边。

黑夜正在消逝。

我们已经为即将到来的一天做好准备。

余芝萍　译

---

①汤姆·李(1907—2001)，美国艺术家和作家，生于得克萨斯州西部城市埃尔帕索。

My friend, the artist Tom Lea of El Paso, captured the way I feel about our great land.

He and his wife, he said, "live on the east side of the mountain."

It is the sunrise side, not the sunset side.

It is the side to see the day that is coming, not the side to see the day that is gone.

Americans live on the sunrise side of mountain.

The night is passing.

And we are ready for the day to come.

2000年大选获胜演讲①

乔治·W.布什

2000年12月13日

晚上好,美国同胞们。我非常珍惜今晚有机会对你们讲话。

议长先生,副州长,朋友们,尊贵的客人们,我们国家度过了一个漫长而难熬的时期,总统选举结果的揭晓过程如此漫长,超出所有人的想象。

戈尔副总统和我都对竞选倾注了全部心血和希望。我们都

---

① 本篇是在得克萨斯州首府奥斯汀发表的电视讲话,宣布竞选获胜。

George W. Bush

December 13, 2000

2000 Victory Speech

Good evening, my fellow Americans. I appreciate so very much the opportunity to speak with you tonight.

Mr. Speaker, Lieutenant Governor, friends, distinguished guests, our country has been through a long and trying period, with the outcome of the presidential election not finalized for longer than any of us could ever imagine.

Vice President Gore and I put our hearts and hopes into

倾尽全力。我们都有相似的感受，因此，我能理解这一时刻对于戈尔副总统和他的一家是多么艰难。

无论作为一名众议员、参议员还是副总统，他都为我们国家作出了卓越贡献。

今晚，我接到来自副总统的亲切电话。我们同意下周初在华盛顿会面，我们将尽力治愈这个经历了激烈竞选国家的伤口。

今晚，我要感谢成千上万为了我而艰苦工作的志愿者和竞选工作人员。

我也要向发起这场猛烈的竞选攻势的副总统和他的支持者们致敬。我要感谢他打来的电话，我知道这是多么困难。劳拉和我向副总统和利伯曼参议员以及他们的家人致以最衷心的祝福。

今晚，我要感谢许多人。感谢美国，感谢我们能够以和平方式解决我们在选举中的分歧。

our campaigns. We both gave it our all. We shared similar emotions, so I understand how difficult this moment must be for Vice President Gore and his family.

He has a distinguished record of service to our country as a congressman, a senator and a vice president.

This evening I received a gracious call from the vice president. We agreed to meet early next week in Washington, and we agreed to do our best to heal our country after this hard-fought contest.

Tonight I want to thank all the thousands of volunteers and campaign workers who worked so hard on my behalf.

I also salute the vice president and his supports for waging a spirited campaign. And I thank him for a call that I know was difficult to make. Laura and I wish the vice president and Senator Lieberman and their families the very best.

I have a lot to be thankful for tonight. I'm thankful for America and thankful that we were able to resolve our electoral differences in a peaceful way.

感谢美国人民,能够成为你们的下一任总统,我感到巨大的荣幸。

感谢我的妻子和女儿的爱。劳拉作为州长夫人的积极工作使德州变得更加美好,她将成为一位出色的美国第一夫人。

我为选择迪克·切尼作为我的竞选伙伴感到骄傲,美国将会为选他作为下一任副总统而感到骄傲。

今晚,我选择得克萨斯州众议院的会议厅发表演讲,因为它已成为两党合作的大本营。在这个民主党占大多数的地方,为了我们代表的人民的利益,共和党和民主党走到了一起。

我们有过激烈的争执。最后,我们找到了建设性的共识。我将永远铭记这一经历,并永远以此为榜样。

感谢我的朋友,皮特·莱尼议长,今天刚刚将我介绍给大家的一位民主党人。

I'm thankful to the American people for the great privilege of being able to serve as your next president.

I want to thank my wife and our daughters for their love. Laura's active involvement as first lady has made Texas a better place, and she will be a wonderful first lady of America.

I am proud to have Dick Cheney by my side, and America will be proud to have him as our next vice president.

Tonight, I chose to speak from the chamber of the Texas House of Representatives because it has been a home to bipartisan cooperation. Here in a place where Democrats have the majority, Republicans and Democrats have worked together to do what is right for the people we represent.

We've had spirited disagreements. And in the end, we found constructive consensus. It is an experience I will always carry with me, an example I will always follow.

I want to thank my friend, House Speaker Pete Laney, a Democrat, who

感谢所有与我共事的两党议员。

穿过得克萨斯州议会大厦大厅是州参议院。我情不自禁想起我们共同的朋友，前任副州长，民主党人鲍伯·布洛克。他对德州的爱和他促进两党合作的才能将继续成为我们的榜样。

我在这个礼堂里所看到的合作精神正是华府所需要的。这是我们当前面临的挑战。在困难的选举结束之后，我们必须将政治抛在一边，齐心协力，让美国的承诺在每个美国人身上都得到实现。

我乐观地相信，我们能够改变华府的氛围。

我相信事情的发生总有理由，并且希望，经过最近5周漫长的等待，力求前进的意愿将会超越过去的痛苦和党派偏见。

我们的国家必须超越家庭分裂。美国人民的共同愿望、目标和价值观远远高

---

introduced me today. I want to thank the legislators from both political parties with whom I've worked.

Across the hall in our Texas capitol is the state Senate. And I cannot help but think of our mutual friend, the former Democrat lieutenant governor, Bob Bullock. His love for Texas and his ability to work in a bipartisan way continue to be a model for all of us.

The spirit of cooperation I have seen in this hall is what is needed in Washington, D.C. It is the challenge of our moment. After a difficult election, we must put politics behind us and work together to make the promise of America available for every one of our citizens.

I'm optimistic that we can change the tone in Washington, D.C.

I believe things happen for a reason, and I hope the long wait of the last five weeks will heighten a desire to move beyond the bitterness and partisanship of the recent past.

Our nation must rise above a house divided. Americans share hopes and

于一切党派分歧。

共和党人爱国,民主党人亦是。我们的得票数不同,但我们的愿望相同。

我知道美国希望和解和团结。我知道美国人民希望国家进步。我们必须抓住这个机会开始吧!

让我们一起,在理智、公德和共同目标的精神指引下,团结和激励全体美国公民。

让我们一起,努力使公立学校更为出色,教育每个学生而不论其背景和种族,不让一个学生掉队。

让我们一起,挽救社会保障,重新给未来几代人一个安全退休的承诺。

让我们一起,加强医疗保险,为所有年长者提供医药。

让我们一起,给美国人民一个应得的、广泛公平的、财政上有保证的减税计

---

goals and values far more important than any political disagreements.

Republicans want the best for our nation, and so do Democrats. Our votes may differ, but not our hopes.

I know America wants reconciliation and unity. I know Americans want progress. And we must seize this moment and deliver.

Together, guided by a spirit of common sense, common courtesy and common goals, we can unite and inspire the American citizens.

Together, we will work to make all our public schools excellent, teaching every student of every background and every accent, so that no child is left behind.

Together, we will save Social Security and renew its promise of a secure retirement for generations to come.

Together, we will strengthen Medicare and offer prescription drug coverage to all of our seniors.

Together, we will give Americans the broad, fair, and fiscally responsible

划。

让我们一起,制定一个忠于我们的信仰、忠于我们的朋友的两党合作的外交政策,我们将拥有一支足以应对任何挑战和任何对手的军队。

让我们一起,通过鼓励和支持美国人民的善良和才干,逐一解决社会最深层次的问题。

这是富有同情心的保守主义的本质,并且它将成为我的执政之本。

上述优先考虑的问题不仅仅是共和党人或是民主党人关注的问题;它们是美国人民肩负的责任。

在秋季大选之时,我们对于这些提议的细节各执其词,但是对于我们面临的重大问题已达成了非凡的共识:卓越的学校、退休和医疗保障、减税、一支强大的军队和一个更好的市民社会。

tax relief they deserve.

Together, we'll have a bipartisan foreign policy true to our values and true to our friends, and we will have a military equal to every challenge and superior to every adversary.

Together, we will address some of society's deepest problems one person at a time, by encouraging and empowering the good hearts and good works of the American people.

This is the essence of compassionate conservatism and it will be a foundation of my administration.

These priorities are not merely Republican concerns or Democratic concerns; they are American responsibilities.

During the fall campaign, we differed about the details of these proposals, but there was remarkable consensus about the important issues before us: excellent schools, retirement and health security, tax relief, a strong military, a more civil society.

我们已经探讨了我们的分歧。现在,寻找我们共同的背景,建立共识,使美国成为21世纪最具发展机会的国家的时候到了。

我对此持乐观态度。我们的未来需要这样做,而我们的历史证明了这一点。200年前,1800年的大选,美国面临着另一个票数接近的选举结果①。选举团中的平局将决定结果的权力交给了国会。

经过6天36次投票,众议员们选举托马斯·杰斐逊担任美国第三任总统。那次选举,第一次在我们新的民主形式下,将权力从一个党移交给了另一个党。

选举后不久,杰斐逊在一封名为"和解与改革"的信中写道:"同胞们的坚定不移的性格是我们可以依靠的磐石;在原则上决不含糊,在方式上通情达理。我们应

---

① 1800年,托马斯·杰斐逊和艾伦·伯尔在总统大选中获得了相同的选票,经众议院投票,杰斐逊以一票的多数当选美国第三任总统。

We have discussed our differences. Now it is time to find common ground and build consensus to make America a beacon of opportunity in the 21st century.

I'm optimistic this can happen. Our future demands it and our history proves it. Two hundred years ago, in the election of 1800, America faced another close presidential election. A tie in the Electoral College put the outcome into the hands of Congress.

After six days of voting and 36 ballots, the House of Representatives elected Thomas Jefferson the third president of the United States. That election brought the first transfer of power from one party to another in our new democracy.

Shortly after the election, Jefferson, in a letter titled Reconciliation and Reform, wrote this: "The steady character of our countrymen is a rock to which we may safely moor; unequivocal in principle, reasonable in manner. We should

当能够期待,在自由与和谐的事业上取得巨大的成功。"

200年的光阴进一步加强了美国人民坚定不移的性格。因此,当我们开始医治国家创伤这一工作之时,今晚,我呼唤这样的精神:尊重彼此,尊重分歧,慷慨大方,愿意努力工作,共同解决问题。

我对每个美国人还有个请求。我请求你们为这个伟大的国家祈祷。我请求你们为两党的领导人祈祷。我感谢你们为我和我的家人祈祷,同时,我也请求你们为戈尔副总统和他全家祈祷。

我坚信,在上帝的帮助下,我们这一民族将作为一个不可分裂的国家向前发展。同时,我们将一起创造一个开放的美国,这样每个公民就都能实现他的美国梦;我们将创造一个教育良好的美国,这样每个孩子就都有能力实现他的美国梦;我们将创造一个统一而多样性的美国,这样,美国价值观将高于民族和政党。

be able to hope to do a great deal of good to the cause of freedom and harmony."

Two hundred years have only strengthened the steady character of America. And so as we begin the work of healing our nation, tonight I call upon that character: respect for each other, respect for our differences, generosity of spirit, and a willingness to work hard and work together to solve any problem.

I have something else to ask you, to ask every American. I ask for you to pray for this great nation. I ask for your prayers for leaders from both parties. I thank you for your prayers for me and my family, and I ask you to pray for Vice President Gore and his family.

I have faith that with God's help we as a nation will move forward together as one nation, indivisible. And together we will create an America that is open, so every citizen has access to the American dream; an America that is educated, so every child has the keys to realize that dream; and an America that is united in our diversity and our shared American values that are larger than race or party.

我当选后不是要服务于某一政党,而是要服务于整个国家。

合众国总统是每个美国人的总统,不论其种族背景。

不管你是否投票给我,我都会尽最大的努力为你的利益服务,并将通过我的工作赢得你的尊重。

我将遵循杰弗逊总统的目标,坚守原则,通情达理,最重要的是,为自由与和谐的事业竭尽全力。

担任总统不仅仅是一项荣誉,也不仅仅是执掌总统办公室。它是一种责任,我将为此奉献所有。

非常感谢,上帝保佑美国。

张衡 译 王建华 校

I was not elected to serve one party, but to serve one nation.

The president of the United States is the president of every single American, of every race and every background.

Whether you voted for me or not, I will do my best to serve your interests and I will work to earn your respect.

I will be guided by President Jefferson's sense of purpose, to stand for principle, to be reasonable in manner, and above all, to do great good for the cause of freedom and harmony.

The presidency is more than an honor. It is more than an office. It is a charge to keep, and I will give it my all.

Thank you very much and God bless America.

巴拉克·奥巴马

2008 年 8 月 28 日

美国的承诺

怀着深深的感激与谦恭,我接受你们的提名,做美国总统的候选人。

四年前,我站在你们面前讲了我的故事———一个来自肯尼亚的男青年和一个来自堪萨斯州的女青年结合在一起,俩人虽不富裕,也不出名,但怀着共同的信念:在美国,他们的儿子只

---

* 美国第 44 任总统(2009—),民主党人。2008 年击败共和党总统候选人约翰·麦凯恩,成为美国第一位黑人总统,四年后获连任。本篇是他在丹佛市民主党代表大会上接受总统候选人提名时发表的演说。

Barrack Obama

August 28, 2008

The American Promise

With profound gratitude and great humility, I accept your nomination for the presidency of the United States.

Four years ago, I stood before you and told you my story—of the brief union between a young man from Kenya and a young woman from Kansas who weren't well-off or well-known, but

要用心,就能事业有成。①

正是这个承诺一直使美国与众不同——通过努力和付出,我们每个人都能追求自己的梦想,但仍然构成一个美利坚大家庭,来保证我们的下一代也能追求自己的梦想。

这就是为什么我今晚站在这里。因为232年来,每当这个承诺遇到危险,平凡的男男女女——学生和士兵、农民和教师、护士和清洁工——都会勇敢地挺身而出,维护这个承诺。

我们相聚在又一个决定性的时刻——在我国处于战争的时刻,在我国经济动荡的时刻,在美国的承诺又一次遭到威胁的时刻。

今晚,更多的美国人失业了,更多的美国人工作得更辛苦,得到的报酬却更少。在你们当中,更多的人失去了住所,更多的人在看着自己的家产迅速地贬值。

---

① 2004年在民主党代表大会上发表主旨演讲,述及家世,支持克里竞选。

shared a belief that in America, their son could achieve whatever he put his mind to.

It is that promise that has always set this country apart—that through hard work and sacrifice, each of us can pursue our individual dreams but still come together as one American family, to ensure that the next generation can pursue their dreams as well.

That's why I stand here tonight. Because for two hundred and thirty two years, at each moment when that promise was in jeopardy, ordinary men and women—students and soldiers, farmers and teachers, nurses and janitors—found the courage to keep it alive.

We meet at one of those defining moments—a moment when our nation is at war, our economy is in turmoil, and the American promise has been threatened once more.

Tonight, more Americans are out of work and more are working harder for less. More of you have lost your homes and even more are watching your home values

在你们当中,更多的人有车付不起油费,有信用卡付不起账单,可以上学却付不起学费。

这些问题并不全是政府造成的。但对这些问题应对不当,却是华盛顿的破烂政治和小布什的失败政策的直接后果。

美利坚呀,我们应该比过去八年过得好,我们的国家应该比现在强!

俄亥俄州有一个妇女,在辛劳了一辈子以后,在退休前夕发现自己患上了重病。我们的国家应该比这做得更体面!

印第安纳州有一个工人,不得不把使用了近20年的机器打包,并看着它们运往中国。当他回到家中告诉家人时,他哽咽了,说他感觉就像遭遇了失败。我们的国家应该比这做得更慷慨!

退伍军人流落街头,许多家庭陷入贫困;美国一座重要的城市在我们的眼前

plummet. More of you have cars you can't afford to drive, credit card bills you can't afford to pay, and tuition that's beyond your reach.

These challenges are not all of government's making. But the failure to respond is a direct result of a broken politics in Washington and the failed policies of George W. Bush.

America, we are better than these last eight years. We are a better country than this.

This country is more decent than one where a woman in Ohio, on the brink of retirement, finds herself one illness away from disaster after a lifetime of hard work.

This country is more generous than one where a man in Indiana has to pack up the equipment he's worked on for twenty years and watch it shipped off to China, and then chokes up as he explains how he felt like a failure when he went home to tell his family the news.

We are more compassionate than a government that lets veterans sleep on our streets and families slide into poverty; that sits on its hands while a major American

被洪水淹没,政府却袖手旁观。①我们的政府应该比这做得更具同情心!

今晚,我要对美国人民说,我要对这片伟大的土地上的民主党人、共和党人和独立人士说:够了!此时此刻——本届选举——是我们在21世纪保持美国承诺的活力的机会。因为在下个星期,在明尼苏达州,曾经给你们带来两届布什和切尼政府的那个党,将会谋求第三届任期。而我们来到这里,是因为我们太热爱这个国家了,绝不能让下一个四年再像过去八年一样!在11月4日②,我们必须站起来说:"八年已经够了!"

毫无疑问,共和党提名的约翰·麦凯恩曾经身穿军装,勇敢而光荣,为此,我们感谢他并尊敬他。下个星期我们还会听到,他在有些场合将与共和党分道扬镳,以此说明他能带来我们所需要的改变。

---

① 2008年6月,中西部爱荷华州锡达拉皮兹市遭遇500年罕见的洪水袭击。
② 美国大选日。

city drowns before our eyes.

Tonight, I say to the American people, to Democrats and Republicans and Independents across this great land—enough! This moment—this election—is our chance to keep, in the 21st century, the American promise alive. Because next week, in Minnesota, the same party that brought you two terms of George Bush and Dick Cheney will ask this country for a third. And we are here because we love this country too much to let the next four years look like the last eight. On November 4th, we must stand up and say: "Eight is enough."

Now let there be no doubt. The Republican nominee, John McCain, has worn the uniform of our country with bravery and distinction, and for that we owe him our gratitude and respect. And next week, we'll also hear about those occasions when he's broken with his party as evidence that he can deliver the change that we need.

但是记录清楚地表明:在过去,麦凯恩把百分之九十的票都投给了乔治·布什。麦凯恩参议员喜欢说判断力,但是,如果你认为乔治·布什百分之九十几都是对的,那么你的判断力在哪里呢?我不知道你们会怎么办,但我不准备把变革的希望寄托在百分之十的机会上。

事实是,在诸如健康医疗、教育和经济等一个个会改变你们的生活的问题上,麦凯恩参议员从来没有独立的判断。他说在现任总统的治理下,我国经济已取得"很大的进步",经济基础很强健。当他的拟定经济计划的主要顾问之一谈到美国人当前的焦虑情绪时,他竟然说,我们只是承受着"精神上的衰退",我们变成了一个"牢骚之邦"——这是他的原话。"牢骚之邦"?去对密歇根州一家汽车厂的自豪的工人们这样说吧!当他们发现工厂就要倒闭,仍然每天上班,一如既往地努力工作,因为他们知道,还有人指望他们生产出来的制动器呢。去对默默挑起重担的军属们这样说吧!他们曾看着自己的亲人,一次又一次离家去履行义务。他们都不是

But the record's clear: John McCain has voted with George Bush ninety percent of the time. Senator McCain likes to talk about judgment, but really, what does it say about your judgment when you think George Bush has been right more than ninety percent of the time? I don't know about you, but I'm not ready to take a ten percent chance on change.

The truth is, on issue after issue that would make a difference in your lives—on health care and education and the economy—Senator McCain has been anything but independent. He said that our economy has made "great progress" under this President. He said that the fundamentals of the economy are strong. And when one of his chief advisors—the man who wrote his economic plan—was talking about the anxiety Americans are feeling, he said that we were just suffering from a "mental recession," and that we've become, and I quote, "a nation of whiners." A nation of whiners? Tell that to the proud auto workers at a Michigan plant who, after they found out it was closing, kept showing up every day and working as hard as ever, because they knew there were people who counted on the brakes that they made. Tell that to the military families who shoulder their burdens silently as they watch their loved ones leave for

满腹牢骚的人,而是努力工作、回报社会、坚持不懈、毫无怨言的人。这就是我所知道的美国人。

其实,我并不相信麦凯恩参议员不关心美国人当今的生活,我只是认为他不懂。否则,他怎么会把中产阶级定义为年收入低于500万美元的人呢?否则,他怎么会提议为大企业和石油公司减税数千亿美元,却不为1亿多美国人减一分钱的税呢?否则,他怎么会提出实际上要对民众福利抽税的健康医疗计划,怎么会提出无助于家庭支付大学学费的教育计划,怎么会拿你们的退休做赌注,提出社会保障的私有化呢?

这不是因为他不关心,而是因为他不懂。

二十多年来,他赞成令共和党名誉扫地的陈旧哲学——将更多的东西给予拥有大部分财富的人,希望繁荣能由上而下惠及每一个人。在华盛顿,他们把这叫作"所有权社会",但它实际上说的是一切全靠你自己。失业了?你不走运。没有医疗

their third or fourth or fifth tour of duty. These are not whiners. They work hard and give back and keep going without complaint. These are the Americans that I know.

Now, I don't believe that Senator McCain doesn't care what's going on in the lives of Americans. I just think he doesn't know. Why else would he define middle-class as someone making under five million dollars a year? How else could he propose hundreds of billions in tax breaks for big corporations and oil companies but not one penny of tax relief to more than one hundred million Americans? How else could he offer a health care plan that would actually tax people's benefits, or an education plan that would do nothing to help families pay for college, or a plan that would privatize Social Security and gamble your retirement?

It's not because John McCain doesn't care. It's because John McCain doesn't get it.

For over two decades, he's subscribed to that old, discredited Republican philosophy—give more and more to those with the most and hope that prosperity trickles down to everyone else. In Washington, they call this the Ownership Society, but what it really means is—you're on your own. Out of work? Tough luck. No health care?

保险？市场会解决这个问题。出身贫寒？努力向上攀升吧，尽管你没有梯子。你完全要依靠自己！

好吧，现在到了他们承认失败的时候了。现在是我们来改变美国的时候了。这就是为什么我要当美国总统。

你们瞧，对于什么才是国家的进步，我们民主党人有着截然不同的量度。

我们衡量进步是看多少人能找到工作以偿付贷款，是看你们能否每个月有所结余，这样，总有一天能看到你们的孩子取得大学的文凭。我们衡量进步是看克林顿执政时产生了2300万个新的工作机会，美国家庭的收入平均提高了7500美元，而布什当政时却下降了2000美元。

我们衡量经济实力不是看有多少个亿万富翁，不是看财富500强企业有多少利润，而是看有创意的人能否冒险开一家公司，是看一个靠小费生活的女招待能否请一天假照顾生病的孩子，而且不必担心失去工作——是看这个经济体制是否

The market will fix it. Born into poverty? Pull yourself up by your own bootstraps—even if you don't have boots. You're on your own.

Well it's time for them to own their failure. It's time for us to change America. And that's why I want to be the President of the United States.

You see, we Democrats have a very different measure of what constitutes progress in this country.

We measure progress by how many people can find a job that pays the mortgage; whether you can put a little extra money away at the end of each month so you can someday watch your child receive her college diploma. We measure progress in the 23 million new jobs that were created when Bill Clinton was President—when the average American family saw its income go up $7,500 instead of down $2,000 like it has under George Bush.

We measure the strength of our economy not by the number of billionaires we have or the profits of the Fortune 500, but by whether someone with a good idea can take a risk and start a new business, or whether the waitress who lives on tips can take a day off to look after a sick kid without losing her job—an economy that honors

尊重劳动的尊严。

我们衡量经济实力的根本原则是，我们是否遵守了使美国变得伟大的根本承诺——正是为了这个承诺，我今天晚上才会站在这里。

因为在那些从伊拉克和阿富汗归来的年轻的退伍军人的脸上，我看到了我祖父的影子。珍珠港事件后，他参加了军队，在巴顿的麾下服役。后来，根据《退伍军人权利法案》，他得到了这个伟大国家的报偿，有机会上了大学。

从那个只睡三个小时就要上夜班的年轻学生的脸上，我想起了我的妈妈。她靠自己抚养了我和妹妹，一边工作，一边取得了学位；她曾领取救济性质的食品券，但仍借助学生贷款和奖学金，把我和妹妹送到美国最好的学校。

当我又听到一个工人告诉我他的工厂倒闭时，我想起了二十多年前芝加哥南部一家钢铁厂倒闭时，我曾经支持并为之战斗过的那些人。

当我听到一个妇女告诉我创业的艰难时，我想起了我的祖母。她努力进取，从

the dignity of work.

The fundamentals we use to measure economic strength are whether we are living up to that fundamental promise that has made this country great—a promise that is the only reason I am standing here tonight.

Because in the faces of those young veterans who come back from Iraq and Afghanistan, I see my grandfather, who signed up after Pearl Harbor, marched in Patton's Army, and was rewarded by a grateful nation with the chance to go to college on the GI Bill.

In the face of that young student who sleeps just three hours before working the night shift, I think about my mom, who raised my sister and me on her own while she worked and earned her degree; who once turned to food stamps but was still able to send us to the best schools in the country with the help of student loans and scholarships.

When I listen to another worker tell me that his factory has shut down, I remember all those men and women on the South Side of Chicago who I stood by and fought for two decades ago after the local steel plant closed.

And when I hear a woman talk about the difficulties of starting her own business, I think about my grandmother, who worked her way up from the secretarial pool

普通秘书升为中层管理人员,尽管这用了很多年,因为她是个女性。她教育我要努力工作。为了让我过得好一些,她推迟买车,推迟买新衣服。她把所有的一切都给了我。虽然她再也不能来到现场,但我知道她一定在看着,因为这个夜晚也属于她。

我不知道麦凯恩认为名人应当过怎样的生活,但我认为这就是我的生活。他们是我的英雄。他们的故事塑造了我。我打算代表他们赢得这次总统选举,并作为美国的总统,使我们的承诺充满活力!

那个承诺是什么?

那个承诺说每个人都可以按照自己的意愿生活,同时又有义务彼此尊重。

那个承诺说市场应该奖励主动和创新,促进增长,但企业应该尽责创造工作机会,聘用美国工人,依照规则行事。

我们的承诺说的是政府虽然不能解决我们所有的问题,但是它应该做我们无

to middle-management, despite years of being passed over for promotions because she was a woman. She's the one who taught me about hard work. She's the one who put off buying a new car or a new dress for herself so that I could have a better life. She poured everything she had into me. And although she can no longer travel, I know that she's watching tonight, and that tonight is her night as well.

I don't know what kind of lives John McCain thinks that celebrities lead, but this has been mine. These are my heroes. Theirs are the stories that shaped me. And it is on their behalf that I intend to win this election and keep our promise alive as President of the United States.

What is that promise?

It's a promise that says each of us has the freedom to make of our own lives what we will, but that we also have the obligation to treat each other with dignity and respect.

It's a promise that says the market should reward drive and innovation and generate growth, but that businesses should live up to their responsibilities to create American jobs, look out for American workers, and play by the rules of the road.

Ours is a promise that says government cannot solve all our problems, but what it should do is that which we cannot do for ourselves—protect us from harm and pro-

法去做的事：保护我们免受伤害，给每个孩子提供像样的教育，保持水质洁净、玩具安全，投资于新的学校、道路和科学技术。

我们的政府应该为我们工作，而不是与我们作对。它应该帮助我们，而不是伤害我们。它应该保证，不仅把机遇给予最有钱有势的人，也给予每一个愿意工作的美国人。

这就是美国的承诺，它是一种理念——我们为自己负责，也与这个国家共同盛衰；它是一个根本信念——我是兄弟姐妹的保护人。

这就是我们应该保持的承诺，这就是我们现在就需要的改变。所以，让我在这里阐明，如果我当选总统，那个改变究竟意味着什么。

改变意味着：免税条款将不再回报那些制定它们的说客，而将回报那些值得回报的美国工人和小企业主。

不同于麦凯恩，我将停止为那些把工作机会转到海外的公司减税，我将开始

vide every child a decent education; keep our water clean and our toys safe; invest in new schools and new roads and new science and technology.

Our government should work for us, not against us. It should help us, not hurt us. It should ensure opportunity not just for those with the most money and influence, but for every American who's willing to work.

That's the promise of America—the idea that we are responsible for ourselves, but that we also rise or fall as one nation; the fundamental belief that I am my brother's keeper; I am my sister's keeper.

That's the promise we need to keep. That's the change we need right now. So let me spell out exactly what that change would mean if I am President.

Change means a tax code that doesn't reward the lobbyists who wrote it, but the American workers and small businesses who deserve it.

Unlike John McCain, I will stop giving tax breaks to corporations that ship jobs

为在美国本土创造良好就业机会的公司减税。

对那些能提供高薪、高技术工作的小企业和新企业,我将取消她们的资本收益税。

我将为95%的工薪家庭减税,因为根据目前的经济状况,最不该做的事就是增加中产阶级的税赋。

为了我们的经济和安全,为了我们这个星球的未来,作为总统我将制定一个明确的目标:在十年内,我们将结束对中东石油的依赖。

华盛顿谈论石油依赖已经有30年之久,麦凯恩也有26年。在此期间,他曾对高效汽车燃油标准说"不",对投资可再生能源说"不",对可再生燃料说"不"。今天,我们进口的石油数量已经是麦凯恩当选参议员时的三倍。

现在是结束这种依赖的时候了,要知道,钻探油井仅为权宜之计,而不是长久之策,根本扯不上关系。

---

overseas, and I will start giving them to companies that create good jobs right here in America.

I will eliminate capital gains taxes for the small businesses and the start-ups that will create the high-wage, high-tech jobs of tomorrow.

I will cut taxes—cut taxes—for 95 percent of all working families. Because in an economy like this, the last thing we should do is raise taxes on the middle-class.

And for the sake of our economy, our security, and the future of our planet, I will set a clear goal as President: in ten years, we will finally end our dependence on oil from the Middle East.

Washington's been talking about our oil addiction for the last thirty years, and John McCain has been there for twenty-six of them. In that time, he's said no to higher fuel-efficiency standards for cars, no to investments in renewable energy, no to renewable fuels. And today, we import triple the amount of oil as the day that Senator McCain took office.

Now is the time to end this addiction, and to understand that drilling is a stop-gap measure, not a long-term solution. Not even close.

作为总统,我将开发天然气储备,投资于洁净煤炭技术,找到安全利用核能的办法。我将帮助汽车公司调整装备,以便在美国本土生产出未来的高效燃油汽车,并让美国人更容易买得起这些新车。未来十年,我将投资1500亿美元用于可再生能源——风能、太阳能和下一代的生物燃料,这笔投资会造就新的工业,带来500万个报酬丰厚的新工作,而且不会被外包。

美利坚呀,现在不是执行微不足道的计划的时候了!

现在终于到了要履行我们的道德义务的时候了——给每一个孩子提供一流的教育,否则我们将难以参与全球经济的竞争。米歇尔和我都曾得到受教育的机会,所以我们今晚才能来到这里。如果有的孩子还得不到这样的机会,我不会满意这样的美国。我将投资于早期教育,招募一支新的教师队伍,并给予高薪和更多的支持。作为交换,我将提出更高的标准,要求有更高的责任心。我们将对每个美国年轻人保证:如果你承诺为社区和国家服务,我们将保证你能付得起大学的学费。

As President, I will tap our natural gas reserves, invest in clean coal technology, and find ways to safely harness nuclear power. I'll help our auto companies re-tool, so that the fuel-efficient cars of the future are built right here in America. I'll make it easier for the American people to afford these new cars. And I'll invest 150 billion dollars over the next decade in affordable, renewable sources of energy—wind power and solar power and the next generation of biofuels; an investment that will lead to new industries and five million new jobs that pay well and can't ever be outsourced.

America, now is not the time for small plans.

Now is the time to finally meet our moral obligation to provide every child a world-class education, because it will take nothing less to compete in the global economy. Michelle and I are only here tonight because we were given a chance at an education. And I will not settle for an America where some kids don't have that chance. I'll invest in early childhood education. I'll recruit an army of new teachers, and pay them higher salaries and give them more support. And in exchange, I'll ask for higher standards and more accountability. And we will keep our promise to every young American-if you commit to serving your community or your country, we will make sure you can afford a college education.

现在终于到了要履行承诺的时候了——为每一个美国人提供能承受的、便捷的医疗保险。如果你已经有医疗保险,我的计划是降低你的费用;如果你还没有,那么你将能得到和国会议员一样的那种医疗覆盖。我曾目睹我的母亲在患癌症奄奄一息之际还在和保险公司争辩,所以,我要确保医疗保险公司不再歧视那些最需要保险的病人。

现在是实行带薪病假和更好的家庭假来帮助每一个家庭的时候了,因为美国不应该有人被迫在保住工作和照看生病的孩子或照看生病的父母之间作出选择。

现在是修改破产法的时候了,这样,你们的养老金就能先于首席执行官的各种奖金得到保护。现在是为子孙后代保护社会保障制度的时候了。

现在是履行同工同酬的承诺的时候了,因为我希望,我的女儿能和你们的儿子一样得到完全相同的机会。

这些计划中有许多都需要花钱,这就是为什么我已经阐明我将如何支付每一

Now is the time to finally keep the promise of affordable, accessible health care for every single American. If you have health care, my plan will lower your premiums. If you don't, you'll be able to get the same kind of coverage that members of Congress give themselves. And as someone who watched my mother argue with insurance companies while she lay in bed dying of cancer, I will make certain those companies stop discriminating against those who are sick and need care the most.

Now is the time to help families with paid sick days and better family leave, because nobody in America should have to choose between keeping their jobs and caring for a sick child or ailing parent.

Now is the time to change our bankruptcy laws, so that your pensions are protected ahead of CEO bonuses; and the time to protect Social Security for future generations.

And now is the time to keep the promise of equal pay for an equal day's work, because I want my daughters to have exactly the same opportunities as your sons.

Now, many of these plans will cost money, which is why I've laid out how I'll

笔钱——堵住公司的漏洞,关闭避税的天堂,因为这些不利于美国的发展。我还将逐项审查联邦的预算,砍掉失效的项目,而让所需要的项目进展得更好、花费更低,因为我们绝不能用20世纪的官僚作风应对21世纪的挑战。

民主党人,我们还必须承认,履行美国的承诺不仅需要钱,还需要每个人都树立一种新的责任感,来恢复肯尼迪总统所说的我们的"思想和道德的力量"。诚然,政府必须领导能源独立的计划,但我们每个人也要尽自己的努力,使家庭和公司更加节能。是的,我们必须为犯罪和绝望的青少年提供更多的成功阶梯;但我们也要承认,政府的各项计划并不能取代家长的位置,政府不能关掉电视,强迫一个孩子去做功课,而父母们必须为关爱和指导孩子承担更多的责任。

个人的责任和共同的责任——这才是美国的承诺的精华。

正如我们在国内为下一代履行承诺一样,我们在国外也要履行美国的承诺。如果麦凯恩要和我辩论,谁具备了担任下一任总司令的素质和判断力,我已经做

---

pay for every dime—by closing corporate loopholes and tax havens that don't help America grow. But I will also go through the federal budget, line by line, eliminating programs that no longer work and making the ones we do need work better and cost less—because we cannot meet twenty-first century challenges with a twentieth century bureaucracy.

And Democrats, we must also admit that fulfilling America's promise will require more than just money. It will require a renewed sense of responsibility from each of us to recover what John F. Kennedy called our "intellectual and moral strength." Yes, government must lead on energy independence, but each of us must do our part to make our homes and businesses more efficient. Yes, we must provide more ladders to success for young men who fall into lives of crime and despair. But we must also admit that programs alone can't replace parents; that government can't turn off the television and make a child do her homework; that fathers must take more responsibility for providing the love and guidance their children need.

Individual responsibility and mutual responsibility—that's the essence of America's promise.

And just as we keep our promise to the next generation here at home, so must we keep America's promise abroad. If John McCain wants to have a debate about who has the temperament, and judgment, to serve as the next Commander-in-Chief,

好了准备。

因为当麦凯恩参议员在"9·11"事件后将目光转向伊拉克时,我已经站起来反对这场战争,我知道,它会分散我们对真正威胁的关注。而当麦凯恩说什么我们在阿富汗不妨"敷衍了事"时,我坚持说需要派更多的力量和军队,来完成对恐怖分子的作战,因为实际上这些恐怖分子在"9·11"事件中攻击过我们。我还表明,一旦看到本·拉登①和他的部属,务必将他们除掉。麦凯恩喜欢说,他会追踪本·拉登直到地狱之门。可是他连本·拉登住的山洞都没去过。

如今,我提出的从伊拉克撤军要有时间表的呼吁,已经得到伊拉克政府、甚至布什政府的响应。然而,即便我们获知伊拉克的贸易顺差为790亿美元,而我们却在赤字中挣扎,麦凯恩还是一意孤行,固执地拒绝结束这场不明智的战争。

那不是我们需要的判断力。那样做不会使美国安全。我们需要一个能面对未

---

① 本·拉登(1957—2011),基地组织头目,被认为是"9·11"事件的幕后总策划。

that's a debate I'm ready to have.

For while Senator McCain was turning his sights to Iraq just days after 9/11, I stood up and opposed this war, knowing that it would distract us from the real threats we face. When John McCain said we could just "muddle through" in Afghanistan, I argued for more resources and more troops to finish the fight against the terrorists who actually attacked us on 9/11, and made clear that we must take out Osama bin Laden and his lieutenants if we have them in our sights. John McCain likes to say that he'll follow bin Laden to the Gates of Hell—but he won't even go to the cave where he lives.

And today, as my call for a time frame to remove our troops from Iraq has been echoed by the Iraqi government and even the Bush Administration, even after we learned that Iraq has a $79 billion surplus while we're wallowing in deficits, John McCain stands alone in his stubborn refusal to end a misguided war.

That's not the judgment we need. That won't keep America safe. We need a

来的威胁、而不是抱住过时观念不放的总统。

你不可能通过占领伊拉克,来挫败一个遍布80个国家的恐怖主义网络。你不可能仅凭在华盛顿发布强硬的措辞,来保护以色列并遏制伊朗。当你和老盟友之间的关系已经搞得很紧张,你也不可能真正地支持格鲁吉亚。如果麦凯恩执意追随布什的强硬口气和糟糕政策,那是他的选择——但不是我们所需要的改变。

我们是罗斯福的党,是肯尼迪的党。所以,别对我说民主党不能保卫这个国家,别对我说民主党不能保证我们的安全!布什和麦凯恩的对外政策已经挥霍了好几代美国人——包括民主党人和共和党人——留下的遗产,现在我们在这里要恢复那笔遗产。

作为总司令,我将毫不犹豫地保卫我们的国家。但是,我只会为一个明确的使命、一个神圣的承诺而派遣军队出征,同时给这些军队所需要的作战装备,当他们回家时,还要给他们应得的照顾和福利。

President who can face the threats of the future, not keep grasping at the ideas of the past.

You don't defeat a terrorist network that operates in eighty countries by occupying Iraq. You don't protect Israel and deter Iran just by talking tough in Washington. You can't truly stand up for Georgia when you've strained our oldest alliances. If John McCain wants to follow George Bush with more tough talk and bad strategy, that is his choice—but it is not the change we need.

We are the party of Roosevelt. We are the party of Kennedy. So don't tell me that Democrats won't defend this country. Don't tell me that Democrats won't keep us safe. The Bush-McCain foreign policy has squandered the legacy that generations of Americans—Democrats and Republicans—have built, and we are here to restore that legacy.

As Commander-in-Chief, I will never hesitate to defend this nation, but I will only send our troops into harm's way with a clear mission and a sacred commitment to give them the equipment they need in battle and the care and benefits they deserve when they come home.

我将负责结束这场伊拉克战争,并结束对基地组织和塔利班的阿富汗战争。我将重建军队,以应付未来的冲突。我还将恢复强硬的、直接的外交策略,防止伊朗获得核武器,并遏制俄罗斯的侵略。我将建立新的伙伴关系,来应对21世纪的威胁,包括恐怖主义和核扩散,贫穷和种族灭绝,气候变化和疾病。我将恢复我们的道德立场,这样,美国将再次成为投身自由事业、渴望和平、期待美好未来的人们的最后和最好的希望。

这些就是我要采取的政策。在未来几个星期里,我期待着和麦凯恩就此展开辩论。

但是,有一件事我不做:我不会暗示麦凯恩参议员采取的立场是出于政治目的。因为我国政治有一个亟须改变之处,那就是一有不同意见,就去质疑对方的人品和爱国心。

当前的历史关头太严峻了,赌注太高昂了,玩不得同样的党派攻略。所以,让

I will end this war in Iraq responsibly, and finish the fight against al Qaeda and the Taliban in Afghanistan. I will rebuild our military to meet future conflicts. But I will also renew the tough, direct diplomacy that can prevent Iran from obtaining nuclear weapons and curb Russian aggression. I will build new partnerships to defeat the threats of the 21st century: terrorism and nuclear proliferation; poverty and genocide; climate change and disease. And I will restore our moral standing, so that America is once again that last, best hope for all who are called to the cause of freedom, who long for lives of peace, and who yearn for a better future.

These are the policies I will pursue. And in the weeks ahead, I look forward to debating them with John McCain.

But what I will not do is suggest that the Senator takes his positions for political purposes. Because one of the things that we have to change in our politics is the idea that people cannot disagree without challenging each other's character and patriotism.

The times are too serious, the stakes are too high for this same partisan play-

我们都能同意,爱国主义不分党派。我爱这个国家,你们也爱,麦凯恩也不例外。在战场上服役的可能是民主党人、共和党人或无党派人士,他们在一起战斗,一起流血,其中一些人死在同一面自豪的军旗下。他们不是为红色美国或是为蓝色美国服役①——他们是为了美利坚合众国。

所以,麦凯恩,我要告诉你:我们都把国家放在第一位。

美利坚呀,我们将来的工作并不容易。我们面临的挑战需要艰难的抉择,而民主党人和共和党人一样,都需要抛弃陈旧的理念和过时的政治。我们过去八年所失去的,不能仅用失去的薪水或者更高的贸易赤字来衡量,我们还失去了共同的目标——更崇高的目标,这才是我们必须恢复的。

关于堕胎问题,我们可能各持己见,但对减少意外怀孕,我们肯定能取得一致。关于持枪问题,俄亥俄州的农村猎户的看法,可能不同于那些为团伙暴力困扰

---

① 美国媒体用红蓝两色标注大选的进程和结果,共和党获胜的州用红色,民主党获胜的州用蓝色。

book. So let us agree that patriotism has no party. I love this country, and so do you, and so does John McCain. The men and women who serve in our battlefields may be Democrats and Republicans and Independents, but they have fought together and bled together and some died together under the same proud flag. They have not served a Red America or a Blue America—they have served the United States of America.

So I've got news for you, John McCain. We all put our country first.

America, our work will not be easy. The challenges we face require tough choices, and Democrats as well as Republicans will need to cast off the worn-out ideas and politics of the past. For part of what has been lost these past eight years can't just be measured by lost wages or bigger trade deficits. What has also been lost is our sense of common purpose—our sense of higher purpose. And that's what we have to restore.

We may not agree on abortion, but surely we can agree on reducing the number of unwanted pregnancies in this country. The reality of gun ownership may be different for hunters in rural Ohio than for those plagued by gang-violence in Cleveland,

的克利夫兰居民，但这并不是说，我们不可能一方面赞同宪法第二条修正案，另一方面不让罪犯持有AK-47步枪。关于同性婚姻问题，我知道还存在异议，但我们肯定都能同意，同性恋兄弟姐妹们应当可以探望住院的爱人，并不受歧视地生活。关于群情激愤的移民问题，我不知道当一个母亲和她的婴儿分离时，或是当一个雇主雇黑工来降低美国人的工资时，究竟有谁能获益。但这同样是美国承诺的一部分——它承诺了一种民主，从中可以找到力量和善意，弥合分歧，团结起来，共同努力。

我知道有些人会摒弃上述信念，把它们当作笑谈。他们声称，我们坚持公众生活中更广义、更坚定、更正直的事物，就像一只特洛伊木马，将会导致更高的税收和抛弃传统的价值。这是意料之中的。因为你如果没有新颖的观念，就只能用陈腐的手段来吓唬选民；而如果你缺乏一份纪录来充当竞选的资本，就会把对手描绘成一个众叛亲离的人。

---

but don't tell me we can't uphold the Second Amendment while keeping AK-47s out of the hands of criminals. I know there are differences on same-sex marriage, but surely we can agree that our gay and lesbian brothers and sisters deserve to visit the person they love in the hospital and to live lives free of discrimination. Passions fly on immigration, but I don't know anyone who benefits when a mother is separated from her infant child or an employer undercuts American wages by hiring illegal workers. This too is part of America's promise—the promise of a democracy where we can find the strength and grace to bridge divides and unite in common effort.

I know there are those who dismiss such beliefs as happy talk. They claim that our insistence on something larger, something firmer and more honest in our public life is just a Trojan Horse for higher taxes and the abandonment of traditional values. And that's to be expected. Because if you don't have any fresh ideas, then you use stale tactics to scare the voters. If you don't have a record to run on, then you paint your opponent as someone people should run from.

你使得一场大选围绕着小事展开。

想知道吗——这种做法以前奏效过。因为它滋养了我们对政府都具有的怀疑情绪。当华盛顿不起作用时,似乎它的所有承诺都成了空话。而如果你的希望一再落空,那么,最好别再抱希望了,接受你已经了解的现实吧。

这一点我懂。我意识到,对于这一职务,我不是最有可能的候选人。我没有典型的家世,也没有在华盛顿工作的经历。

然而,我今晚站在你们面前,因为有一件事正在轰动全美国。摇头派人士不会明白,本届选举从来不是关于我,而是关于你们!

漫长的18个月以来,你们一个个站起来对过去的政治说"够了"!你们知道,在本届选举中, 最大的风险莫过于指望同样的政策和同样的官员能带来不同的结果。你们已经展示了历史的教诲——在当前这个决定性的时刻,我们需要的改变不会来自华盛顿,而是改变来到了华盛顿!之所以发生了改变,是因为美国人民需

You make a big election about small things.

And you know what—it's worked before. Because it feeds into the cynicism we all have about government. When Washington doesn't work, all its promises seem empty. If your hopes have been dashed again and again, then it's best to stop hoping, and settle for what you already know.

I get it. I realize that I am not the likeliest candidate for this office. I don't fit the typical pedigree, and I haven't spent my career in the halls of Washington.

But I stand before you tonight because all across America something is stirring. What the nay-sayers don't understand is that this election has never been about me. It's been about you.

For eighteen long months, you have stood up, one by one, and said enough to the politics of the past. You understand that in this election, the greatest risk we can take is to try the same old politics with the same old players and expect a different result. You have shown what history teaches us—that at defining moments like this one, the change we need doesn't come from Washington. Change comes to Washing-

要改变——因为他们起来反抗了,他们坚持要求新的观念、新的领导和新时代的新政治。

美利坚呀,那样的时刻再次来临!

我相信,不管有多么艰难,我们所需要的改变正在来临。因为我已经看到它了,因为我已经经历过它了。我在伊利诺伊州看到它了——我们为更多的儿童提供医疗保健,使更多的家庭从依靠救济走向就业。我在华盛顿看到它了——我们打破党派的界线,让政府变得开放,使院外游说集团变得更加负责,给退役军人更好的待遇,阻止恐怖主义者拥有核武器。

我在本届竞选中看到了改变。在第一次参加投票的年轻选民中,在隔了很久又参加投票的老选民中,我看到了改变;在从未想过会为民主党投票、却为它投了票的共和党人中,我看到了改变。从宁愿减少自己的工作时间,也不愿看到朋友们失业的工人身上,从那些再次应征的断肢士兵身上,从那些当暴风和洪水袭来时

ton. Change happens because the American people demand it—because they rise up and insist on new ideas and new leadership, a new politics for a new time.

America, this is one of those moments.

I believe that as hard as it will be, the change we need is coming. Because I've seen it. Because I've lived it. I've seen it in Illinois, when we provided health care to more children and moved more families from welfare to work. I've seen it in Washington, when we worked across party lines to open up government and hold lobbyists more accountable, to give better care for our veterans and keep nuclear weapons out of terrorist hands.

And I've seen it in this campaign. In the young people who voted for the first time, and in those who got involved again after a very long time. In the Republicans who never thought they'd pick up a Democratic ballot, but did. I've seen it in the workers who would rather cut their hours back a day than see their friends lose their jobs, in the soldiers who re-enlist after losing a limb, in the good neighbors who take

收容陌生人的善良同胞身上,我看到了改变。

我们这个国家拥有的财富比任何国家都多,但并不是这个原因我们才富有。我们有地球上最强大的军队,但并不是这个原因我们才坚强。我们的大学、我们的文化为全世界所羡慕,但并不是这个原因各国移民才涌向美国的海岸。

其实,是美国的精神——美国的承诺——它推着我们向前,即使道路尚不确定;它让我们团结起来,尽管我们各持己见;它使我们不要盯着眼前,而要放眼未来,放眼弯道后面的美妙世界。

这个承诺是我们最伟大的遗产。它是我在晚上为女儿塞被子时所作的承诺,也是你们为你们的孩子所作的承诺——这个承诺曾使移民们漂洋过海,使拓荒者走向西部;这个承诺曾使工人们走上街头,使妇女们拿起选票。

45年前的今天,正是这个承诺把这片土地上各个角落的美国人聚集起来,站

a stranger in when a hurricane strikes and the floodwaters rise.

This country of ours has more wealth than any nation, but that's not what makes us rich. We have the most powerful military on Earth, but that's not what makes us strong. Our universities and our culture are the envy of the world, but that's not what keeps the world coming to our shores.

Instead, it is that American spirit—that American promise—that pushes us forward even when the path is uncertain; that binds us together in spite of our differences; that makes us fix our eye not on what is seen, but what is unseen, that better place around the bend.

That promise is our greatest inheritance. It's a promise I make to my daughters when I tuck them in at night, and a promise that you make to yours—a promise that has led immigrants to cross oceans and pioneers to travel west; a promise that led workers to picket lines, and women to reach for the ballot.

And it is that promise that forty five years ago today, brought Americans from every corner of this land to stand together on a Mall in Washington, before Lincoln's

在华盛顿的广场上和林肯纪念碑前,听一个年轻的佐治亚州牧师①讲述他的梦想。

聚在那里的人们可能听到了很多。他们可能听到了愤怒和争论。他们也可能听到了劝说——这么多梦想都推迟了,向恐惧和挫折低头吧。

但是,他们听到的正好相反——不同信仰、不同肤色、不同行业的人们听到的是:在美国,我们的命运紧密相连;我们抱成团,就可以有共同的梦想。

"我们不能单独行动,"那个牧师呼喊着,"当我们行动时,就必须保证勇往直前。我们不能倒退。"

美利坚呀,我们不能倒退。我们还有这么多事业未完成,我们不能倒退。我们还有这么多孩子需要教育,这么多退伍军人需要关爱,我们不能倒退。我们还要修复经济,重建城市,拯救农场,我们不能倒退。我们还有这么多家庭需要保护,这么

---

① 指马丁·路德·金(1929—1968),美国民权运动领袖,1963年在"向华盛顿进军"的集会上发表《我有一个梦想》的演说。1964年获诺贝尔和平奖。

Memorial, and hear a young preacher from Georgia speak of his dream.

The men and women who gathered there could've heard many things. They could've heard words of anger and discord. They could've been told to succumb to the fear and frustration of so many dreams deferred.

But what the people heard instead—people of every creed and color, from every walk of life—is that in America, our destiny is inextricably linked. That together, our dreams can be one.

"We cannot walk alone," the preacher cried. "And as we walk, we must make the pledge that we shall always march ahead. We cannot turn back."

America, we cannot turn back. Not with so much work to be done. Not with so many children to educate, and so many veterans to care for. Not with an economy to fix and cities to rebuild and farms to save. Not with so many families to protect and

多人的生活需要弥补。美利坚呀,我们不能倒退!我们不能单独行动!此时此刻,在这次选举中,我们必须再次保证勇往直前!让我们履行这个承诺——美国的承诺——如《圣经》所说,毫不动摇地坚守我们所认同的希望①。

谢谢你们,上帝保佑你们,上帝保佑美利坚合众国!

井 力 译

---

① 参见圣经《希伯来书》第10章第23节。

so many lives to mend. America, we cannot turn back. We cannot walk alone. At this moment, in this election, we must pledge once more to march into the future. Let us keep that promise–that American promise–and in the words of Scripture hold firmly, without wavering, to the hope that we confess.

Thank you, God Bless you, and God Bless the United States of America.

在选举夜庆祝胜利集会上的讲话*

巴拉克·奥巴马

2012年11月7日

今晚,这个前殖民地在赢得决定自己命运的权利200多年后,完善我们的联邦的任务又向前推进了。

这个任务能向前推进,是因为有了你们。因为你们重申了一种能打赢战争和战胜萧条的精神,一种能使这个国家走出绝望的深渊来到希望的高地的精神——这是一种信念:尽管我们每个人都追求自己的梦想,却构成了一个美利坚大家庭,并作

---

* 奥巴马以较大优势击败共和党总统候选人罗姆尼而获得连任。本篇是他在芝加哥著名的麦考密克广场庆祝胜利集会上发表的演说。

Barrack Obama

November 7, 2012

Remarks at the Election Night Rally Celebrating Victory

Tonight, more than 200 years after a former colony won the right to determine its own destiny, the task of perfecting our union moves forward.

It moves forward because of you. It moves forward because you reaffirmed the spirit that has triumphed over war and depression; the spirit that has lifted this country from the depths of despair to the great heights of hope—the belief that while each of

为一个国家和民族,一起兴盛和衰落。

今晚,在本届选举中,你们——美国人民——提醒我们,虽然道路艰辛,虽然征途漫长,但我们振作起来进行了反击,而我们从心里知道,对美利坚合众国来说,最美好的前景尚未到来。

我要感谢每一个参加本次选举的美国人。无论你是第一次投票,还是排队等了很久才投上一票——顺便说一句我们必须解决排队的问题——无论你是上门投的票,还是用电话投票;无论你是投奥巴马的票,还是投罗姆尼的票,你们都已表达了自己的意愿,从而带来了改变。

我刚刚和罗姆尼州长通过电话,祝贺他和保罗·瑞安①经历了一场艰苦的竞选。我们的选战也许很激烈,但这只是因为我们都深爱这个国家,并且非常强烈地关心她的未来。从罗姆尼的父亲乔治、母亲莱诺到他们的儿子米特,罗姆尼家族选

---

①罗姆尼的竞选搭档。

us will pursue our own individual dreams, we are an American family, and we rise or fall together, as one nation, and as one people.

Tonight, in this election, you, the American people, reminded us that while our road has been hard, while our journey has been long, we have picked ourselves up, we have fought our way back, and we know in our hearts that for the United States of America, the best is yet to come.

I want to thank every American who participated in this election. Whether you voted for the very first time or waited in line for a very long time, by the way, we have to fix that. Whether you pounded the pavement or picked up the phone, whether you held an Obama sign or a Romney sign, you made your voice heard, and you made a difference.

I just spoke with Governor Romney, and I congratulated him and Paul Ryan on a hard-fought campaign. We may have battled fiercely, but it's only because we love this country deeply, and we care so strongly about its future. From George to Lenore to their son Mitt, the Romney family has chosen to give back to America through

择担任公职来回报美国，这种传统，我们今晚要引以为荣和为之喝彩。

在未来几个星期里，我期待着能和罗姆尼坐下来探讨，我们可以在哪些方面共同努力，推动国家的发展。

我要感谢过去四年来我的朋友和搭档、美国最快乐的勇士、任何人都梦寐以求的最优秀的副总统乔·拜登。

要是没有那个20年前同意嫁给我的女人，我就不可能是今天的我了。让我公开地表明：米歇尔，我从来没有比现在这样更爱你。我看到全美国也爱你，爱我们的第一夫人，我感到从未有过的自豪。萨莎和玛莉亚，你们在我们的眼前长大了，长成了两个坚强、聪明和漂亮的大姑娘，就像你们的母亲一样。我为你们感到非常骄傲。不过，我觉得你们目前养一条宠物狗就够了。

我要感谢我的竞选团队和志愿者，你们是最棒的，政治史上最棒的！有些人是

public service, and that is a legacy that we honor and applaud tonight.

In the weeks ahead, I also look forward to sitting down with Governor Romney to talk about where we can work together to move this country forward.

I want to thank my friend and partner of the last four years, America's happy warrior, the best Vice President anybody could ever hope for—Joe Biden.

And I wouldn't be the man I am today without the woman who agreed to marry me 20 years ago. Let me say this publicly—Michelle, I have never loved you more. I have never been prouder to watch the rest of America fall in love with you, too, as our nation's First Lady. Sasha and Malia, before our very eyes, you're growing up to become two strong, smart, beautiful young women, just like your mom. And I'm so proud of you guys. But I will say that for now, one dog is probably enough.

To the best campaign team and volunteers in the history of politics, the best, the

新成员,这次刚刚来,有些人从一开始就站在我的一边。但你们都是大家庭的一员。你们离开这里后,无论你们做什么、去哪里,你们都会记得我们共同创造过历史,都会得到一个心怀感激的总统对你们的终生感谢。谢谢你们一路上的信任,使我们跨过了高山、越过了峡谷。在整个征途上,你们提振了我的士气。对于你们所做的一切和所有令人难以置信的工作,我将永远心存感激。

我知道,政治竞选可能有时候显得小家子气,甚至很愚蠢。这就给玩世不恭者提供了充足的弹药。他们告诉我们,政治只不过是自负者们的竞赛,属于特殊利益的范畴。然而,如果你一旦有机会和我们集会上的小伙子聊聊,或者在中学的体育馆里,你沿着绳子拉出的警戒线挤在人群中,或者在离家很远的小县城的竞选办公室里,你看见了工作到深夜的年轻人,那么,你就会另有发现。

你能从一个年轻的现场组织者的声音里听到决心——他从校园一路走来,想

best ever. Some of you were new this time around, and some of you have been at my side since the very beginning. But all of you are family. No matter what you do or where you go from here, you will carry the memory of the history we made together, and you will have the lifelong appreciation of a grateful President. Thank you for believing all the way, through every hill, through every valley. You lifted me up the whole way. And I will always be grateful for everything that you've done and all the incredible work that you put in.

I know that political campaigns can sometimes seem small, even silly. And that provides plenty of fodder for the cynics who tell us that politics is nothing more than a contest of egos, or the domain of special interests. But if you ever get the chance to talk to folks who turned out at our rallies, and crowded along a rope line in a high school gym, or saw folks working late at a campaign office in some tiny county far away from home, you'll discover something else.

You'll hear the determination in the voice of a young field organizer who's

确保每一个孩子都有同样的机会。你能从一个女志愿者的声音里听到自豪——她挨家挨户地送喜讯,因为当地的汽车厂增加了一班活儿,她的兄弟终于有工作了。你能从一个军属的声音里听到深深的爱国主义——他打电话直到深夜,为的是确保为国而战的人,回家后不必再为工作或为住房而烦恼。

这就是我们为什么要这样做。这就是政治可能的内容。这就是选举为什么如此重要;它不是小事,而是大事,是重要的事。

在一个三亿人口的国家里实行民主,有可能是喧闹的、乱糟糟的和复杂的。每个人都有自己的观点,每个人都有深深的信仰。当我们经历艰难的时刻,当我们作为一个国家作出重要的决定,民主必然会引起群情激昂和争论不休。这种情形今晚以后不会改变——也不应该改变。这些争论标志着我们的自由,我们在说话时永远不能忘记这一点。现在,遥远的国家里的人民正在冒着生命的危险,为的就是

---

worked his way through college, and wants to make sure every child has that same opportunity. You'll hear the pride in the voice of a volunteer who's going door to door because her brother was finally hired when the local auto plant added another shift. You'll hear the deep patriotism in the voice of a military spouse who's working the phones late at night to make sure that no one who fights for this country ever has to fight for a job, or a roof over their head when they come home.

That's why we do this. That's what politics can be. That's why elections matter. It's not small; it's big. It's important.

Democracy in a nation of 300 million can be noisy and messy and complicated. We have our own opinions. Each of us has deeply held beliefs. And when we go through tough times, when we make big decisions as a country, it necessarily stirs passions, stirs up controversy. That won't change after tonight—and it shouldn't. These arguments we have are a mark of our liberty, and we can never forget that as we speak, people in distant nations are risking their lives right now just for a chance

有机会争辩事关重大的问题,为的就是有机会像我们今天这样投票。

但是,尽管我们有各种分歧,我们大多数人对美国的未来都有一定的希望。我们都想要孩子们在这样一个国家里长大,在那里,他们能够上最好的学校,有最好的教师——这个国家不会辜负自己的遗产,它要在技术、发现和创新等方面做全球的领袖,并且源源不断地创造出优秀的就业岗位和崭新的企业。

我们想要我们的孩子们生活在这样一个美国:它不受债务的拖累,不被不公平所削弱,不为渐渐变暖的星球上的恐怖势力所威胁。

我们想把这样一个国家传下去:它安全、受人尊敬、举世仰慕,有地球上最强大的军队和世界上最优秀的部队保卫,正满怀信心地度过当前的战争年代,为每个人塑造一种在自由和尊严的承诺的基础上建立起来的和平。

我们信奉一个慷慨的美国,一个充满同情心的美国,一个具有宽容精神的美

to argue about the issues that matter, the chance to cast their ballots like we did today.

But despite all our differences, most of us share certain hopes for America's future. We want our kids to grow up in a country where they have access to the best schools and the best teachers—a country that lives up to its legacy as the global leader in technology and discovery and innovation, with all the good jobs and new businesses that follow.

We want our children to live in an America that isn't burdened by debt; that isn't weakened by inequality; that isn't threatened by the destructive power of a warming planet.

We want to pass on a country that's safe and respected and admired around the world; a nation that is defended by the strongest military on Earth and the best troops this world has ever known—but also a country that moves with confidence beyond this time of war to shape a peace that is built on the promise of freedom and dignity for every human being.

We believe in a generous America; in a compassionate America; in a tolerant

国。这个美国向一个移民的女儿的梦想开放,她正在我们的一所学校里读书,并向国旗宣誓;这个美国向芝加哥南部的一个男青年开放,他在距离最近的大街拐角处找到了生计;这个美国向北卡罗莱纳州一个家具厂工人的孩子开放,他想成为一个医生、科学家、工程师、企业家、外交官,甚至一个总统。这就是我们所希望的未来,这就是我们共享的愿景,这就是我们需要去的地方。向前进,这就是我们需要去的地方!

对于怎样才能到达目的地,我们的意见并不统一,有时还存在着严重的分歧。二百多年来的情况表明,进步的来临是一阵一阵的,不完全沿着一条直线,不完全是一条平坦的道路。认识到我们拥有共同的希望和梦想,本身并不能打开所有的僵局,解决所有的问题,或取代辛苦的、建立共识的工作,并达成困难的、推动本国前进所需的妥协。但这一共同的契约,正是我们必须开始的地方。

America, open to the dreams of an immigrant's daughter who studies in our schools and pledges to our flag. To the young boy on the South Side of Chicago who sees a life beyond the nearest street corner. To the furniture worker's child in North Carolina who wants to become a doctor or a scientist, an engineer or entrepreneur, a diplomat or even a President. That's the future we hope for. That's the vision we share. That's where we need to go. Forward. That's where we need to go.

Now, we will disagree, sometimes fiercely, about how to get there. As it has for more than two centuries, progress will come in fits and starts. It's not always a straight line. It's not always a smooth path. By itself, the recognition that we have common hopes and dreams won't end all the gridlock, or solve all our problems, or substitute for the painstaking work of building consensus, and making the difficult compromises needed to move this country forward. But that common bond is where we must begin.

我国的经济正在复苏。长达十年的战争正在终结。漫长的竞选已经成为过去。无论我是否赢得了你们的选票,我都已倾听了你们的声音,并从你们那里学到了很多。你们已经使我成为一名更好的总统。我会带着你们的故事和抗争返回白宫,对白宫要做的工作和前方的未来更加信心百倍,更加充满豪情。

今晚,你们是为了行动而投票,而不像以往是为了政治而投票。你们选举我们,是要聚焦你们的、而不是我们的工作。在今后的几个星期和几个月里,我期待着欢迎两党领导人并与他们一起工作,来应对我们只能共同应对的挑战:减少赤字,改革税则,修改完善移民制度,减少对外国石油的依赖,等等。

但是,这并不意味着你们的工作完成了。在民主社会中,公民的作用并不以投票而终止。美国从来不是能为我们做些什么,而是通过艰苦的、令人沮丧的、也是必需的自治工作,我们能一起做些什么。这是我们的建国原则。

Our economy is recovering. A decade of war is ending. A long campaign is now over. And whether I earned your vote or not, I have listened to you. I have learned from you. And you've made me a better President. With your stories and your struggles, I return to the White House more determined and more inspired than ever about the work there is to do, and the future that lies ahead.

Tonight, you voted for action, not politics as usual. You elected us to focus on your jobs, not ours. And in the coming weeks and months, I am looking forward to reaching out and working with leaders of both parties to meet the challenges we can only solve together: reducing our deficit; reforming our tax code; fixing our immigration system; freeing ourselves from foreign oil. We've got more work to do.

But that doesn't mean your work is done. The role of citizen in our democracy does not end with your vote. America has never been about what can be done for us. It's about what can be done by us, together, through the hard and frustrating but necessary work of self-government. That's the principle we were founded on.

我们这个国家拥有的财富比任何国家都多,但并不是这个原因我们才富有。我们有历史上最强大的军队,但并不是这个原因我们才坚强。我们的大学、我们的文化为全世界所羡慕,但并不是这个原因各国移民才涌向美国的海岸。

美国变得特殊的原因在于,通过契约把地球上最多样化的民族凝聚起来——我们都相信:我们有共同的命运;我们只有彼此之间承担一定的义务,并承担对子孙后代的义务,这个国家才能运转;这么多美国人为之奋斗、为之牺牲的自由,不但意味着权利,而且意味着责任,其中包括爱心、慈善、责任和爱国心。这些就是使美国变得伟大的东西。

今晚我满怀希望,因为我已经看到这种精神正在美国起作用。我从宁愿少领薪水也不愿解雇邻居的家庭企业主的身上看到了这种精神;我从宁愿减少自己的工作时间,也不愿看到朋友们失业的工人身上看到了这种精神。

This country has more wealth than any nation, but that's not what makes us rich. We have the most powerful military in history, but that's not what makes us strong. Our university, culture are the envy of the world, but that's not what keeps the world coming to our shores.

What makes America exceptional are the bonds that hold together the most diverse nation on Earth—the belief that our destiny is shared; that this country only works when we accept certain obligations to one another, and to future generations; that the freedom which so many Americans have fought for and died for comes with responsibilities as well as rights, and among those are love and charity and duty and patriotism. That's what makes America great.

I am hopeful tonight because I have seen this spirit at work in America. I've seen it in the family business whose owners would rather cut their own pay than lay off their neighbors, and in the workers who would rather cut back their hours than see a friend lose a job.

我从再次应征的断肢士兵们身上看到了这种精神;我从海豹突击队队员身上看到了这种精神,他们冲上台阶,消失在黑暗和危险中,因为他们知道,他们的队友就在身后,照顾着他们的后方。

我在新泽西州和纽约州的沿岸看到了这种精神,在那里,各党派和各级政府的领导人抛开分歧,帮助一个遭到特大暴风雨蹂躏的社区重建家园。

有一天,我从俄亥俄州门托市看到了这种精神,在那里,一个父亲讲述了他的八岁女儿的故事:她与白血病进行了漫长的斗争,几乎花掉家中的一切,幸运的是,就在保险公司准备停付保健费的前几个月,医保改革方案通过了。我不仅有机会与这位父亲交谈,而且见到了他的那个不可思议的女儿。当他对着人群讲述时,房间里每一个聆听的父母亲都噙着热泪,因为我们知道,那个小女孩也可能是我们自己的。而我知道,每一个美国人都会祝福她有光明的未来。

I've seen it in the soldiers who re-enlist after losing a limb, and in those SEALs who charged up the stairs into darkness and danger because they knew there was a buddy behind them, watching their back.

I've seen it on the shores of New Jersey and New York, where leaders from every party and level of government have swept aside their differences to help a community rebuild from the wreckage of a terrible storm.

And I saw it just the other day in Mentor, Ohio, where a father told the story of his eight-year-old daughter, whose long battle with leukemia nearly cost their family everything, had it not been for health care reform passing just a few months before the insurance company was about to stop paying for her care. I had an opportunity to not just talk to the father, but meet this incredible daughter of his. And when he spoke to the crowd, listening to that father's story, every parent in that room had tears in their eyes, because we knew that little girl could be our own. And I know that every American wants her future to be just as bright.

这就是我们美国人。这就是我作为总统如此自豪地领导的国家。今晚,尽管我们度过了所有的艰难困苦,尽管华府经历了种种沮丧,但我对未来、对美国从未像现在这样满怀希望。我要求你们支持这个希望。

我不是在谈盲目的乐观主义,无视前方任务的艰巨性和道路上的障碍。我不是在谈一厢情愿的理想主义,让我们坐在一旁,逃避战斗。我一直认为,希望是我们内心固有的品质,尽管有种种相反的证据,它仍然坚持还有更好的结果在等着我们,只要我们勇于坚持探索、工作和战斗。

美利坚呀,我相信我们能在取得成就的基础上继续进行建设,继续为中产阶级获得新的工作、新的机会和新的安全而战斗。我相信,我们能实现开国元勋们许下的承诺——只要你愿意努力工作,其他都无所谓,包括你是谁、你从哪里来、你

①美国媒体用红蓝两色标注大选的进程和结果,共和党获胜的州用红色,民主党获胜的州用蓝色。

That's who we are. That's the country I'm so proud to lead as your President. And tonight, despite all the hardship we've been through, despite all the frustrations of Washington, I've never been more hopeful about our future. I have never been more hopeful about America. And I ask you to sustain that hope.

I'm not talking about blind optimism—the kind of hope that just ignores the enormity of the tasks ahead or the roadblocks that stand in our path. I'm not talking about the wishful idealism that allows us to just sit on the sidelines or shirk from a fight. I have always believed that hope is that stubborn thing inside us that insists, despite all the evidence to the contrary, that something better awaits us, so long as we have the courage to keep reaching, to keep working, to keep fighting.

America, I believe we can build on the progress we've made, and continue to fight for new jobs, and new opportunity, and new security for the middle class. I believe we can keep the promise of our founding—the idea that if you're willing to work hard, it doesn't matter who you are, or where you come from, or what you look

长得什么样、你在哪里恋爱等等——无论你是黑人还是白人,西班牙裔、亚裔还是美国土著,青年还是老年,富有还是贫穷,健全人还是残疾人,同性恋者还是非同性恋者,一切都不要紧——只要你愿意尝试,都可以在这里、在美国实现承诺。

我相信,我们能一起抓住这样的未来——因为我们并非像我们的政治所说的那样四分五裂;我们并非像学究们认为的那样愤世嫉俗;我们大于个人雄心的总和;我们不只是红色州和蓝色州的集合①。我们是、永远是美利坚合众国!有了你们的帮助和上帝的恩惠,我们将一起继续我们的旅程,不断向前,并提醒世界我们为什么会屹立于最伟大的民族之林!

谢谢你,美国!上帝保佑美国!上帝保佑合众国!

井 力 译

like, or where you love—it doesn't matter whether you're black or white, or Hispanic or Asian, or Native American, or young or old, or rich or poor, abled, disabled, gay or straight—you can make it here in America if you're willing to try.

I believe we can seize this future together—because we are not as divided as our politics suggest; we're not as cynical as the pundits believe; we are greater than the sum of our individual ambitions; and we remain more than a collection of red states and blue states. We are, and forever will be, the United States of America. And together, with your help, and God's grace, we will continue our journey forward, and remind the world just why it is that we live in the greatest nation on Earth.

Thank you, America. God bless you. God bless these United States.

附录

美国历届总统谈竞选

迄今为止,选举中的腐败已摧毁了所有的民选政府。将来能采取何种规章制度或预防措施来防止腐败,这个问题就留给后人去考虑吧。我坚信,你我两人将怀着纯洁的心灵和干净的双手,在选举中不为营私舞弊所累,走向正义的王国。

——第2任总统约翰·亚当斯,1796年4月6日致托马斯·杰斐逊

我感到,若能摆脱激烈而烦人的、旷日持久的竞选活动,就可省去许多麻烦,不然我就要大伤脑筋。

——第6任总统约翰·昆西·亚当斯,1800年12月20日致托马斯·亚当斯

这种拉选票的竞选方式,既不符合我的情趣,也不符合我的原则。我想,它同样不符合我的性格和所担当的职位。

——1827年6月29日约翰·昆西·亚当斯《日记》

一个陌生人也许会想,美国人除了竞选,无所事事。

——1828年8月5日约翰·昆西·亚当斯《日记》

我大概已经和好几千人握过手。有人问我手疼不疼,我回答

说,我发现握手是大有讲究的。如果被动地伸出手让别人握,那就会吃苦头。但如果采取主动,去握别人而不是被别人握,对方使多大劲,你就使多大劲,那就不会有任何不适。

——第11任总统詹姆斯·波尔克,1849年1月1日《日记》

对自由人民而言,选票是解决分歧的最可靠的仲裁人。

——第15任总统詹姆斯·布坎南,1860年12月3日第4篇国情咨文

政界对我的名字还不熟悉,所以我认为,我不会是大多数人的首选提名。这样,我们的方针应当是不冒犯别人——让他们感到,他们如果被迫放弃首选,可以加入我们的行列。

——第16任总统亚伯拉罕·林肯,1860年致共和党人的信

现在是人民向世界展示自己的时候:凡能公正举行选举的人民,也能够镇压叛乱;选票可以合法而和平地取代子弹;一旦由选票公正而合法地作出决定,任何诉诸武力的行径将不会取得成功;在未来选举中,除了选票本身,诉诸任何其他手段均属无效。这将成为一堂伟大的和平课:从选举中得不到的东西,从战争中也休想得到,这对所有发动战争的蠢人也是一个教育。

——亚伯拉罕·林肯,1861年7月4日在国会特别会议上的演说

我不能自以为共和党大会或全国联盟党大会都已经得出结论,说我是美国最伟大或最出类拔萃的人物。与此相反,他们的结论是,骑到河中最好别换马,而他们的进一步结论则是,我这匹马还不算太坏,所以如果换马将会搞得一团糟。

——亚伯拉罕·林肯,1864年6月9日在获得连任提名后对全国联盟党代表团说的话

据我所知,迄今只有两个总统候选人肆无忌惮地拉选票。两人都是大演说家,但结果都大败而归。我不是演说家,而我也不想被击败!

——第18任总统尤利塞斯·格兰特,1872年竞选演说

我们切不可墨守毫无意义的、荒唐的成规旧习,说什么肤色是选举权的基础和自由的护身符。让我们不分肤色,把选举权扩大到每一个适龄公民吧。

——第20任总统詹姆斯·加菲尔德，1865年7月4日在俄亥俄州拉文纳市的演说

　　侵犯自由和侵犯选举权的神圣性不仅是堕落，而且是犯罪。这种恶习如果延续，必将摧毁政府本身。自杀绝不是一种补救。
　　——詹姆斯·加菲尔德，1881年3月4日就职演说

　　我对第一批来访的代表团说过，这是崇高的原则之争。因此，只能在真理的高原，而不能在诋毁的沼泽地决出胜负。在沼泽地安营扎寨的军队，必定会把胜利果实供手奉给高原的军队。
　　——第23任总统本杰明·哈里森，1888年10月25日在印第安纳波利斯的竞选演说

　　对你们这些聚集一堂、献身于向邪恶开战的人，对你们这些坚定不移、满怀信心面向未来的人，对你们这些以四海之内皆兄弟的精神为指导、为改善我国而奋斗的人，我现在把6星期前在这里说过的话再说一遍：我们正站在哈米吉多顿，我们是在为上帝而战。
　　——西奥多·罗斯福，1912年8月5日在进步党代表大会上接受总统候选人提名时的演说

　　总统竞选很容易蜕化成纯粹的个人之争，因而失去了尊严。必不可少的人物并不存在。
　　——第28任总统伍德罗·威尔逊，1912年8月7日在民主党代表大会上接受总统候选人提名时的演说

　　万万不可去谋杀一个正在自杀的人。
　　——伍德罗·威尔逊在其竞争对手失败后所作的评论，引自约翰·帕索斯《威尔逊先生的战争》

　　"哈里，这太糟了。"
　　"什么太糟了？"
　　"在全国巡回游说，自吹自擂。"
　　——第29任总统沃伦·哈定，1914年对哈里·多尔蒂竞选参议员所作的评论

最好不要对提名过程施加太多的压力,而要顺其自然,避免人为刺激。人民需要谁,就会提名谁,而如果不需要某人,那么此人最好把机会让给别人。
　　——第30任总统卡尔文·柯立芝,《卡尔文·柯立芝自传》1929年版

美国人在作出像选举总统这样的重大决定时,并不倾心于出价最高的人。仅有诺言和良好的愿望是不够的。
　　——卡尔文·柯立芝,1932年说过的话

在职业政客看来,选票是众神存放在肉桶里的食品。
　　——第31任总统赫伯特·胡佛,引自尤金·莱昂斯《赫伯特·胡佛传》

我向你们保证,也向自己保证,我要为美国人民实施新政。
　　——第32任总统富兰克林·罗斯福,1932年7月2日在民主党代表大会上接受总统候选人提名时的演说

在古老的日子里,竞选是在乐队和彩灯的包围中进行的。随着教育的普及,报刊的广泛阅读,尤其是随着无线电的出现,仅仅靠演讲术和表情来决定重大问题的做法已经过时。如今,人们的常识起到了关键作用,而最终意见则是在家庭里平静的气氛中形成的。
　　——富兰克林·罗斯福,1932年7月30日广播演说

我们竞选预算的最大一笔开支是购买广播时间。
　　——富兰克林·罗斯福,1932年说过的话

我认为,用事实来回答歪曲是一种社会责任。我不必装模作样,说什么这会令我不快。我是竞选老手了,我喜爱真正的战斗。
　　——富兰克林·罗斯福,1940年10月23日在费城的演说

我们不妨把伟大的重量级拳王刘易斯说过的话铭记在心。在不久前的一次决赛中,为了赶上对手,他有过难熬的时刻。但他终于赶上了对手,并把对手击倒在地。刘易斯在赛后如是说:"哦,他可以逃,但他无处躲。"
　　——第33任总统哈里·杜鲁门,1948年10月6日在费城会议厅的演说

无论选举还是赛马,谁暂时领先并不重要。最先到达终点的马才是大赢家。
　　——哈里·杜鲁门,1948年10月17日的声明

就个人而言,我一生中经历过10次总统竞选的盛事。但我必须说,这第11次却使我仿佛觉得,我已经经历过25次。
　　——约翰·肯尼迪,1960年9月14日在纽约市的演说

年纪这么小,错误那么大。
　　——约翰·肯尼迪,1960年在伊利诺伊州看到一个举着支持尼克松标牌的女孩时说的话

要求诸位在将来的选举中支持我,这样做为时太早;感谢诸位在过去的选举中支持我,这样说却未必正确。
　　——约翰·肯尼迪,1960年当选后不久对一批实业家说的话

如果你逢人就说喜欢我胜过喜欢尼克松,那我回国后可就要遭殃了。
　　——约翰·肯尼迪,1961年6月在维也纳对赫鲁晓夫说的话

选票是人类迄今发明的最有力的工具,它可以打倒不公正,并且摧垮禁锢人们的可怕的高墙。
　　——林登·约翰逊,1965年8月6日的演说

竞选真不容易,而对夫人们而言就更惨了。她们必须老是听你发表同样的演说,却又要装出津津有味的样子。
　　——第37任总统查德·尼克松,1960年9月29日在堪萨斯城记者招待会上说的话

8年前,我输掉了一场势均力敌的竞选,今年我赢得了一场势均力敌的竞选;因此我可以说:赢的滋味要美妙得多。
　　——第37任总统查德·尼克松,1972年赢得竞选后在纽约市的演说

至于电视辩论,总的来说,我怀疑它们对于阐明竞选中的重大问题能否起到

可靠的作用。新闻媒体由于其性质关系，必然更为重视表演才能，而不是重视治国才能。

——理查德·尼克松，《理查德·尼克松回忆录》1978年版

我要在这里承认，我首次参加总统竞选时——当时我在密歇根州大拉皮兹市的南方高级中学读书——我选择了进步党的政纲，结果我失败了。也许，这就是为什么我成了共和党人的缘由。

——第38任总统杰拉尔德·福特，1974年8月12日在国会的演说

对现代竞选来说，拿报酬的竞选策划人是一个大问题。他们拿的是高报酬，干的却是错事。

——杰拉尔德·福特，引自美国公共广播公司1988年11月21日《麦克尼尔·莱雷尔报道》

千百万美国人认为，今年是他们给予我们这个制度以最后一次机会的一年。他们不愿意再次失望。他们要研究各位候选人，审查我们的政治记录、个人能力和品质，然后确定哪一位候选人能最好地使我们的政府恢复能力、眼光和诚实。

——第39任总统吉米·卡特，1976年7月15日在民主党代表大会接受总统候选人提名时的演说

来吧，在11月6日那一天，我希望你们中的千百万人，用你们选择未来的选票去创造历史——为机会而投票，为你们信任的领导人而投票，为你们梦寐以求的权利而投票。

——第40任总统罗纳德·里根，1984年10月27日广播演说

在1940年，当时我还是个大孩子，富兰克林·罗斯福说我们不应该在中途换马。朋友们，近来世界变化得更快了，现在经过两个任期后，将进行一次换班。但是当你们必须在中途换马时，就换乘一匹走着同一道路的马，不也很明智吗？

——第41任总统乔治·H. 布什，1988年8月18日在共和党代表大会上接受总统候选人提名时的演说。

我是中层阶级的儿子。我若当选为总统，你们就不再会被人遗忘了。

——第42任总统比尔·克林顿,1992年7月16日在民主党全国代表大会上的讲话

许多人把选举当作分裂我们的机会。但是,我相信,此次选举将使我们团结在一起,共同前进。当我们齐聚一处,找到共同的立场,作为一个国家,我们将更为强大,战无不胜。

——第42任总统比尔·克林顿,1996年11月2日广播演说。

我有一个明确而积极的竞选纲领,那就是建设一个更安全的世界和一个更有希望的美国。我秉持富有同情心的保守哲学,那就是,政府应当帮助人们改善生活,而不是统治人们的生活。

——第43任总统乔治·W. 布什,2004年9月2日在共和党全国代表大会上的讲话

王建华　编译

世界名人演说系列

《美国 20 世纪经典演讲 100 篇·社会卷》
[美]马丁·路德·金　富兰克林·罗斯福等著
ISBN 978-7-210-03569-5/I·455
定价:32.00元
2007 年 4 月第 1 版

《美国 20 世纪经典演讲 100 篇·政治卷》
[美]马丁·路德·金　富兰克林·罗斯福等著
ISBN 978-7-210-03569-5/I·455
定价:32.00元
2007 年 4 月第 1 版

《美国总统就职演说精选》

王建华　主编
ISBN 978-7-210-03751-4
定价：35.00元
2009年5月第2版

《美国常春藤名校校长演说精选》

[美]朱易主编　王建华等译
ISBN 978-7-210-03998-3
定价：30.00元
2009年3月第1版